Shakespeare's Audiences

Shakespeare wrote for a theater in which the audience was understood to be, and at times invited to be, active and participatory. How have Shakespeare's audiences, from the sixteenth century to the present, responded to that invitation? In what ways have consumers across different cultural contexts, periods, and platforms engaged with the performance of Shakespeare's plays? What are some of the different approaches taken by scholars today in thinking about the role of Shakespeare's audiences and their relationship to performance? The chapters in this collection use a variety of methods and approaches to explore the global history of audience experience of Shakespearean performance in theater, film, radio, and digital media. The approaches that these contributors take look at Shakespeare's audiences through a variety of lenses, including theater history, dramaturgy, film studies, fan studies, popular culture, and performance. Together, they provide both close studies of particular moments in the history of Shakespeare's audiences and a broader understanding of the various, often complex, connections between and among those audiences across the long history of Shakespearean performance.

Matteo Pangallo is Assistant Professor of English at Virginia Commonwealth University.

Peter Kirwan is Associate Professor of Early Modern Drama at the University of Nottingham.

Routledge Studies in Shakespeare

For more information about this series, please visit: www.routledge.com/
Routledge-Studies-in-Shakespeare/book-series/RSS

Shakespeare's Audiences

Edited by Matteo Pangallo
and Peter Kirwan

Routledge
Taylor & Francis Group

NEW YORK AND LONDON

First published 2021
by Routledge
605 Third Avenue, New York, NY 10158

and by Routledge
2 Park Square, Milton Park, Abingdon, Oxon OX14 4RN

Routledge is an imprint of the Taylor & Francis Group, an informa business

© 2021 Taylor & Francis

The right of Matteo Pangallo and Peter Kirwan to be identified as the authors of the editorial material, and of the authors for their individual chapters, has been asserted in accordance with sections 77 and 78 of the Copyright, Designs and Patents Act 1988.

Library of Congress Cataloging-in-Publication Data
Names: Pangallo, Matteo A., editor. | Kirwan, Peter, editor.
Title: Shakespeare's audiences / edited by Matteo Pangallo and Peter Kirwan.
Description: New York, NY : Routledge, 2021. |
Series: Routledge studies in Shakespeare |
Includes bibliographical references and index.
Identifiers: LCCN 2020043944 (print) | LCCN 2020043945 (ebook) |
ISBN 9780367715465 (hardback) | ISBN 9781003152538 (ebook)
Subjects: LCSH: Shakespeare, William, 1564–1616–Dramatic production |
Shakespeare, William, 1564–1616–Stage history. | Theater audiences–Psychology.
Classification: LCC PR3091 .S675 2021 (print) |
LCC PR3091 (ebook) | DDC 822.3/3–dc23
LC record available at https://lccn.loc.gov/2020043944
LC ebook record available at https://lccn.loc.gov/2020043945

ISBN: 978-0-367-71546-5 (hbk)
ISBN: 978-0-367-71548-9 (pbk)
ISBN: 978-1-003-15253-8 (ebk)

Typeset in Sabon
by Newgen Publishing UK

Contents

Illustrations

Contributor Biographies

Pascale Aebischer is Professor of Shakespeare and Early Modern Performance Studies at the University of Exeter. She works on the performance of early modern drama on stage and in various media. Her most recent book, *Shakespeare, Spectatorship and The Technologies of Performance*, was published in 2020. Prior to that, she was one of the editors of *Shakespeare and the "Live" Theatre Broadcast Experience* (2018) and the author of *Screening Early Modern Drama: Beyond Shakespeare* (2013), and *Shakespeare's Violated Bodies: Stage and Screen Performance* (2004).

Koel Chatterjee is a lecturer in Integrated English at Trinity Laban Conservatoire of Music and Dance. She specializes in Global Shakespeares and Academic English in Higher Education. She has interests in crossover pedagogical practices in the classroom and in applying literary and pedagogical research to affect policy change. She was awarded her PhD in Shakespeare and Bollywood in 2018 from Royal Holloway, University of London, and is currently coediting a collection of essays on the impact of Indian Shakespeares in the West as part of the new Arden Global Shakespeare Inverted series, edited by Bi-qi Beatrice Lei, David Schalkwyk, and Silvia Bigliazzi.

Miles Drawdy is a PhD candidate in English at The University of California, Berkeley, where he researches and teaches courses on early modern drama, disability, and contemporary American theater. His dissertation is focused on deformity as both a formal and aesthetic feature of English drama and performance throughout the long seventeenth century.

Joe Falocco (Texas State University) is the author of *Reimagining Shakespeare's Playhouse: Early Modern Staging Conventions in the Twentieth Century* (Boydell and Brewer, 2010) as well as several journal articles. Joe's essay, "Tommaso Salvini's Othello and Racial Identity in Late Nineteenth-Century America" (*New England Theatre Journal*, 2012) won the ATDS's Vera Mowry Roberts Outstanding Essay

Award. Joe is a member of Actors' Equity and has worked for many regional Shakespeare companies. He has also directed professional and university productions of *Richard III, Antony and Cleopatra, The Merry Wives of Windsor, The Comedy of Errors, Hamlet, Henry V,* and *Macbeth*.

Valerie M. Fazel, PhD, teaches at Arizona State University. She is co-author (with Louise Geddes) of *The Shakespeare Multiverse: Fandom as Literary Praxis,* and coeditor (with Geddes) of *The Shakespeare User: Critical and Creative Appropriation in a Networked Culture* and *Variable Objects: Shakespeare and Speculative Appropriation.* Valerie's essays on Shakespeare, social media, and fandom appear in *Borrowers and Lenders, The Sundial,* and *Shakespeare* (with Geddes).

Louise Geddes is Associate Professor of English at Adelphi University. She is the author of *Shakespeare in Appropriation: A Cultural History of Pyramus and Thisbe.* Her work has also been published in *Shakespeare Survey, Shakespeare,* and *Shakespeare Bulletin.* With Valerie M. Fazel, she is the editor of *The Shakespeare User: Creative and Critical Appropriation in a Networked Culture* and the co-author of the forthcoming *The Shakespeare Multiverse: Fandom as Literary Praxis.* She is the co-general editor of the open-access, online journal, *Borrowers and Lenders: A Journal of Shakespearean Appropriation,* and the co-editor of Palgrave's Fan Studies book series.

Peter Kirwan is Associate Professor of Early Modern Drama at the University of Nottingham. He researches early modern drama in text and performance from the early modern period to the present. His books include *Shakespeare in the Theatre: Cheek by Jowl* (Bloomsbury, 2019), *Shakespeare and the Idea of Apocrypha* (Cambridge, 2015), *The Arden Research Handbook of Shakespeare and Contemporary Performance* (with Kathryn Prince: Bloomsbury, 2021), *Canonising Shakespeare* (with Emma Depledge: Cambridge, 2017), and *Shakespeare and the Digital World* (with Christie Carson: Cambridge, 2014). He is a general editor of the Revels Plays Companion Library and editor of *Shakespeare Bulletin.*

Edel Lamb is a Senior Lecturer in Renaissance Literature at Queen's University Belfast. She is the author of *Performing Childhood in the Early Modern Theatre* (2009) and *Reading Children in Early Modern Culture* (2018), both published by Palgrave Macmillan, and co-editor of a special issue of *Shakespeare* on Shakespeare and Riot (2018). Her work on early modern theater, Shakespeare, and performance has been published in *Australian Studies, Ben Jonson Journal, Renaissance Drama, The Edinburgh Companion to Shakespeare and the Arts* (Edinburgh University Press, 2012), and *The New Companion to Renaissance Literature and Culture* (Blackwell, 2010).

Emily Lathrop is a PhD candidate in the Department of English at The George Washington University. She holds a Bachelor's degree in English from the University of Iowa and a Master's degree in early modern literature from King's College London. Her current work is concerned with how modern Shakespeare theaters construct and enact paratheatrical audience programming. Her work has appeared in *The Rambling* and in the Renaissance volume of Bloomsbury's *A Cultural History of Disability* series, and she has contributed performance reviews to *Shakespeare Bulletin* and *Cahiers Élisabéthains*. Emily is also a theater practitioner and member of Actors' Equity.

Jennifer A. Low, professor emerita at Florida Atlantic University, is the author of *Manhood and the Duel: Masculinity in Early Modern Drama and Culture* (Palgrave, 2003) and *Dramatic Spaces: Scenography and Spectatorial Perceptions* (Routledge, 2016), as well as coeditor with Nova Myhill of the essay collection *Imagining the Audience in Early Modern Drama 1558–1642* (Palgrave, 2011). Low's articles have appeared in *Philological Quarterly, Comparative Drama*, *The Centennial Review*, and *Poetics Today*. Her work has been translated into Hungarian for publication in *Apertúra*, and her most recent essay appeared in the *Actes des congrès de la Société française Shakespeare*.

Rachael Nicholas recently completed a PhD at the University of Roehampton. Her thesis explores the reception of digitally distributed Shakespeare performances in cinemas, schools, and online. She is currently a Postdoctoral Research Fellow at the University of Exeter working on a UKRI-funded COVID-19 rapid response project investigating audience response to live Zoom performances during lockdown. She has also written about Shakespeare's digital audiences for chapters in *Shakespeare and the "Live" Theatre Broadcast Experience* (2018), edited by Pascale Aebischer, Susanne Greenhalgh, and Laurie E. Osborne, and in *King Lear: Shakespeare on Screen* (2019), edited by Victoria Bladen, Sarah Hatchuel, and Nathalie Vienne-Guerrin.

Romola Nuttall is an Associate Research Fellow at King's College London and visiting unit tutor at the Royal Central School of Speech and Drama. She is currently working on her first monograph, *Shakespeare, Print, and Patronage*, which explores the interplay between different forms of theatrical and textual patronage and their impact on early modern drama.

Matteo Pangallo is an Assistant Professor of English at Virginia Commonwealth University. His monograph, *Playwriting Playgoers in Shakespeare's Theater*, was published by the University of Pennsylvania Press in 2017, and he has published widely in collections, including the *Oxford Handbook of Shakespeare* (2012) and *A New Companion to Renaissance Drama* (2017), and journals, such as *ELR*, *RES*, and *Early Theatre*. He is general editor of the *Database of English Manuscript*

Drama and an editor for the Malone Society, Digital Renaissance Editions, New Variorum Shakespeare, and the Oxford *Collected Works of Thomas Heywood*. He is coeditor of the forthcoming *Teaching the History of the Book* (MLA) and is completing his second monograph, *Strange Company: Foreign Performers in Medieval and Early Modern England*.

Adam Sheaffer is an independent educator/scholar currently living and working in Milwaukee, Wisconsin. His publications have appeared in *Theater History Studies, Theatre Journal,* and the edited collection *Shakespeare's Hamlet in the Era of Textual Exhaustion*. In addition to his scholarly pursuits, Adam continues to perform with outdoor Shakespeare companies in New York City and Milwaukee, while exploring the dynamics of this ubiquitous—but endlessly fascinating—performance mode and milieu.

Stephanie Shirilan is Associate Professor of English at Syracuse University, where she teaches courses on early modern literature, Western and trans-Atlantic histories of science and medicine, and performance. She is the author of *Robert Burton and the Transformative Powers of Melancholy* (Ashgate 2015, Routledge 2016). She is currently working on a series of articles on the literary history of early modern respiratory medicine and writing her second monograph, a study of respiratory and pneumatic themes in Shakespeare's plays, provisionally titled, *The Breathing World: A Natural History of Air in Shakespeare*.

Acknowledgments

When we began working on this book in late 2018, we could not have anticipated what the following two years would have in store. The impact of the events of 2020 on physical and mental health, on working conditions, on institutions—especially theaters, which at the time of writing in September 2020 are only just beginning to explore possibilities of reopening—and on day-to-day life, has been incalculable. We want to pay tribute, first and foremost, to the contributors to this volume for their grace, patience, commitment, and generosity in helping us complete this book under difficult conditions.

We are grateful to Routledge for its support and guidance at all times. Bryony Reece has been an exemplary and supportive editor, and we are especially grateful for her support and that of Michelle Salyga and our project manager Sarah Green and the team at Newgen. We would like to offer our shared thanks to Annalisa Castaldo, Ashley Hendricks, Haley Lancaster, Amanda Lang, Amber Luttig-Buonodono, Ben Naylor, Anthony Guy Patricia, Andrea Smith, Lindsey Snyder, and Geoffrey Way for their insights and conversations, and to our anonymous readers at the press, whose suggestions were instrumental in helping shape the book at an early stage.

Peter would like to thank Matteo for inviting him to join this project and for his scrupulous attention to detail as we have edited the final manuscript. His thanks go to his colleagues in the Drama section at the University of Nottingham, where the embeddedness of audience theory in the team's work has been formative on his approach to editing this book. He'd also particularly like to thank past and present PhD students Hannah Manktelow, Beth Sharrock, and Josh Caldicott (and co-supervisors Jo Robinson, Erin Sullivan, and Simon Smith) for invaluable conversations about past and present audience behaviors, and Kathryn Prince and the contributors to *The Arden Research Handbook to Shakespeare and Contemporary Performance* for conversations and insights that helped shape the thinking here, as well as for sharing advance work with contributors to this volume. The friends and colleagues who have offered support/advice at crucial stages are too many to name, but particular thanks to Pascale Aebischer, Mark Thornton Burnett, Emma

Depledge, Diana Henderson, Georgie Lucas, Emer McHugh, Eoin Price, Ellie Rycroft, Emma Smith, Nora Williams, and Ramona Wray. Closer to home, as always, this book couldn't have been completed without the love and support of Susan Anderson (and, of course, Peppermint, the toughest audience of all).

Matteo is grateful to Peter for his patience, diligence, and, above all, expertise, without which this volume would not have been possible. He extends thanks, also, to the contributors for generously sharing their insights and knowledge, and for their spirit of collaboration over two years of conversations carried out in emails, in the margins of Word documents, and over coffees at several Shakespeare Association of America conferences. He is grateful to the mentors and colleagues who have helped inform and enrich his thinking about early modern playgoing and theater history, particularly Arthur Kinney, Ros Knutson, Pierre Hecker, Grace Ioppolo, Farah Karim-Cooper, Jess Landis, Nathaniel Leonard, Gordon McMullan, Philip Palmer, William Proctor Williams, and Adam Zucker. Thanks are also due to those theater artists with whom he has worked and who have helped inform his practical understanding of audiences, including Amy George Brown, Keri Ellis Cahill, John Fogle, and Dominick Pangallo. Matteo is particularly grateful to the late Cristina Malcolmson for her years of support, advice, and friendship; he dedicates his work on this book to her memory. Finally, he extends his perpetual thanks to his most important, and indulging, of audiences: Toby, Atticus, and Nettie.

A Note on Quotations

Unless otherwise stated, all quotations from Shakespeare's works are taken from stand-alone volumes in the third series of the Arden Shakespeare.

Introduction

Matteo Pangallo and Peter Kirwan

> I turned my head and looked around an immense but dilapidated great hall. Inches from my face was Hamlet himself, reciting his famous "To be, or not to be" monologue while sitting in a bathtub, reflecting on his life and contemplating its end. Suddenly he submerged himself into the water, and before I had the chance to understand what had happened, I was underwater with him.[1]

An inescapable proximity to performance characterizes Sofía Barrell's account of being an audience member for the 2019 Commonwealth Shakespeare Company (CSC) production *Hamlet 360*. This "immersive theatre experience," as Barrell puts it, involved a collaboration between CSC and Google's AR/VR Lens team in which a seventeen-lens, 360-degree Yi Halo camera was used to record a stage production of Shakespeare's tragedy.[2] In *Hamlet 360*, the camera, and thus the audience, is not merely an observer of the performance, however; rather, the camera/audience stands in the position of the Ghost of Hamlet's father—the spectator as specter. "When the ghost speaks," Barrell observes, "the stereoscopic and spherical sound reverberates through your headphones." If we, as spectators, look into a mirror within the world of the play, we see, in a profoundly uncanny conjunction between what Susan Bennett terms the "outer frame" that constitutes our world and the "inner frame" that constitutes the world within the dramatic production, the ghostly figure of Hamlet's father (played by Jay O. Sanders) looking back at us.[3] Indeed, not merely "looking back" at us but actually *being* us. It is audience–play proximity of perhaps the most intense kind.

Part of the decision to record *Hamlet 360* this way was to eliminate inequities of sightline experienced by spectators in different parts of the audience and to impose a heightened degree of control over perspective: as CSC artistic director Steve Maler explained, "It puts every viewer in the best seat in the house, the seat that *we've chosen them to be in*, as opposed to in a theatre where your perspective is not always optimized."[4] Like the Ghost—bound to obey specific paranormal laws about when it may walk abroad and for how long—the spectator–specter is constrained to a specific perspective (where the camera was placed on the stage during the recording) and can only "speak" the lines spoken for us by the actor playing the Ghost. As Barrell notes, following Hamlet's contemplation of suicide, we are subjected immediately to an involuntary sense of drowning as the camera goes underwater with the prince (a pointed literalization of virtual reality's (VR) promise of "immersive" theater), even, she mentions, "before I had the chance to understand." Besides having the freedom to look about the space, in fact, the only real agency the audience member has is removing the VR headset and ending the performance.

Besides control over the audience's perspective, an equally important reason for recording the CSC production in this way was, according to Maler, to eliminate the perceived boundary between play and playgoer— that is, to produce that sense of *proximity* by eliding the two frames of the audience's experience: "You're not watching the art, you're *in* the art."[5] This impetus to collapse the boundary between play and play-goer was not merely an attempt to transform the individual spectator's experience; rather, a broader political objective lay behind the choice, an attempt, Maler hopes, to "truly democratize Shakespeare and theater."[6] In this motivation, *Hamlet 360* speaks to one of the more familiar tensions that exists for Shakespeare productions across media and periods: producers' desire to provide a recognizably "Shakespearean" performance but also remove potential barriers that might intimidate new audiences or disincentivize them from experiencing that performance. The solution to that problem as pursued by *Hamlet 360* was to use new technologies to erase the literal barrier between the audience and the play, between the spaces of production and reception. As Maler put it, "what gives this project so much potential [is that] it changes the experience of a story that has been told for 400 years" because it puts the audience "in the space where it's happening."[7]

Hamlet 360's use of technology to collapse the boundaries between performance and audience foregrounds the dynamic relationship between these two entities that was at the heart of early theatrical performance, as influentially theorized by Robert Weimann (see Valerie Fazel's Chapter 11 in this volume).[8] In fact, *Hamlet 360* recalls the very nature of the word "audience" itself in the two main senses that Shakespeare himself used. The more familiar usage today, though the one he uses least often, describes one or more people who pay attention to an event. This includes specifically theatrical audiences, as in *A Midsummer Night's Dream*—when Bottom warns, "let the audience look to their eyes" (1.2.22)—and in *Love's Labour's Lost*—when Moth is worried "if any of the audience [will] hiss" (5.1.129) at the pageant of the Nine Worthies. The most prevalent use of "audience" in the plays, however, is not as a noun describing a person or group of people who observe an event but as a noun describing a quality *given* by those people. Repeatedly, Shakespeare frames the granting of "audience"—that is, formal attention to or engagement with another's words and actions—as an active gesture in which the person or people who "give" the audience are the ones empowered with agency: "Give me audience," insists Celia in *As You Like It* (3.2.231); "We'll give them present audience," accedes the King of France in *Henry V* (2.4.67); "Then follow me, and give me audience, friends," invites Brutus in *Julius Caesar* (3.2.2); "Let me have audience," demands Philip the Bastard in *King John* (5.2.119). As Stephen Purcell notes of these usages, for Shakespeare, "'audience' is something that one can give and receive, promise or withhold. It is active. It is processual. It is an item of exchange and part of a transaction … [It] is the first act in a pact of complicity."[9] This sense of "audience" as something actively given, rather than just passively "experienced," captures the dialogic nature of the relationship between playmaker and playgoer, between producer and consumer, in Shakespeare's theatrical context. Shakespeare wrote for a theater in which the audience was understood to be, and at times invited to be, dynamic and participatory, and performances of his plays after his time and in very different media have to engage with that genetic identity in the plays. As Sarah Werner so precisely puts it, "audiences are made by performers, and … performances are made by audiences."[10] Put another way, the conventional, transactional view of the playmaker as the "giver" and the playgoer as the "receiver" is too unidirectional and unilateral: to Shakespeare, it was the playgoer who was the "giver" of "audience" and the playmaker who was the "receiver."

This idea of "audience" as something given presumes, then, a particular bond or shared identity between the giver and the receiver in the theatrical event—Shakespeare's use of the term "audience," after all, requires that the two categories of "giver" and "receiver" themselves collapse into one another. Shakespeare implies this sense of shared identity, for example, when the Gentleman in *The Winter's Tale* reports that the reconciliation of Sicilia and Bohemia "was worth the audience of kings and princes, for by such was it acted" (5.2.78–9). In this, then, *Hamlet 360* simply makes manifest in a particularly vivid way the underlying presumption of audience–play proximity underwriting all performances of Shakespeare's plays. This understanding of the audience and its encounter with the play animates many of the questions pursued by scholars of Shakespeare's audiences, both in the early modern period and since. How have Shakespeare's audiences, from the sixteenth century to the present, responded to the invitation, or expectation, to be active, participatory, and proximal? In what ways have consumers, across different cultural contexts, periods, and platforms, engaged with the performance of Shakespeare's plays in ways that relate to their status as participants? What are some of the different approaches taken by scholars in thinking about the role of Shakespeare's audiences and their relationships to performance?

In order to show how some scholars have responded to these, and related, questions, *Shakespeare's Audiences* brings together a wide-ranging collection of chapters exploring Shakespeare's audiences from the sixteenth through the twenty-first centuries and across a range of platforms, including theater, radio, film, and online. The chapters in this volume turn a spotlight on the consumers of Shakespearean productions, their understanding of and engagements with those productions, and the relationships between production choices and audience experience. Written by a diverse group of scholars, teachers, and practitioners, the chapters draw upon a variety of methods and approaches, including theater history, dramaturgy, fan studies, popular culture, and performance studies. They provide both close analysis of particular moments and people in the history of Shakespeare's audiences and a broader perspective on the various, often complex, connections between and among those audiences. Some of the contributors employ an empirical approach, drawing on data from audience surveys, interviews, observation, and other tools, while others turn to the historical record, reviews, and the plays themselves. This diversity of topics and methodologies is intentional: rather than presume there is only one way to study Shakespeare's audiences, this volume highlights how different approaches can yield different but equally important insights. As Purcell argues, the different ways scholars go about studying audiences are "not so much in opposition to one another as in negotiation."[11] Besides responding to different performance platforms, periods, and cultural contexts, this diversity of scholarship in the study of Shakespeare's audiences (explored further below) reflects the nature of audience experience itself. Even in a production like *Hamlet 360*, in which the audience is constrained to a particular position on stage, each audience member is free to look about the space and, in doing so, to choose to attend to or ignore the place where the action is occurring. There are as many different ways of understanding or making meaning out of a performance as there are spectators watching it. This multiplicity is reflected in the perennial challenge of audience studies in distinguishing between the audience as an individual entity and the audience as a collective entity. It is a primary contention of this volume that only by giving voice to a diversity of scholarly approaches to the study of Shakespeare's audiences can we hope to understand something that is itself as fundamentally diverse as Shakespeare's audiences.

Studying Shakespeare's Audiences

In 2009, Helen Freshwater lamented that scholarly studies of theater audiences were "relatively few and far between," but there now exists a compelling and ever-growing body of work on the subject, surveyed most recently by Kirsty Sedgman in two important articles.[12] Scholars in the field are developing innovative ways to confront the various hurdles such work faces, including the scarcity and idiosyncratic nature of evidence, as well as what Christopher Balme identifies as the different kinds of disciplinary expertise required to analyze that evidence:

To study the spectator individually or collectively implies a shift from interpreting an aesthetic object to studying the cognitive and emotional responses of actual human beings. This is the field of empirical psychology and sociology, and most theatre scholars do not possess this kind of scholarly background and training.

However, as Balme goes on to argue, and as we concur, "the gulf is not ... unbridgeable."[13] As the various methodologies adopted by the contributors to this volume show, the study of Shakespeare's audiences is influenced by the same multiplicity that informs all studies of audiences and is engaged in the kind of disciplinary bridging called for by Balme. As Ben Walmsley notes, "audience research remains a loose and fragmented field that lacks not only a scholarly home but also a coherent set of questions and principles around which scholars might cohere;" though, as Sedgman observes, the 2017 formation of the International Network for Audience Research in the Performing Arts is just one indication of the increasing importance of audience research as an interdisciplinary field that combines different forms of expertise.[14] We embrace that multivalence as one of the particular strengths of the field. Audience studies remains diffuse and diverse because of the many different ways by which scholars carry out such studies and the subjects and questions around which such studies can focus. As Walmsley urges, no matter where scholars position themselves in the "currently fractured community of academics cohered loosely around audience research," it is essential that we all "engage more authentically and rigorously with audiences" through scholarship "that respects audiences and engages with them actively and on equal terms."[15]

The study of Shakespeare's audiences as a specific subset has overlapped with, but has frequently not learned enough from, audience studies scholarship, and it is worth briefly interrogating the other word in this book's title. The anachronistic exceptionalism of Shakespeare, in both academia and cultural industries, leads to the works of Shakespeare and their afterlives often being discussed and reinvented primarily in relation to themselves and dominated by the critical methodologies of the literary-historical disciplines within which Shakespeare is still primarily taught. But while Shakespeare's plays certainly had audiences in their own time, there was (and remains) no such thing as a "Shakespearean audience," insofar as Shakespeare's works made up (and continue to make up) only a tiny proportion of the cultural offerings available to audiences. Even to speak of "early modern audiences" is to risk engaging in homogenization. The global cultural ubiquity of Shakespeare, however, has produced an extraordinary body of work across centuries and media, locales and communities, genres and forms, that requires the expertise and tools of multiple disciplines to comprehend fully. Our choice to focus on "Shakespeare" allows us to bring together approaches from multiple disciplines to audiences across a wide spectrum of performance, providing the volume with one—indeed, the only—consistent variable across all of its contributions. It is not our contention that there is some singular transcendent experience shared by all of Shakespeare's audiences. Indeed, quite the opposite: the very ubiquity that qualifies Shakespeare's audiences as the subject of our study renders it impossible to claim for those audiences some totalizing or universalizing quality; rather, Shakespeare's audiences can only be understood in their specific, diverse, and localized contexts.

The study of Shakespeare's audiences has undergone tremendous shifts and developments over the past century, reflecting changes in how scholars understand and analyze different kinds of evidence as well as the increasing range of contexts, periods, and platforms of performance they address. Not surprisingly, the earliest aspect of Shakespeare's audience investigated by scholars—such as Alfred Harbage, Michael Neill, Ann Jennalie Cook, Martin Butler, Andrew Gurr, and Leo Salingar—centered on trying to determine who comprised Shakespeare's original audiences and what their playgoing experience involved.[16] These historical studies typically turn to textual references and archival records to answer questions such as: What type of people attended what playhouse? How often? In what numbers? What did they do there? Even drawing on largely the same limited body of evidence to answer these questions, these scholars often arrived at very different conclusions. Cook was correct when she noted that the task of understanding who was in the original audience remains a "vexed" one: "Part of the difficulty derives from lack of evidence, part from inadequate interpretation of the limited evidence available, and part from the subordination of evidence to preconceptions about those who attended performances."[17] The work of these scholars, and others who have taken up such questions, resulted in debates about the extent to which socioeconomic status, educational background, and other factors shaped which playhouses particular audience members attended and thus the nature of the plays that were written for those audiences. While some scholars maintain that variables such as status or education corresponded with particular theatrical tastes or capacities to understand or appreciate certain kinds of content, others challenge such interpretations as reductive, and still others contend that the paucity of evidence renders any general conclusions about the audience unreliably idiosyncratic or speculative.[18]

Growing caution over generalizations based on the limited historical accounts of audience behavior has led in recent years to more focused micro-histories of specific subsets of audience behavior and what that behavior might reveal about the audience's expectations and experiences, as in Matteo Pangallo's study of plays written by dedicated playgoers who had no prior experience as playwrights or actors, or Tiffany Stern's consideration of note-taking done by particular playgoers, as well as to carefully contextualized analysis of documented responses, as in the work of Charles Whitney and Richard Preiss.[19] On the other hand, much work on audiences has looked instead to evidence in the plays themselves. Literary critics, particularly those trained in New Historicism, have long turned to claims about audience response that depend upon the imagined or desired audience of the playwright—or, more precisely, the critic. This was in part component to New Historicism's objective of recuperating literary texts as sources of historical agency. In this approach, the audience is taken to be reflected in, or even controlled by, the play, which suits well if the subject of study is the text and its assumptions about the audience rather than the person or people who actually experienced a performance of the text. Scholars who adopt this approach, however, typically assume that in a commercial playhouse, such as Shakespeare's, there must be considerable similarity between, on the one hand, what the play reveals about audience experience and response, and, on the other, what the actual audience experienced and how they responded: a savvy playwright like Shakespeare, who had a financial interest in satisfying the audience and providing it with an experience it could understand, might reasonably be expected to write plays that would reflect the desires, expectations, and experiences of that audience. This is an approach that, as Purcell puts it, is "concerned not with what audiences *usually* do but with what they *ought* to do."[20] It empowers the playwright as an agent exercising some manner of manipulation or, more generously, "orchestration" over the audience to control and constrain its responses to and understanding of the play. In Shakespeare studies, such engagement with the imagined, or anticipated, audience is one of the oldest approaches to studying the "audience," with roots in the work of Arthur Colby Sprague and Maynard Mack.[21] The key value of this strand of work—exemplified in books like E. A. J. Honigmann's *Shakespeare: Seven Tragedies: The Dramatist's Manipulation of Response*, Jean Howard's *Shakespeare's Art of Orchestration: Stage Technique and Audience Response*, Jeremy Lopez's *Theatrical Convention and Audience Response in Early Modern Drama*, and Darlene Farabee's *Shakespeare's Staged Spaces and Playgoers' Perceptions*—is their interrogation of how the structures and conventions of the drama seek to shape their own reception, and work of this kind has done much to recuperate the plays as theatrical texts that have their audience in mind from inception.[22]

A focus on the text can risk rendering audiences themselves passive, however, and throughout history and scholarship the audience has frequently been a convenient scapegoat for narratives of failure and blame, as demonstrated by Bettina Boecker.[23] Indeed, deprecation of an unappreciative audience seems to have been a selling point for early publishers of plays by Francis Beaumont, Shakespeare, John Webster, and other early modern playwrights, where audiences are described as having "want of iudgement" or are characterized as "the vulger" or "ignorant asses."[24] No playwright perhaps did more to cultivate a hostile relationship with the theatrical audience, and so distinguish it from the reading public, than Ben Jonson, who, for example, famously characterized the audience of his failed *The New Inn* (1629) as "malicious spectators" who "squeamishly beheld" the play but could not, in his view, understand it because they were preoccupied with their intention to "possesse the Stage, against the Play": as the epigraph on the octavo's title-page proclaims (borrowing from Horace), "*me lectori credere mallem: / Quàm spectatoris fastidia ferre superbi*" ("I prefer to entrust myself to a reader rather than to bear the disdain of a scornful spectator").[25] In the hands of a writer or publisher with a narrative to pursue, the unseen and imagined audience becomes a malleable projection of desire. It was Jonson's style of disdain for the theatrical audience, after all, that implicitly underwrote many modern literary critics' use of the generalized, abstract term "audience" to justify their own, individual approaches to the dramatic texts. As Freshwater cautions, such generalizations "project the subjective responses of the critic on to the rest of the audience, discursively producing the audience the critic would like to imagine rather than accurately reflecting the complexity and potential diversity of collective and individual response."[26] Starting with Moody Prior's 1951 characterization of such "reconstructions" of the audience as "at best an act of embalming," many scholars have argued that, while we might be able to extrapolate from a play what the playwright imagined about the audience, its experiences, and its responses, these are not necessarily the same as what actual audiences experience as that play or how they respond to and understand it and its performance.[27] Or, put another way, there is a distinction between how plays anticipate, solicit, appeal to, or even construct audiences, and the assertion that they therefore also manipulate or orchestrate audiences. Nova Myhill and Jennifer Low offer a useful rubric for understanding the distinction between the two approaches by returning to the question of whether we are attempting to understand a collective unit ("audience") or a variegated mass of individuals ("audiences"): "These terms, then, represent fundamentally different understandings of what happens in the theater, with the former privileging the performative authority of the play and the latter the interpretive authority of the playgoer."[28] The work of recuperating a sense of how particular audience members—Low and Myhill's "audiences"—responded to and actively engaged with early modern performances characterizes the work of Preiss, Pangallo, and others, including the contributors to Low and Myhill's *Imagining the Audience in Early Modern Drama, 1558–1642*, as well as Allison Hobgood in her *Passionate Playgoing in Early Modern England*, which explicitly responds to New Historicism's "sometimes inflexible demand for archival documentation of literary-historical phenomena" by addressing the kinds of experience that are not part of textual record.[29] Such approaches seek to understand the effects that audience members have on plays and their performances, the ways in which those effects are produced, and the extent to which they are *understood* to be produced.

These methodological debates continue to characterize research on later audiences for Shakespeare performance, and the tension between the projected experience of an idealized/imagined audience, the critical generalization and often dismissal of audiences as collectives, and the experience of real individual audience members drives many of the most important questions.[30] The opening of Shakespeare's Globe in 1997 generated a fresh wave of interest in audience research for several reasons. That theater's extensive documentation of audience response and investment in embedded audience researchers generated substantial bodies of archival material and case studies that sought to understand audience members' experiences in their own words.[31] But the visibility of the audiences in that open-air, shared-light theater also made visible assumptions and prejudices about audiences. Paul Prescott analyzes the ways in which theater reviewers speak disparagingly of other audience members in the space of the Globe, critiquing observed behavior as an assertion of their own cultural superiority.[32] These overt critiques expose a previously much more concealed set of assumptions about how audiences (should) behave in the theater. The classist, sexist, racist, and ableist underpinnings of these assumptions have been tackled most recently by Sedgman.[33] This renewed attention to the ways in which audience behaviors influence the theatrical event, and how these behaviors are in turn read and used to uphold entrenched prejudices, have added urgency to the need for rigor in the ways in which we discuss audiences.

At a fundamental level, this fresh attention to actual audiences has led to more specificity about who is speaking as the audience and on behalf of the audience. Anthony Dawson and Paul Yachnin's *The Culture of Playgoing in Shakespeare's England: A Collaborative Debate* is framed as a debate over whether playgoing was an individualized experience (Yachnin's view) or a collectivized one (Dawson's) in the early modern period, and that debate continues.[34] Not only is every production different from every other, every live performance of that production is different from every other performance of that production, and every member of the audience of those performances experiences and therefore understands that performance in different ways; the journal *Cahiers Élisabéthains* even asks its theater reviewers to specify from which area of the auditorium they viewed the performance. Werner observes,

> One of the hallmarks of live theatre is that we experience it collectively: as a collective of performers and a collective of spectators ... The presence of other spectators and their audible responses shapes how we, in turn, respond, whether our reactions are the same or different from those surrounding us.[35]

At the same time, despite this collective nature, as Freshwater points out, "the responses of theatre audiences are rarely unified or stable" and, indeed, even "a single person can experience multiple responses to a show."[36] A small but significant shift in scholarly practice has been increased caution of the use of the pronoun "we" to refer to an audience of which one is a part, acknowledging that while "we" may be watching the same performance, allowing "my" interpretation of that performance to stand for "our" interpretation risks co-opting the collective to support an individual view without basis. This is especially important in the use of historical reviews as representative of audience experience, when (as Paul Prescott's important study demonstrates), the reviewer is only one kind of audience member, and a specialized rather than representative one at that.[37]

Much recent work on audiences, including that in this volume, has thus pursued increasing specificity about how it speaks for and about audiences. For many scholars, this involves positioning oneself more clearly as a subjective theatergoer, as modeled by Bridget Escolme's work, which uses the experience of contemporary performance of Shakespeare as a guide to understanding how the plays seek to engage the faculties of the spectator.[38] Other work has seen Shakespeare performance scholars embracing more fully empirical methods of performance studies through surveys, observations, and other forms of data gathering, as in the work of John Tulloch, Penelope Woods, Stephen Purcell, Rachael Nicholas, Erin Sullivan, and the contributors to Fiona Banks's *Shakespeare: Actors & Audiences*.[39] Quantitative data, of course, is not neutral, and Ayanna Thompson has argued for the importance of deep engagements and open dialogues alongside "larger and more systematic comparative analyses [of] audience surveys."[40] Increasing attention to the ways in which audience members describe their own experiences, and to the compilation of substantial sets of data, enables deeper studies of specific subsets of audiences, as in Evelyn O'Malley's work on audiences of outdoor Shakespeare and in the ever-growing body of work on the local reception of global Shakespeare productions, including in many of the contributions to Tina Krontiris and Jyotsna Singh's *Shakespeare Worldwide and the Idea of an Audience*, Aneta Mancewicz and Alexa Alice Joubin's *Local and Global Myths in Shakespearean Performance*, and Christy Desmet, Sujata Iyengar, and Miriam Jacobson's *The Routledge Handbook of Shakespeare and Global Appropriation*.[41] Finally, the advent of new technologies for the performance and reception of Shakespeare—on screens and online—has catalyzed scholarship about Shakespeare's audiences beyond the theatrical context and furthered the shift from treatments of the audience as receptors of performance to the audience as an active "user," in the preferred term of Louise Geddes and Valerie Fazel.[42] Works such as those of Aneta Mancewicz and Pascale Aebischer have examined the ways in which the integration of new technologies in theatrical performance has dramatically altered the relationship of audiences to performances, while attention to the behaviors of viewers and fans in digital spaces, as in the work of Fazel, Geddes, and the contributors to Stephen O'Neill's *Broadcast Your Shakespeare*, has expanded the definitions of audience agency to include creativity and re-performance.[43]

As this tremendous and dynamic body of work suggests, to speak of a singular "Shakespearean audience" is a fallacy—hence the plural form in our title. Shakespeare's audiences vary by venue, cultural context, performance medium, demographic, historical period, and a host of other factors. Audience experiences of and responses to Shakespeare in performance are also inherently self-aware and performative themselves, shaped in significant ways by preconceptions about the cultural role of a "Shakespearean audience" and assumptions about what that role involves in a given context of performance; Pauline Kiernan, W. B. Worthen, and Sarah Werner, for example, note this phenomenon in audiences at the reconstructed Globe, while Purcell has argued that it characterizes the experiences of all audiences.[44] Because of this diversity of audiences, then, and the diversity of variables that combine to produce the experiences of audiences and individual audience members, the study of Shakespeare's audiences requires a complementary diversity of approaches, methods, and techniques. While acknowledging that, for this reason, no one book can be exhaustive, *Shakespeare's Audiences* aims to model the kinds of conversations that can emerge by bringing some of these approaches and interests together.

Structure of the Volume

The chapters of this book are organized into four sections, each defined broadly by one particular focus or approach rather than by period or performance media. This design allows us to place in proximity the work of scholars who study audiences in different media and across different periods but who share common sets of questions or come to similar conclusions about those audiences. Our intention with this arrangement is to highlight some of the continuities and discontinuities that arise not only across audiences in different historical moments and of different performance platforms but also across different approaches to the study of those audiences. In keeping with the disciplinary variety described above, some of the following chapters explore how audiences shape the performance, while others explore how the performance shapes—or aspires to shape—the audience. Some chapters consider the aspirational audiences for whom performances are created and others consider the actual audiences who responded to those performances. In all of these sections, our authors consider audiences as both active and responsive participants—as both producers who shape plays and consumers whose experiences are shaped by plays—because audiences are both of these at once. The contributors' methodologies are varied in order to demonstrate some of the different approaches that can be taken to studying the audience and include empirical case studies from direct observation, analyses of audience feedback and response, extrapolations of audiences from textual references, historical reconstructions based on archival evidence, and the application of multidisciplinary concepts in fields cognate and relevant to audience studies.

The first section, "Embodied Audiences," features three chapters that draw upon different categories of evidence to re-create the bodily experiences of Shakespeare's audiences, including the pneumatic, the sensory, and the spatial and kinetic. In this, the authors in this section contribute to an approach to audience studies that recognizes how, as Freshwater puts it, "audience members bring their whole bodies with them into the auditorium, not just their eyes."[45] Stephanie Shirilan considers the embodied bond between playgoer and player, as well as between playgoer and playgoer, through the medium of the very air they collectively inhale and exhale in the playhouse, proposing that the connection formed by that shared, breathed atmosphere mattered to Shakespeare and matters to his audience, and that the audience itself plays an essential role in defining and discerning that atmosphere and its effects. The audience member's embodied experience is also central to Joe Falocco's chapter, in which ideas about audience involvement often associated with modern "original practices" performances are connected to early modern humoral theory through the use of new and emerging research in affect studies and cognitive neuroscience—a disciplinary linkage that scientists and scholars such as Richard Ralley, Roy Connolly, and Bruce McConachie have shown to be particularly effective in discerning audience experience and understanding.[46] Finally, drawing on a 2011 performance of *Macbeth* at Joan Brehms's revolving theater in the Czech town of Český Krumlov, Jennifer Low observes the challenge to the border of performance created by a physical arrangement of audience and stage in which the seated audience turns about and the "stage" is the indefinite circumference of space around it. Low uses her own embodied experience to call attention to the various ways mobility, stability, and sensory experiences such as momentum and nausea inflect the dramatic and political meanings audiences might make from a play. All three chapters remind us that Shakespeare's audiences experience the plays in physical ways that complicate the simplistic and oft-repeated etymological binary of *audiences* as "hearers" and *spectators* as "seers"; as Bernard Beckerman puts it, "an audience does not see with its eyes but with its lungs, does not hear with its ears but with its skin."[47]

The subsequent three sections offer a broad progression from the audiences anticipated by a text or production to the experiences of actual audience members. Section 2, "Constructing Audiences," features four chapters exploring performances and performance contexts that anticipate and seek to shape both the composition of the audience and the nature of its response. In this, these chapters build upon the media studies idea of "audiencing"— introduced by John Fiske and advanced and modified by Pertti Alasuutari—which recognizes how audiences are themselves discursive products of, and responses to, particular social, cultural, commercial, and aesthetic systems.[48] The section opens with a return to Shakespeare's original audiences in Romola Nuttall's investigation of the role played by the Inns of Court as centers of literary and theatrical taste, as well as commercial patronage, that helped shape plays written for the professional London theaters, including Shakespeare's

Titus Andronicus. Nuttall demonstrates the ways in which playwrights sought to capitalize on the desires of specific communities of interest and, in doing so, cultivate new and returning audiences. The cultivation of audiences is central also to Miles Drawdy's chapter, which turns to radio audiences of the early twentieth century. Looking to casting strategies, marketing, reviews, and listeners' responses, Drawdy explores how the competing CBS and NBC 1937 radio productions of Shakespeare attempted—and failed—to construct two mutually exclusive audiences. In a transcultural approach to the study of Shakespeare's audiences that recalls John Tulloch's point that audiences form processual relationships with the performance "across a changing temporality before, during, and (sometimes long) after the performance," Koel Chatterjee turns to Indian, especially Bollywood, film adaptations of *Romeo and Juliet* in order to understand how traditions of reception, informed by popular media and postcolonial legacies, can shape audience responses to Shakespeare.[49] Finally, Pascale Aebischer closes the section with the broadcast of Phyllida Lloyd's 2017 Donmar Warehouse production of *Julius Caesar*, taking up Walter Benjamin's concept of the "aura" in mechanical reproductions of art, as well as other performance and audience theories, to critique the use of particular camera angles and shot compositions as methods for encoding and framing performances of Shakespearean femininity for a majority female broadcast audience. Across a range of historical periods, these chapters demonstrate how an audience's "horizon of expectations," to use the term adapted by Susan Bennet from the work of Hans Robert Jauss, might be shaped consciously and subconsciously by the choices and strategies of cultural industries.[50]

The contributors to the third section, "Performing Audiences," expose some of the creative and disruptive ways audiences respond independently of a production's intentions. In looking at traces left by audiences in property destruction and event disruption, newspaper and stage management reports, and discursive creative play, these chapters feature audiences who stake a claim to their own identity and agency, reminding us of the limited extent to which audience behavior can be anticipated. Audience disruption and disorder often feature in studies that see the audience as a site for both public debate and aesthetic creativity.[51] As scholars such as Richard Rowland and Eric Dunnum have shown, troublesome audience behavior resulting in productive, if unanticipated, meaning dates back to the early modern playhouses.[52] The section begins with Edel Lamb revisiting the infamous 1849 Astor Place riots to unpack the ways disorderly audience responses do not merely interrupt performance but also interact with and shape the presentation of the play and thus function as a crucial part of the theatrical event. The audience's ability to stop the show, and to appropriate elements of the performance for its own ends, speaks to a counter-history of co-option of Shakespeare. Looking at a similar history of contests over the Shakespearean performance in the twentieth century, Adam Sheaffer draws upon theories about the ecology of performance and play, as well as the phenomenology of performance spaces and their topographies, to read the volatile audience responses encountered by the New York Shakespeare Festival's Mobile Theater unit as it toured neighborhood and community spaces around the city between 1964 and 1968. Sheaffer's work is a timely reminder that outreach and community work must understand the needs and desires of its stakeholders to be effective. The section ends by shifting to the creative behaviors of audiences, as Louise Geddes explores how digital culture has encouraged creative practices in which Shakespeare fans imagine and circulate speculative performances that combine the plays' characters with references to wider popular culture, effectively producing new, fan-made performative iterations of the plays. In these chapters, the playgoer whom the authors bring to the center of our attention is Bennett's "productive and emancipated spectator" whose agency ensures that "it is the audience which finally ascribes meaning and usefulness to any cultural product."[53]

In the final section, "Observing Audiences," we move to chapters that demonstrate how direct observation can provide insights into the nature of the reception-response of members of Shakespeare's audiences as well as their capacity to transform the reception experience of other members of the audience through those responses. Valerie Fazel starts the section with a digital studies approach that bridges with performance studies. Mapping Robert Weimann's critical terms for the imaginative (*locus*) and interactive (*platea*) spaces of the early modern theater onto YouTube's dynamic interface, Fazel explores how viewers' comments on YouTube videos of Shakespeare performances influence other viewers' reception of those videos and, by extension, of Shakespeare as well. Fazel's approach allows her to observe responses from global audiences; by contrast, Rachael Nicholas's chapter provides a deep exploration of a localized performance, watching the students of a UK secondary school audience as they watch the 2018 RSC Schools' Broadcast of the company's 2017 production of *Twelfth Night*. Nicholas uses observations of those audience members and their social media reactions to the broadcast to call attention to the different agents exercising control—or failing to exercise control—over the reception experience of the student audience and thus to how these novice audiences might be learning to understand and ultimately value Shakespeare. Finally, taking up an essential conversation that includes Ayanna Thompson, Lauren Eriks Cline, and others, Emily Lathrop brings our attention to the effect for audiences of considerations of race in the casting of Shakespeare performances through a case study of the Public Theatre's 2019 Mobile Unit production of *Measure for Measure*, performed by a cast of Black women.[54] Drawing on primary evidence from audience observation and interviews, as well as reviews, marketing materials, and production member interviews, Lathrop unpacks how the shift from "colorblind" to "color-conscious" casting practices affected audience experience of and response to the production. These chapters thus demonstrate different ways of observing Shakespeare's audiences as they both incorporate dominant cultural values and meanings encoded in performances and also resist those values and meanings through oppositional readings of their own.[55]

Each of these sections is not mutually exclusive of the others, and readers will find many productive overlaps between and across the sections. For example, though separated by over four hundred years, both Nicholas and Nuttall consider the role that educational contexts have upon student audiences of Shakespeare in performance. Both Low and Fazel engage with the relationship of space to the dynamics of audience experience and engagement—Low in a theatrical setting and Fazel in the digital domain. Lathrop and Sheaffer examine audience responses to productions by one company—the Mobile Unit of what was once the New York Shakespeare Festival and later became The Public Theater—at two very different points in the company's history. In addition, many of the chapters could fit into a different section of the book than the one in which they appear; for example, Falocco's argument regarding "emotional contagion" in the audiences of original practice performances is another example of the kind of audience member influence upon other audience members discussed elsewhere in the volume. Similarly, the violent, physical audience responses described by Lamb in her analysis of the Astor Place riots also speaks to a kind of embodied audience experience similar to those explored by the contributors to the first section.

Such intersections demonstrate some of the ways that different scholarly approaches to Shakespeare's audiences can speak to each other across such a diverse subject. In this, *Shakespeare's Audiences* considers how we can bring, to use Purcell's terms, "practical research" about the audience off "the periphery of Shakespeare studies" and situate it as a central part of the field.[56] As the scholarly body of literature surveyed in this introduction and drawn upon by our contributors suggests, much has changed since Tulloch asserted that "Shakespeare scholars have been surprisingly shy of devising methodologies and concepts to approach the actual audience."[57] In place of such shyness, by the start of the second decade of the twenty-first century, Shakespeare scholars have employed a robust, diverse, and rich range of approaches to engage with and better understand Shakespeare's audiences, whether contemporary or historical, conceptual or actual. Our hope is that *Shakespeare's Audiences* will serve as an invitation for future scholarship in this important, ever-growing, and wide-ranging field of study.

Postscript

During the final stages of preparing this volume, the world was upended by the global COVID-19 pandemic. The nature of audience experience—whether of Shakespeare's plays or those of any dramatist—radically and instantly changed as live theaters closed their doors. A pervasive refrain in the press and on social media became the comparison of these closures to the closures of playhouses in early modern London during plague outbreaks. Theater historians have a fairly good understanding of how players and playwrights survived those sudden stoppages: downsizing troupes, going on tours of the provinces, pawning off props and costumes, selling scripts to stationers, pleading with patrons for a subsistence gift, writing poetry or pamphlets rather than plays. What we do not know—indeed, cannot know—is what the *audience* response was to those closures.[58] How did early modern playgoers register the abrupt and indefinite lack of one of their customary, if not primary, forms of recreation and entertainment?

While it is impossible, without more evidence, to answer such a question, we might find a parallel audience experience to our own historical moment by looking to the provinces, where the London troupes went on tour. Just as audiences during the present pandemic closures are turning to recorded online broadcasts of past performances or livestreams of physically distanced performers over videoconferencing platforms such as Zoom, provincial audiences suddenly found London performers on their very doorsteps. Thanks to the work of scholars and historians, such as the editors of the *Records of Early English Drama*, we know that audiences consumed and interacted with those performances in a wide range of spaces and contexts around their localities, from the churchyard to the local inn and from the mayor's house to the marketplace. It would be extending the metaphor too far to claim that such closeness between the provincial playgoer and the play replicates what, for example, Sofía Barrell experienced while watching *Hamlet 360*, with Hamlet "inches from [her] face." Nonetheless, in both situations, the quick and unexpected transition to new performance platforms brought about a further development in what it means for Shakespeare's audiences to be in fundamental and meaningful proximity to Shakespeare's plays. The contributors to a special issue of *Shakespeare Bulletin* on "Lockdown Shakespeare" speak eloquently of experiences of togetherness in isolation, of being part of an online audience community while wearing pajamas, of experiencing intimacy and proximity with a screen while being separated from both performers and other audience members in both space and time.[59] Such juxtapositions and paradoxes, experienced intellectually, emotionally, and bodily, attest to the importance of the kind of attention shown by the contributors to *Shakespeare's Audiences* to the dynamic and symbiotic relationship between audiences and performances. As Shakespeare's audiences have changed and continue to change, Shakespeare's works themselves, always in proximity with the audience even when "socially distant," likewise transform. No understanding of those works can therefore be complete without an understanding also of their audiences—their needs, their experiences, and their contributions to the performance of Shakespeare's plays.

Notes

1 Sofía Barrell, "What Dreams May Come: A VR *Hamlet* Puts Us in the Room," *American Theatre*, January 25, 2019. www.americantheatre.org/2019/01/25/what-dreams-may-come-a-vr-hamlet-puts-us-in-the-room/.

2 The interactive video of *Hamlet 360* can be viewed, with or without a VR headset, at www.wgbh.org/hamlet360. *Hamlet 360* is not the first production to use immersive virtual reality to present a theatrical performance; indeed, an earlier VR *Hamlet*, "To Be With Hamlet," was produced in 2017 (http://hamletvr.org).

3 On "outer" and "inner" frames of audience experience, and how the audience makes meaning at the "points of intersection" between the two, see Susan Bennett, *Theatre Audiences*, 2nd ed. (London: Routledge, 1997), 1–2 and 139.

4 Quoted in Barrell, "What Dreams May Come." Emphasis added.

5 Quoted in Barrell, "What Dreams May Come."

6 Quoted in Elizabeth Harris, "*Hamlet* in Virtual Reality Casts the Viewer in the Play," *The New York Times*, January 25, 2019.

7 Quoted in Harris, "*Hamlet* in Virtual Reality."

8 Robert Weimann, *Shakespeare and the Popular Tradition,* trans. Robert Schwartz (Baltimore: Johns Hopkins University Press, 1978).

9 Stephen Purcell, *Shakespeare & Audience in Practice* (Basingstoke: Palgrave Macmillan, 2013), xiii.

10 Sarah Werner, "Audiences," in *Shakespeare and the Making of Theatre*, eds. Stuart Hampton-Reeves and Bridget Escolme (New York: Palgrave Macmillan, 2012), 179.

11 Purcell, *Shakespeare & Audience*, 41.

12 Helen Freshwater, *Theatre & Audience* (Basingstoke: Palgrave Macmillan, 2009), 11; Kirsty Sedgman, "Audience Experience in an Anti-Expert Age: A Survey of Theatre Audience Research," *Theatre Research International* 42, no. 3 (2017): 307–22; Sedgman, "On Rigour in Theatre Audience Research," *Contemporary Theatre Review* 29, no. 4 (2019): 462–79.

13 Christopher Balme, *The Cambridge Introduction to Theatre Studies* (Cambridge: Cambridge University Press, 2008), 34–5.

14 Ben Walmsley, *Audience Engagement in the Performing Arts* (Cham: Palgrave Macmillan, 2019), 25; Sedgman, "On Rigour," 463.

15 Walmsley, *Audience Engagement*, 20.

16 Alfred Harbage, *Shakespeare's Audience* (New York: Columbia University Press, 1941); Michael Neill, "'Wit's Most Accomplished Senate': The Audience of the Caroline Private Theaters," *Studies in English Literature, 1500–1900* 18, no. 2 (Spring 1978): 341–60; Ann Jennalie Cook, *The Privileged Playgoers of Shakespeare's London, 1576–1642* (Princeton: Princeton University Press, 1981); Martin Butler, *Theatre and Crisis, 1632–1642* (Cambridge: Cambridge University Press, 1984); Leo Salingar, "Jacobean Playwrights and 'Judicious' Spectators," *Renaissance Drama* 22 (1991): 209–34; Andrew Gurr, *Playgoing in Shakespeare's London*, 3rd ed. (Cambridge: Cambridge University Press, 2004).

17 Ann Jennalie Cook, "Audiences: Investigation, Interpretation, Invention," in *A New History of Early English Drama*, eds. John Cox and David Scott Kastan (New York: Columbia University Press, 1997), 305.

18 On the debate about the "two audiences" idea of the early modern audience, see Cook, "Audiences," 315–20, and Eoin Price, *"Public" and "Private" Playhouses in Renaissance England* (Basingstoke: Palgrave Macmillan, 2015); on the problems caused by the fragmentary nature of evidence about playgoers and playgoing, see Nova Myhill and Jennifer Low, "Audience and Audiences," in *Imagining the Audience in Early Modern Drama, 1558–1642*, eds. Jennifer Low and Nova Myhill (New York: Palgrave Macmillan, 2011), 9.

19 Matteo Pangallo, *Playwriting Playgoers in Shakespeare's Theater* (Philadelphia: University of Pennsylvania Press, 2017); Tiffany Stern, "Sermons, Plays and Note-Takers: *Hamlet* Q1 as a 'Noted' Text," *Shakespeare Survey* 66 (2013): 1–23; Charles Whitney, *Early Responses to Renaissance Drama* (Cambridge: Cambridge University Press, 2006); Richard Preiss, *Clowning and Authorship in Early Modern Theatre* (Cambridge: Cambridge University Press, 2014), 18–47.

20 Purcell, *Shakespeare & Audience*, 42; Purcell engages with this in more detail (see 66–73); on its use in studies of the early modern audience, see Pangallo, *Playwriting Playgoers*, 4–8.

21 Arthur Colby Sprague, *Shakespeare and the Audience* (Cambridge, MA: Harvard University Press, 1935); Maynard Mack, "Engagement and Detachment in Shakespeare's Plays," in *Essays on Shakespeare and Elizabethan Drama in Honor of Hardin Craig*, ed. Richard Hosley (Columbia: University of Missouri Press, 1962), 275–96.

22 E. A. J. Honigmann, *Shakespeare: Seven Tragedies* (New York: Barnes and Noble, 1976); Jean Howard, *Shakespeare's Art of Orchestration* (Chicago: University of Illinois Press, 1984); Jeremy Lopez, *Theatrical Convention and Audience Response in Early Modern Drama* (Cambridge: Cambridge University Press, 2002); Darlene Farabee, *Shakespeare's Staged Spaces and Playgoers' Perceptions* (Basingstoke: Palgrave Macmillan, 2014).

23 Bettina Boecker, *Imagining Shakespeare's Original Audience, 1660–2000* (Basingstoke: Palgrave Macmillan, 2015).

24 Francis Beaumont, *The Knight of the Burning Pestle* (London, 1613), A2^r; William Shakespeare, *The famous historie of Troylus and Cresseid* (London, 1609), ¶2; John Webster, *The White Divel* (London, 1612), A2^r.

25 Ben Jonson, *The New Inn* (London, 1631), H1v, *1r, *2v; epigraph translated by Julie Sanders, *"The New Inn*: Textual Essay," in *The Cambridge Edition of the Works of Ben Jonson Online*, eds. David Bevington, Martin Butler, and Ian Donaldson (Cambridge: Cambridge University Press, 2014), accessed September 7, 2020, universitypublishingonline.org/cambridge/benjonson/k/essays/New_Inn_textual_essay/1/.

26 Freshwater, *Theatre & Audience*, 8–9.

27 Moody Prior, "The Elizabethan Audience and the Plays of Shakespeare," *Modern Philology* 49, no. 2 (November 1951): 104.

28 Myhill and Low, "Audience and Audiences," 2.

29 Allison P. Hobgood, *Passionate Playgoing in Early Modern England* (Cambridge: Cambridge University Press, 2013), 3.

30 For an overview of current work on audience research in relation to contemporary Shakespeare performances, see Margaret Jane Kidnie, "The Audience: Receiving and Remaking Experience," in *The Arden Research Handbook to Shakespeare and Contemporary Performance*, eds. Peter Kirwan and Kathryn Prince (London: Bloomsbury, 2021), 38–48.

31 See Christie Carson and Farah Karim-Cooper, eds. *Shakespeare's Globe: A Theatrical Experiment* (Cambridge: Cambridge University Press, 2007); Penelope Woods, *Globe Audiences: Spectatorship and Reconstruction at Shakespeare's Globe* (PhD thesis: Queen Mary, University of London, 2012).

32 Paul Prescott, "Inheriting the Globe: The Reception of Shakespearean Space and Audience in Contemporary Reviewing," in *A Companion to Shakespeare and Performance*, eds. Barbara Hodgdon and W. B. Worthen (Malden, MA: Blackwell, 2005), 359–75.

33 Kirsty Sedgman, *The Reasonable Audience* (Cham: Palgrave, 2018).

34 Anthony Dawson and Paul Yachnin, *The Culture of Playgoing in Shakespeare's England* (Cambridge: Cambridge University Press, 2001).

35 Werner, "Audiences," 177.

36 Freshwater, *Theatre & Audience*, 3, 6.

37 Paul Prescott, *Reviewing Shakespeare* (Cambridge: Cambridge University Press, 2013).

38 Bridget Escolme, *Talking to the Audience: Shakespeare, Performance, Self* (Abingdon: Routledge, 2005).

39 John Tulloch, *Shakespeare and Chekhov in Production and Reception* (Iowa City: University of Iowa Press, 2005); Woods, *Globe Audiences*; Purcell, *Shakespeare & Audience*; Rachael Nicholas, *Encountering Shakespeare Elsewhere* (PhD thesis: University of Roehampton, 2019); Erin Sullivan, "Live to Your Living Room: Streamed Theatre, Audience Experience, and the Globe's *A Midsummer Night's Dream*," *Participations* 17, no. 1 (2020): 92–119; Fiona Banks, ed., *Shakespeare: Actors and Audiences* (New York: Bloomsbury Publishing, 2018).

40 Ayanna Thompson, "(How) Should We Listen to Audiences? Race, Reception, and the Audience Survey," in *The Oxford Handbook of Shakespeare and Performance*, ed. James C. Bulman (Oxford: Oxford University Press, 2017), 168.

41 Evelyn O'Malley, *Weathering Shakespeare* (London: Bloomsbury, 2021); Tina Krontiris and Jyotsna Singh, eds., *Shakespeare Worldwide and the Idea of an Audience* (Thessaloniki: Aristotle University, 2007); Aneta Mancewicz and Alexa Alice Joubin, eds., *Local and Global Myths in Shakespearean Performance* (Cham: Palgrave, 2018); Christy Desmet, Sujata Iyengar, and Miriam Jacobson, eds., *The Routledge Handbook of Shakespeare and Global Appropriation* (London: Routledge, 2020).

42 Valerie M. Fazel and Louise Geddes, eds., *The Shakespeare User* (Cham: Palgrave, 2017).

43 Pascale Aebischer, *Shakespeare, Spectatorship and Technologies of Performance* (Cambridge: Cambridge University Press, 2020); Aneta Mancewicz, *Intermedial Shakespeares on European Stages* (Basingstoke: Palgrave Macmillan, 2014); Valerie M. Fazel and Louise Geddes, *The Shakespeare Multiverse* (London: Routledge, 2021); Stephen O'Neill, ed., *Broadcast Your Shakespeare* (London: Bloomsbury, 2018). See also Pascale Aebischer, Susanne Greenhalgh, and Laurie E. Osborne, eds., *Shakespeare and the "Live" Theatre Broadcast Experience* (London: Bloomsbury, 2018).

44 Pauline Kiernan, *Staging Shakespeare at the New Globe* (Basingstoke: Macmillan, 1999), 28; W. B. Worthen, *Shakespeare and the Force of Modern Performance* (Cambridge: Cambridge University Press, 2003), 25; Werner, "Audiences," 172; Purcell, *Shakespeare & Audience*, 147 and 150.

45 Freshwater, *Theatre & Audience*, 18. On embodied experience in the-
    ater studies research, see Simon Shepherd, *Theatre, Body and Pleasure*
    (Abingdon: Routledge, 2006); Sally Banes and André Lepecki, eds., *The
    Senses in Performance* (Abingdon: Routledge, 2007); Peter Eversmann, "The
    Experience of the Theatrical Event," in *Theatrical Events: Borders, Dynamics,
    Frames*, eds., Vicki Ann Cremona et al. (New York: Rodopi, 2004), 139–74.

46 Richard Ralley and Roy Connolly, "In Front of Our Eyes: Presence and
    the Cognitive Audience," *About Performance* 10 (2010), 51–66; Bruce
    McConachie, *Engaging Audiences* (New York: Palgrave Macmillan, 2008).

47 Bernard Beckerman, *Dynamics of Drama* (New York: Alfred A. Knopf,
    1970), 150.

48 John Fiske, "Audiencing: A Cultural Studies Approach to Watching Television,"
    Poetics 21, no. 4 (August 1992): 345–59; Pertti Alasuutari, "Introduction:
    Three Phases of Reception Studies," in *Rethinking the Media Audience*, ed.
    Pertti Alasuutari (London: Sage, 1999), 6; see also Tulloch, *Shakespeare and
    Chekhov*, 15.

49 Tulloch, *Shakespeare and Chekhov*, 7.

50 Bennett, *Theatre Audiences*, 141.

51 Freshwater, *Theatre & Audience*, 26. On the socially and dramatically pro-
    ductive nature of audience riots, see Neil Blackadder, *Performing Opposition*
    (Westport, CT: Praeger, 2003).

52 Richard Rowland, "(Gentle)Men Behaving Badly: Aggression, Anxiety,
    and Repertory in the Playhouses of Early Modern London," *Medieval and
    Renaissance Drama in England* 25 (2012): 17–41; Eric Dunnum, *Unruly
    Audiences and the Theater of Control in Early Modern London* (London:
    Routledge, 2019).

53 Bennett, *Theatre Audiences*, 1, 156.

54 Ayanna Thompson, *Passing Strange* (Oxford: Oxford University Press, 2011),
    69–96, and "(How) Should We Listen"; Lauren Eriks Cline, "Audiences
    Writing Race in Shakespeare Performance," *Shakespeare Studies* 47 (2019),
    112–19.

55 On these reception strategies, see Stuart Hall, "Encoding/Decoding," in
    Culture, Media, Language, eds. Stuart Hall et al (London: Hutchinson, 1980),
    128–38. On "resistance reading" in the context of Shakespeare's audiences,
    see Tulloch, *Shakespeare and Chekhov*, especially 4–6.

56 Purcell, *Shakespeare & Audience*, 60.

57 Tulloch, *Shakespeare and Chekhov*, 20.

58 For one approach to this problem, however, see Nichole DeWall, "'Sweet rec-
    reation barred': The Case for Playgoing in Plague-Time," in *Representing the
    Plague in Early Modern England*, eds. Rebecca Totaro and Ernest B. Gilman
    (London: Routledge, 2011), 133–49.

59 Peter Kirwan and Erin Sullivan, eds., "Shakespeare in Lockdown," *Shakespeare
    Bulletin* 38, no. 3 (2020).

Bibliography

Aebischer, Pascale. *Shakespeare, Spectatorship and Technologies of Performance.*
    Cambridge: Cambridge University Press, 2020.

Aebischer, Pascale, Susanne Greenhalgh, and Laurie E. Osborne, eds. *Shakespeare
    and the "Live" Theatre Broadcast Experience.* London: Bloomsbury, 2018.

Alasuutari, Pertti. "Introduction: Three Phases of Reception Studies." In *Rethinking the Media Audience: The New Agenda*, edited by Pertti Alasuutari, 1–21. London: Sage, 1999.

Balme, Christopher. *The Cambridge Introduction to Theatre Studies*. Cambridge: Cambridge University Press, 2008.

Banes, Sally, and André Lepecki, eds. *The Senses in Performance*. Abingdon: Routledge, 2007.

Banks, Fiona, ed. *Shakespeare: Actors and Audiences*. New York: Bloomsbury, 2018.

Barrell, Sofía. "What Dreams May Come: A VR *Hamlet* Puts Us in the Room." *American Theatre*, January 25, 2019.www.americantheatre.org/2019/01/25/what-dreams-may-come-a-vr-hamlet-puts-us-in-the-room/.

Beaumont, Francis. *The Knight of the Burning Pestle*. London, 1613.

Beckerman, Bernard. *Dynamics of Drama: Theory and Method of Analysis*. New York: Alfred A. Knopf, 1970.

Bennett, Susan. *Theatre Audiences: A Theory of Production and Reception*, 2nd ed. London: Routledge, 1997.

Blackadder, Neil. *Performing Opposition: Modern Theater and the Scandalized Audience*. Westport, CT: Praeger, 2003.

Boecker, Bettina. *Imagining Shakespeare's Original Audience, 1660–2000: Groundlings, Gallants, Grocers*. Basingstoke: Palgrave Macmillan, 2015.

Butler, Martin. *Theatre and Crisis, 1632–1642*. Cambridge: Cambridge University Press, 1984.

Carson, Christie, and Farah Karim-Cooper, eds. *Shakespeare's Globe: A Theatrical Experiment*. Cambridge: Cambridge University Press, 2007.

Cline, Lauren Eriks. "Audiences Writing Race in Shakespeare Performance." *Shakespeare Studies* 47 (2019): 112–19.

Cook, Ann Jennalie. *The Privileged Playgoers of Shakespeare's London, 1576–1642*. Princeton, NJ: Princeton University Press, 1981.

Cook, Ann Jennalie. "Audiences: Investigation, Interpretation, Invention." In *A New History of Early English Drama*, edited by John Cox and David Scott Kastan, 305–20. New York: Columbia University Press, 1997.

Dawson, Anthony, and Paul Yachnin, *The Culture of Playgoing in Shakespeare's England*. Cambridge: Cambridge University Press, 2001.

Desmet, Christy, Sujata Iyengar, and Miriam Jacobson, eds. *The Routledge Handbook of Shakespeare and Global Appropriation*. London: Routledge, 2020.

DeWall, Nichole. "'Sweet recreation barred': The Case for Playgoing in Plague-Time." In *Representing the Plague in Early Modern England*, edited by Rebecca Totaro and Ernest B. Gilman, 133–49. London: Routledge, 2011.

Dunnum, Eric. *Unruly Audiences and the Theater of Control in Early Modern London*. London: Routledge, 2019.

Escolme, Bridget. *Talking to the Audience: Shakespeare, Performance, Self*. Routledge: Abingdon, 2005.

Eversmann, Peter. "The Experience of the Theatrical Event." In *Theatrical Events: Borders, Dynamics, Frames*, edited by Vicki Ann Cremona, Peter Eversmann, Hans van Maanen, Willmar Sauter, and John Tulloch, 139–74. New York: Rodopi, 2004.

Farabee, Darlene. *Shakespeare's Staged Spaces and Playgoers' Perceptions*. Basingstoke: Palgrave Macmillan, 2014.

Fazel, Valerie M., and Louise Geddes, eds. *The Shakespeare User*. Cham: Palgrave, 2017.

Fazel, Valerie M., and Louise Geddes, *The Shakespeare Multiverse: Fandom as Literary Praxis*. London: Routledge, 2021.

Fiske, John. "Audiencing: A Cultural Studies Approach to Watching Television." *Poetics* 21, no. 4 (August 1992): 345–59.

Freshwater, Helen. *Theatre & Audience*. Basingstoke: Palgrave Macmillan, 2009.

Gurr, Andrew. *Playgoing in Shakespeare's London*, 3rd ed. Cambridge: Cambridge University Press, 2004.

Hall, Stuart. "Encoding/Decoding." In *Culture, Media, Language*, edited by Stuart Hall, Dorothy Hobson, Andrew Lowe, and Paul Willis, 128–38. London: Hutchinson, 1980.

Harbage, Alfred. *Shakespeare's Audience*. New York: Columbia University Press, 1941.

Harris, Elizabeth. "*Hamlet* in Virtual Reality Casts the Viewer in the Play." *The New York Times*, January 25, 2019.

Hobgood, Allison P. *Passionate Playgoing in Early Modern England*. Cambridge: Cambridge University Press, 2013.

Honigmann, E. A. J. *Shakespeare: Seven Tragedies: The Dramatist's Manipulation of Response*. New York: Barnes and Noble, 1976.

Howard, Jean. *Shakespeare's Art of Orchestration: Stage Technique and Audience Response*. Chicago: University of Illinois Press, 1984.

Jonson, Ben. *The New Inn*. London, 1631.

Kidnie, Margaret Jane. "The Audience: Receiving and Remaking Experience," in *The Arden Research Handbook to Shakespeare and Contemporary Performance*, edited by Peter Kirwan and Kathryn Prince, 38–48. London: Bloomsbury, 2021.

Kiernan, Pauline. *Staging Shakespeare at the New Globe*. Basingstoke: Macmillan, 1999.

Kirwan, Peter, and Erin Sullivan, eds. "Shakespeare in Lockdown." *Shakespeare Bulletin* 38, no. 3 (2020).

Krontiris, Tina, and Jyotsna Singh, eds. *Shakespeare Worldwide and the Idea of an Audience*. Thessaloniki: Aristotle University, 2007.

Lopez, Jeremy. *Theatrical Convention and Audience Response in Early Modern Drama*. Cambridge: Cambridge University Press, 2002.

Mack, Maynard. "Engagement and Detachment in Shakespeare's Plays." In *Essays on Shakespeare and Elizabethan Drama in Honor of Hardin Craig*, edited by Richard Hosley, 275–96. Columbia: University of Missouri Press, 1962.

Mancewicz, Aneta. *Intermedial Shakespeares on European Stages*. Basingstoke: Palgrave Macmillan, 2014.

Mancewicz, Aneta, and Alexa Alice Joubin, eds. *Local and Global Myths in Shakespearean Performance*. Cham: Palgrave, 2018.

McConachie, Bruce. *Engaging Audiences: A Cognitive Approach to Spectating in the Theatre*. New York: Palgrave Macmillan, 2008.

Myhill, Nova, and Jennifer Low. "Audience and Audiences." In *Imagining the Audience in Early Modern Drama, 1558–1642*, edited by Jennifer Low and Nova Myhill, 1–17. New York: Palgrave Macmillan, 2011.

Neill, Michael. "'Wit's Most Accomplished Senate': The Audience of the Caroline Private Theaters." *Studies in English Literature, 1500–1900* 18, no. 2 (Spring 1978): 341–60.

Nicholas, Rachael. *Encountering Shakespeare Elsewhere: Digital Distribution, Audience Reception, and the Changing Value of Shakespeare in Performance.* PhD thesis, University of Roehampton, 2019.

O'Malley, Evelyn. *Weathering Shakespeare: Audiences and Open-Air Performance.* New York: Bloomsbury Academic, 2021.

O'Neill, Stephen, ed. *Broadcast Your Shakespeare: Continuity and Change across Media.* London: Bloomsbury, 2018.

Pangallo, Matteo. *Playwriting Playgoers in Shakespeare's Theater.* Philadelphia: University of Pennsylvania Press, 2017.

Prescott, Paul. "Inheriting the Globe: The Reception of Shakespearean Space and Audience in Contemporary Reviewing." In *A Companion to Shakespeare and Performance*, edited by Barbara Hodgdon and W. B. Worthen, 359–75. Malden: Blackwell, 2005.

Prescott, Paul. *Reviewing Shakespeare: Journalism and Performance from the Eighteenth Century to the Present.* Cambridge: Cambridge University Press, 2013.

Preiss, Richard. *Clowning and Authorship in Early Modern Theatre.* Cambridge: Cambridge University Press, 2014.

Price, Eoin. *"Public" and "Private" Playhouses in Renaissance England: The Politics of Publication.* Basingstoke: Palgrave Macmillan, 2015.

Prior, Moody. "The Elizabethan Audience and the Plays of Shakespeare." *Modern Philology* 49, no. 2 (November 1951): 101–23.

Purcell, Stephen. *Shakespeare & Audience in Practice.* Basingstoke: Palgrave Macmillan, 2013.

Ralley, Richard, and Roy Connolly. "In Front of Our Eyes: Presence and the Cognitive Audience." *About Performance* 10 (2010): 51–66.

Rowland, Richard. "(Gentle)Men Behaving Badly: Aggression, Anxiety, and Repertory in the Playhouses of Early Modern London." *Medieval and Renaissance Drama in England* 25 (2012): 17–41.

Salingar, Leo. "Jacobean Playwrights and 'Judicious' Spectators." *Renaissance Drama* 22 (1991): 209–34.

Sanders, Julie. "*The New Inn*: Textual Essay." In *The Cambridge Edition of the Works of Ben Jonson Online*, edited by David Bevington, Martin Butler, and Ian Donaldson (Cambridge: Cambridge University Press, 2014). Accessed September 8, 2020. universitypublishingonline.org/cambridge/benjonson/k/essays/New_Inn_textual_essay/1/.

Sedgman, Kirsty. "Audience Experience in an Anti-Expert Age: A Survey of Theatre Audience Research." *Theatre Research International* 42, no. 3 (2017): 307–22.

Sedgman, Kirsty. *The Reasonable Audience: Theatre Etiquette, Behaviour Policing, and the Live Performance Experience.* Cham: Palgrave, 2018.

Sedgman, Kirsty. "On Rigour in Theatre Audience Research." *Contemporary Theatre Review* 29, no. 4 (2019): 462–79.

Shakespeare, William. *The famous historie of Troylus and Cresseid.* London, 1609.

Shepherd, Simon. *Theatre, Body and Pleasure.* Abingdon: Routledge, 2006.

Sprague, Arthur Colby. *Shakespeare and the Audience.* Cambridge, MA: Harvard University Press, 1935.

Stern, Tiffany. "Sermons, Plays and Note-Takers: *Hamlet* Q1 as a 'Noted' Text." *Shakespeare Survey* 66 (2013): 1–23.

Sullivan, Erin. "Live to Your Living Room: Streamed Theatre, Audience Experience, and the Globe's *A Midsummer Night's Dream*." *Participations* 17, no. 1 (2020): 92–119.

Thompson, Ayanna. *Passing Strange: Shakespeare, Race, and Contemporary America*. Oxford: Oxford University Press, 2011.

Thompson, Ayanna. "(How) Should We Listen to Audiences? Race, Reception, and the Audience Survey." In *The Oxford Handbook of Shakespeare and Performance*, edited by James C. Bulman, 157–69. Oxford: Oxford University Press, 2017.

Tulloch, John. *Shakespeare and Chekhov in Production and Reception*. Iowa City: University of Iowa Press, 2005.

Walmsley, Ben. *Audience Engagement in the Performing Arts: A Critical Analysis*. Cham: Palgrave Macmillan, 2019.

Webster, John. *The White Divel*. London, 1612.

Weimann, Robert. *Shakespeare and the Popular Tradition*, translated by Robert Schwartz. Baltimore: Johns Hopkins University Press, 1978.

Werner, Sarah. "Audiences." In *Shakespeare and the Making of Theatre*, edited by Stuart Hampton-Reeves and Bridget Escolme, 165–79. New York: Palgrave Macmillan, 2012.

Whitney, Charles. *Early Responses to Renaissance Drama*. Cambridge: Cambridge University Press, 2006.

Woods, Penelope. *Globe Audiences: Spectatorship and Reconstruction at Shakespeare's Globe*. PhD thesis, Queen Mary, University of London, 2012.

Worthen, W. B. *Shakespeare and the Force of Modern Performance*. Cambridge: Cambridge University Press, 2003.

Embodied Audiences

1 Respiratory Sympathy and Pneumatic Community in Shakespeare

Stephanie Shirilan

Modern Shakespeare scholarship has followed various contemporary turns and trends to theorize audience experience in the early modern theater. The bodily turn emphasized disciplinary responses to the ways such experience exceeded the individual's control,[1] while cognitive studies have offered the language of distribution and network to describe the embeddedness of mind and body within extended cognitive and affective systems or environments.[2] These models have probed the language and logics of humoral and brain physiology but have paid little attention to the ways in which early modern affect was shaped by respiratory experience and the pneumatic principles through which the breath was understood.[3] Recent work in atmospheric philosophy and respiratory phenomenology offers us new tools to observe something old about the relationship between air and affect that Aby Warburg once described in regards to the pictorial arts.[4] The challenges inherent in the visual representation of air, he argued, are suggestively analogous to the challenge of representing divine spirit.[5] The solution, both in painting, as Warburg observed, and in theater, as I am arguing, lies in the paradox that we "see" air only in the way it *affects*—or moves—objects and subjects. Especially, but not exclusively, in live performance, Shakespeare's pneumatic themes suggest that air, and the divine spirit that dwells in it, is knowable only through its affective capacity—that is, through the movement or stirring of the audience.

In his groundbreaking work on early modern acoustic phenomenology, Bruce Smith has historicized the "charged, pulsating [air] medium" through which sound moves.[6] Penelope Woods writes that "the attuned audience member is conscious of the air being 'full' when an audience is attending, receiving, and returning the performers' energy."[7] Like Woods, I wish to emphasize the ways that the labile and porous early modern body extended into its affective surroundings. I argue, however, that this extension needs to be considered more broadly in pneumatic and respiratory terms, both of which have been largely overlooked in accounts of early modern atmosphere, cognition, and affect.[8] Human respiratory experience, in all its diversity and contextual specificity, provides us with vital information about audience experience, past and present. It offers us a tool for thinking transhistorically about the phenomenality of theatergoing, not by reducing the complexity and situatedness of respiratory experience to biological determinism but, quite the opposite, by foregrounding the responsiveness of the breath to local and contextual stimuli.[9] Pneumatic atmosphere in the theater is the complex and dynamic effect of shared physiological, cognitive, and affective processes that may be harnessed or intensified, even as they exceed conscious control. This chapter shows how Shakespeare's plays prompt and prime their intended and future audiences for pneumatic community, respiratory sympathy, and, in climactic moments, respiratory catharsis through techniques of mimetic amplification that work precisely because of the ways that the breath responds to the power of suggestion. At the time of this chapter's initial writing in 2019, few might have anticipated the global pandemic that would make Shakespeare's respiratory and pneumatic themes seem so suddenly conspicuous. But for early modern audiences, whose lives were constantly overthrown by airborne diseases and who simultaneously understood thought, feeling, and divine spirit itself to be communicated atmospherically, the risks and rewards of breathing together would have necessarily shaped the mimetic representation and experience of air and breath in the plays.

Pneumatic Ecology and Community

When critics refer to the ambience, the "charged" or "electric" atmosphere of the theater, they invoke a phenomenon that was, and arguably remains, rooted in shared breathing and immersive pneumatic experience. Early modern religious and philosophical systems understood air to connect living things to one another and to the divine. The relationship between god and air is central to Western cosmologies, from the Hebrew *ruach elohim*, the divine wind or breath that hovered over the waters in Genesis and was breathed into the nostrils of Adam ("man of the dust of the ground")[10] to make him a living breath (*nishmat hayyim*),[11] to the pre-Socratic *pneuma*, or divine wind that suffuses all living things,[12] to the Christian personification of divine wind as *spiritus sanctus*, the Holy Ghost that yoked divine breath to word in the insemination of the Virgin. Medieval and Renaissance art commonly depicts the annunciation as a breeze or beam of light irradiating the air as the inseminating message travels from the mouth of an angel or dove to the Virgin's ear or womb.[13] This iconic scene is key to our understanding of the power of words as agential matter in the air that works in spiritually and physically transformative, but only partially conscious, ways upon the audience.[14]

Pneuma is central to both Hippocratic medicine (air is one of the six non-natural determinants of health and illness) and the Stoic philosophical systems that persisted in and through medieval and early modern faculty psychology.[15] For the Renaissance Neoplatonists, pneumatic principles explained how air worked as the medium of natural magic. Agrippa describes the air as "a vitall spirit, passing through all Beings, giving life, and subsistence ... binding, moving, and filling all things" so that the "Hebrew Doctors ... count it as a Medium or glew, joyning things together ... as the resounding spirit of the worlds instrument."[16] This instrument evokes the lute that served as the primary example of sympathetic resonance in both Renaissance natural magic and natural philosophy.[17] Faculty psychology understood spirits and "species" of information to travel through the air where they are received by the organs of sense and processed by imaginative faculties that function as psychic prostheses in an extended, distributed ecology of sense, thought, and affect.[18]

Early modern audiences were immersed in pneumatic atmospheres that were believed to be full of sense-data, especially of the audible kind, which was deemed to move "more manifestly thorow the *Aire* than the *Species* of *Visibles*."[19] Agrippa likens air to "a divine Looking-glass" that "receives into it self ... the species of all things ... as also of all manner of speeches, and retains them."[20] By this logic, dramatic speech would have been understood to persist in the atmosphere of the theater as pneumatically activated linguistic material that enters, via the species-laden air, "into the bodies of Men, and other Animals, through their pores" and "makes an Impression upon them, as well when they sleep, as when they be awake."[21] Such impressions are both potentially involuntary and communal, as species of sensory data move "by a certain kind of flowings forth of bodies from bodies ... gather[ing] strength in the air."[22] The proximity of bodies in the theater creates the potential for an atmosphere thick not only with noise and odor but with thought, feeling, and spirit, multiplied through the concentration of the air and respiratory exchange therein.

Of course, early modern medical and religious writers understood the physical atmosphere of the theater and its surroundings to pose increased risks of pestilential infection.[23] The air of the "sinfully-polluted suburbs"[24] was deemed to be both physically and morally corrupt. Physical pollution (especially human, animal, and industrial waste) and moral pollution (sin and vices such as gambling and prostitution, tolerated in the suburbs) were held to be co-constitutive and to produce breeding grounds for infection.[25] Then, as now, breathing infected air was held to be the primary mechanism for transmission of pestilence.[26] Clergymen took pains to allay fears about church attendance in times of infection, distinguishing the bad air of the theater from the saving air of the church. Lionel Gatford cautions those who dwell "near infected suspected houses ... such as are all *whore-houses* and *play-houses*" to "keepe thy *Windowes* and thy *doors* towards those places ... close shut."[27] However, he prohibits "forsaking or absenting thy selfe from the *publike assemblies* in the house of God," counseling his readers to attend church more frequently, "provided that thou goe prepared with some inward and outward *antidotes* and *preservatives* ... the bible ... and something in thy purse for the poore."[28] Faith, prayer, and charity were not like pomanders worn around the neck to protect the individual wearer; they worked collectively upon the shared atmosphere, like the herbal fumigations used to cleanse the air of pestilence and the ritual censing these sanitary measures evoked.

Thomas Playfere likens the redemptive power of prayer to the fragrant incense that draws down God's spirit through sympathetic action. He expounds upon what might have seemed a curious prayer in Canticles (4:16) for southern wind (regarded in antiquity as the harbinger of disease):

> We wish the southerne winde would blowe vpon vs that our spices might flowe forth, when as we wish the holy Ghost would worke vpon vs, that our praiers might flowe forth. That as God breatheth his spirit into vs, by the inspiration of grace: so we might breath out our spirit vnto God, by the respiration of praier.[29]

Prayer acts as a bellows, increasing spirit through pneumatic and respiratory exchange: "where there is much prayer, there is much spirit; where there is little praier, there is little spirit; and where there is no prayer, there is no spirit."[30] In John Donne's terms, we breathe or "suck" in the air of spiritual congregation that is materially full of mercy:

> The aire is not so full of Moats, of Atomes, as the Church is of Mercies; and as we can suck in no part of aire, but we take in those Moats, those Atomes; so here in the Congregation we cannot suck in a word from the preacher, we cannot speak, we cannot sigh a prayer to God, but that that whole breath and aire is made of mercy.[31]

No-one is cut off from such mercy, no-one an island, in such a sea of air.

Congregational prayer increases pneumatic spirit through a collective exercise of faith that resembles collective imagining in the playhouse. Pneumatic community in the theater is rooted in the audience's collective faith (or suspension of disbelief) in the stage's fictions, to which its members literally *con-spire*, or breathe together. The mimetic and diegetic representation of suspended and released breath in early modern plays amplifies this effect, particularly in and through the language and performance of sighing.[32] Amidst Protestant debates over the power and purpose of religious works, the sigh remained, as Donne says, an "acceptable sacrifice."[33] In the early modern theater, sighing operated within the generic and psychic matrices of catharsis understood by both classical dramatic theory and Hippocratic medicine as a purging of corrupt spirits.[34] But the sigh is productive as well as purgative, "reorganiz[ing] the state of the organism+environment," as L. O. Aranye Fradenburg observes: "When we sigh, we affect the atmosphere, it affects us, and through the actions of opening and breathing, we transform the affect that initiated the sigh in the first place, as well as the *Umwelt* in which it arose."[35]

Choral invocations in Shakespeare call the audience into being through the power of collective inspiration and respiration. Scholars have largely understood these invocations to appeal to the internal, imaginative faculties of the individual percipient, overlooking the way they are themselves composed of breath, engineered to gather pneumatic force both sonically, as they are bellowed across the playhouse (frequently in stressed monosyllable and open vowels: "O for a muse of Fire;" "Two households"[36]), and by the suggestive power of pneumatic imagery: airy elements and spirits and figures of their quickening and ascent: "behold the swelling scene ... Thus with imagined wing our swift scene flies / In motion of no less celerity / Than that of thought" (*Henry V* Prologue 4; 3.0.1–3). In *Henry V,* the audience is petitioned to raise the "flat unraised spirits that have dared ... bring forth" the play by allowing the actors, "ciphers to this great accompt / On your imaginary forces [to] work" (Prologue 9–10, 17–18). The conjuring is reciprocal. The audience lends "imaginary puissance" (25) in order to deck kings and "[p]iece out imperfections" with its "thoughts" (23). In turn, these ciphers (literally, valueless characters that multiply the figures to which they are attached) amplify the audience.[37] The plays repeatedly measure the success of this exchange by evidence of the audience's pneumatic and respiratory sympathy, its sighing and weeping, or its laughter and applause. The latter is figured in *The Tempest* as a literal bellows that fills the sails of the play's project and drives it home. In what follows, I examine some of the more subtle ways in which the plays produce pneumatic community in and through such respiratory sympathy.

Respiratory Mimesis (Gestures, Attention, and Enactivism)

Scholars of cognition and affect have explored the physiology of sympathetic mimicry mainly in relation to mirror neuron theory, though with greater attention to visual (and to a lesser extent auditory) stimulus. The neurology of respiration and sympathetic breathing has been largely overlooked in cognitive and literary studies.[38] Recent literary research on movement and gesture, however, may help us to remake the connection between brain and breath that was key to early modern audience experience.[39] Hannah Chapple-Wojciehowski and Raphael Lyne consider the "vitality effects" in Shakespeare's "revival scenes" as studies in what Ellen Spolsky calls "kinesic intelligence": "our sense of the muscular forces that produce bodily movement and of the effect of that movement on other parts of the body and on objects within the environment."[40] We might consider the theatricality of respiratory themes and gestures in Shakespeare's plays as prompts to mimetic respiration that offer us new (or perhaps very old) ways of thinking about pneumatic community in the theater.[41]

Shakespeare's plays cue actors and audiences to the oft-made point that the play is a thing of air, as thoughts are made of and communicated by the breath of which they are materially consubstantial. Our attention is repeatedly drawn to the breath as an index of apparent feeling. We learn about the actor's respiratory technique from characters who remark the contrivance of deliberately altered breathing. Shylock offers to "bate" his "breath" (giving us the OED's first instance of "bated" as adjective) in order to play the abject bondsman more convincingly (*Merchant of Venice* 1.3.120). Richard would know if Buckingham can "[m]urder thy breath in middle of a word / And then begin again, and stop again," to make it seem he is "distraught and mad with terror" (*Richard III* 3.5.2–4). Juliet accuses the nurse of feigning breathlessness in order to prolong her torment by withholding her news: "How art thou out of breath when thou has breath / To say to me that thou art out of breath?" (*Romeo and Juliet* 2.5.31–2). To stay in character is, in a visceral way that Shakespeare frequently makes political, to stay, as contemporary actors say, "on breath."[42] The deposed Henry VI, demanding recognition asks: "Do I not breathe a man?" (*3 Henry VI* 3.1.81).

While research on respiratory synchrony and asynchrony and mimetic or sympathetic breathing and breath-holding is only just emerging, these phenomena are routinely probed in dramatic representation in Shakespeare's plays.[43] This is most explicit in scenes wherein the representation of death (or inanimateness) hinges upon the illusion of breathlessness. Representations of breathlessness or seeming breathlessness on stage invite sympathetic and parasympathetic mimesis in response to their affective intensity, an effect that is carefully anticipated and orchestrated by the dramatic action and language. When Paulina announces Hermione's death in *The Winter's Tale*, she depicts her already as the unbreathing statue of the play's finale, challenging her listeners to bring "Tincture or lustre in her lip, her eye, / Heat outwardly or breath within" (3.2.202–3). And when Hermione's "statue" is revealed in Act 5, Paulina baits Leontes, and the audience, with a kind of burlesque of the breath:

> PAULINA. I am sorry, sir, I have thus far stirred you; but
>   I could afflict you farther.
> LEONTES. Do, Paulina,
>   For this affliction has a taste as sweet
>   As any cordial comfort. Still methinks
>   There is an air comes from her. What fine chisel
>   Could ever yet cut breath?
>
>   (5.3.74–9)

Like Leontes, who is "almost transported" to think the "image" lives, the theater audience is "stirred" by the actor's apparent breathlessness. Leontes tastes the air that "comes from her" and invites the audience to do the same. The fiction of Hermione's death is belied by "the air [that] comes from her" as if "cut" from stone. This theatrical trick works not despite but because of its impossibility. The breathing of the actor playing Hermione becomes the object of both the stage audience's and theater audience's focus, as Leontes and Paulina fix our attention on the possibility of dramatic failure (the actor's insuppressible breath) that evokes the possibility of dramatic transcendence (that stone might in fact breathe or the dead reanimate).

Witnessing the Breath in *King Lear*

The stage performance of death calls for the illusory absence (or suspension) of the breath, the paradox being that *enargeia*, vividness or liveliness, calls here for its seeming opposite. The typical sympathetic respiratory responses to dramatic action in the theater (gasping, gaping, sighing, breath-holding) are intensified as audiences strain to see (or not see) the breath of the living actor that belies his/her performance of inanimateness. The literal and figurative suspense of the breath in such climactic scenes is amplified through a set of formal techniques and generic procedures that arouse pneumatic consciousness. Let us consider an illustrative case: the word pair breathe/breed in *King Lear*. The play begins with Gloucester's reluctant acknowledgment of his bastard's *breeding* (1.1.8) and ends with Lear's refusal to accept that his rejected daughter is no longer *breathing*. The word pair breed/breathe establishes a dialectical relationship through a tuning or "priming" of the ear to observe pneumatic analogy in sound.[44] Shakespeare's plays prime us for such attunement through techniques of linguistic echo and dilation, among other patterns of association, repetition, and evocation. This is perhaps most conspicuous in Shakespeare's uses of homonymy, homophony, and "near" species of both that blur what Wilma Koutstaal calls the "edges of words," producing atmospheres thick with material for making eerie/airy associations between things heard or heard like.[45] The blurry punning of phonological neighbors, or "minimal pairs," exerts a different kind of associative pressure on the mind's ear than the closer analogies of more exact rhymes or puns, demanding that we hear relationships across greater temporal and semantic distances. When these echoes "land" (a modern performance term that bears witness to the endurance of materialist psychology in the theater), they produce a kind of resonance not unlike the sympathetic vibration of the natural magicians' exemplary lutes. The audience demonstrates attention as sympathetic attunement by "picking" up these echoes and resonances.

As a kind of bookending word pair for the play, "breed/breathe" tethers *King Lear*'s many sounds and images of suffocated or strangled breaths and speech acts to the last breaths of parents and children, the dramatic intensity of these moments, and the frustration of our efforts to predict or control them. It evokes experiences of watching and listening for the breath of loved ones, not just in times of sickness or death but as part of the routine care for the very young and old, whose respiratory vulnerability was consistently remarked upon in period medical literature. The advice dispensed in these texts reflects the close living, working, and sleeping quarters of most early modern households, reminding us both of the different architectures and sociologies of early modern inhabited spaces as well as the kinds of respiratory experience and consciousness that were made possible by them.[46]

Edgar returns us to the word pair breed/breathe in his gloss on Gloucester's survival (after a moment's ambiguity as to whether "conceit" has indeed robbed his father of the "treasury of life" as he falls from the imaginary cliffs of Dover). He observes the signs of this miracle in Gloucester's unlikely breath, the "sound" and "substance" of which we are cued to by transposition:

> Hadst thou been aught but gossamer, feathers, air,
> So many fathom down precipitating,
> Thou'dst shivered like an egg; but thou dost breathe,
> Hast heavy substance, bleed'st not, speak'st, art sound.
> (4.5.49–52)

This hypothetical egg recalls the egg of the Fool's riddle, where it serves up a queer image of the King's cloven wit as womb, emptied (cannibalized) of its best part, leaving nothing but the "parings" (1.4.179) of his ungrateful daughters. Edgar's egg redeems the bad egg in multiple senses but most urgently by preserving his father from suicidal dissipation. Such "shivering" would have been Gloucester's fate had he been made only of feathers, or air. "But thou," he says, priming us for the contrast of Cordelia's breathlessness, "dost breathe." The redemptive sign of the father's breath here substitutes for the unseen last breaths and words (of forgiveness begged and granted) between father and son.

Edgar's hypothetical feathers return in Lear's fleeting hope for his daughter's miraculous respiration. The climactic scene of the play is enacted over the question of Cordelia's breath: whether Lear sees it and whether we share in this beatific vision. Lear oscillates between certainty in her death and her breath. First, he "know[s] when one is dead, and when one lives; / She's dead as earth." Then: "Lend me a looking-glass; / If that her breath will mist or stain the stone, / Why then she lives" (5.3.258–61). Albany tells Kent and Edgar to "Fall, and cease," in order to behold what Edgar calls the "image of that horror" (262) of the father searching the dead child for signs of life. Albany simultaneously directs Lear's on-stage audience and the theater audience to assume respiratory gestures of attention—holding our breath, as Francis Bacon observes we are wont to do when we strain to hear something. Bacon reasons that this is because "in all Expiration, the Motion is Outwards; And therefore, rather driveth away the voice, than draweth it."[47] In other words, when we would "take something in," we hold our breath so as not to blow it away. In a striking inversion of the conventional topos of theater as mirror, and one that recalls Agrippa's occult figure of the "divine looking-glass," the audience is asked to serve as mirror in order to register the "stain" or vapor of Cordelia's breath and "mist" over, that is, be moved to tears.

The play's fiction demands that we see nothing, hear nothing, but that would make us "men of stones" (255). Pathos invites the audience to see "feelingly" (4.6.145) for Lear, to make "something" of "nothing," allowing the actor's breath to argue if not for the life of the dead child then for the material endurance of her spirit.[48] Lear's feather supports this work in two crucial ways. Its delicate filaments stir at the subtlest movements of air, making it rather useless as a respiratory wind vane but a powerful reminder that Cordelia's breath persists in the spirit-laden theater air where it mingles with the audience's breath. This is the promise of pneumatic community, and our redemption hangs with Lear's upon our witness of it: "This feather stirs, she lives: if it be so, / It is a chance which does redeem all sorrows / That ever I have felt" (263–5). The near homonymy of feather and father remind us that what's at stake here is the redemptive potential of affective stirring; the feather stands for the father's stirring and our redemptive stirring as well.

We can surmise a thousand things about the quintupled "never" with which Lear concludes (in the Folio) that Cordelia has "no breath at all" (306–7). We might note that its perfect trochaic pentameter inverts the more familiar iambic rhythm, placing weight (literally, *gravitas*) on the endings rather than the beginnings.[49] But the line is followed by another respiratory prompt or gesture, "Pray you undo this button. Thank you, sir," that argues again for hope (308). There's some variety of interpretation in contemporary productions as to whether Lear gestures toward his button or Cordelia's. Ian McKellen's fumbling at his collar seems to suggest his own mimetic asphyxiation, recalling his earlier *hysterica passio* and unbuttoning in the storm.[50] But this staging contradicts Lear's demand that we attend to Cordelia's breath, at least in the Folio: "Do you see this? Look on her: look, her lips, / Look there, look there!" (309–10). In the Quarto, Lear's bid for help with the button is followed by four "O"s—last gasps, perhaps, that precede his final words: "Break heart, I prithee break" (311). The Folio gives this line to Kent, exchanging the Quarto's "O"s for the beatific vision of Cordelia's breath. Edgar directs Lear to "look up" (311) urging him to take comfort in heaven, to imagine Cordelia's spirit up there, not "*there*" on her lips. Such spiritual physic, commonplace in the period's literature of consolation (especially for grieving parents) repeats Edgar's direction to his blind father to "look up" (4.6.58, 59) and see the miracle of his survival from his imaginary leap. Cruel as that line may seem in place, the exhortation feels crueler here in the absence of Edgar's willingness to cure by delusion. Kent makes a kindlier handmaid to Lear's expiry: "Vex not his ghost. O, let him pass" (5.3.312). In so doing, he seems to offer dispensation to both Lear and the audience to find redemption not in the fretted heavens but in the shared air of the theater (indeed, *the air* homophonously substitutes for "there"). The "weight of this sad time" that compels us to "Speak what we feel, not what we ought to say" (322–3) marks the affective pressure of the scene in atmospheric and respiratory terms. The audience holds its breath in sympathetic reenactment of the drama of respiratory suspense, and this pressure compels the cathartic release of that same breath as sighs that fill the air with spirit.[51]

Notes

1 See Gail Kern Paster, *The Body Embarrassed* (Ithaca: Cornell University Press, 1993); Gail Kern Paster, *Humoring the Body* (Chicago: University of Chicago Press, 2010); Gail Kern Paster, Kathleen Rowe, and Mary Floyd-Wilson, eds., *Reading the Early Modern Passions* (Philadelphia: University of Pennsylvania Press, 2004); Michael Carl Schoenfeldt, *Bodies and Selves in Early Modern England* (Cambridge: Cambridge University Press, 1999).

2 See, especially, Miranda Anderson, *The Renaissance Extended Mind* (Houndmills: Palgrave, 2015); Miranda Anderson and Michael Wheeler, eds., *Distributed Cognition in Medieval and Renaissance Culture* (Oxford: Oxford University Press, 2019); Evelyn Tribble, *Cognition in the Globe* (New York: Palgrave, 2011).

3 Scholarship on air in Shakespeare has emphasized representations of its sensory imperceptibility: Carla Mazzio, "The History of Air: Hamlet and the Trouble with Instruments," *South Central Review* 26, no. 1 (2009): 153–96; Steve Mentz, "A Poetics of Nothing: Air in the Early Modern Imagination," *Postmedieval* 4 (2013): 30–41. Two recent studies have emphasized the animism and vitality of air and breath in Shakespeare: Elizabeth D. Harvey, "Passionate Spirits," in *The Oxford Handbook of Shakespeare and Embodiment*, ed. Valerie Traub (Oxford: Oxford University Press, 2016), 369–84; and Steven Swarbrick, "In the Anthropocene Air: Deleuze's Encounter with Shakespeare," *Early Modern Culture* 13, no. 1 (2018): 103–14. More phenomenological approaches have focused on sound and smell: Bruce R. Smith, "Within, Without, Withinwards: The Circulation of Sound in Shakespeare's Theater," in *Shakespeare's Theaters and the Effects of Performance*, eds. Farah Karim-Cooper and Tiffany Stern (London: Bloomsbury, 2013), 171–94; Carolyn Sale, "Eating Air, Feeling Smells: Hamlet's Theory of Performance," *Renaissance Drama* 35 (2006): 145–68; Jonathan Gil Harris, "The Smell of 'Macbeth,'" *Shakespeare Quarterly* 58, no. 4 (2007): 465–86; Amy Kenny, "'A Deal of Stinking Breath': The Smell of Contagion in the Early Modern Playhouse," in *Contagion and the Shakespearean Stage*, eds. Darryl Chalk and Mary Floyd-Wilson (Cham: Palgrave, 2019), 47–61. More sustained accounts of pneumatic and/or atmospheric spirit and respiration can be found in Gina Bloom, *Voice in Motion* (Philadelphia: University of Pennsylvania Press, 2013), chap. 2; Leah Knight, *Reading Green in Early Modern England* (Farnham: Ashgate, 2014), chap. 2.

4 See Lenart Škof and Petri Berndtson, eds., *Atmospheres of Breathing* (Albany: State University of New York Press, 2019); Tonino Griffero, *Atmospheres: Aesthetics of Emotional Spaces* (Abingdon: Routledge, 2016). Developments

in respiratory philosophy have drawn especially on Irigary and Levinas in theorizing an intersubjective ethics of breathing. See Lenart Škof, *Breath of Proximity* (Dordrecht: Springer, 2015). Social geographers and disability scholars have contributed to this field in their work on the colonial and racial contexts of atmospheric violence, justice, and injustice, and on generational poverty, industrial violence, and respiratory illness/injury. See, for instance, Marijn Nieuwenhuis, "Atmospheric Governance: Gassing as Law for the Protection and Killing of Life," *Environment and Planning D: Society and Space* 36, no. 2 (2017): 78–95; Jasbir K. Puar, *The Right to Maim* (Chapel Hill: Duke University Press, 2017). Together with recent work on breath in black liberation theology (see Ashon T. Crawley, *Blackpentecostal Breath* [New York: Fordham University Press, 2016]), these approaches provide important frameworks for research (especially in response to COVID-19 and the 2020 Black Lives Matter protests) on the unequal protection of respiratory freedom and unequal exercise of state violence to the breath of black and indigenous bodies.

5 Georges Didi-Huberman, "The Imaginary Breeze: Remarks on the Air of the Quattrocento," *Journal of Visual Culture* 2, no. 3 (2003): 275–89.

6 See Bruce R. Smith, *The Acoustic World of Early Modern England* (Chicago: University of Chicago Press, 1999) and "Within, Without, Withinwards."

7 Penelope Woods, "The Audience of the Indoor Theater," in *Moving Shakespeare Indoors*, eds. Andrew Gurr and Farah Karim-Cooper (Cambridge: Cambridge University Press, 2014), 152–67.

8 For recent exceptions, and important updates to the bibliography on Renaissance imagination, see discussions of air in Anderson, *The Renaissance Extended Mind*, and Suparna Roychoudhury, *Phantasmatic Shakespeare* (Ithaca: Cornell University Press, 2018). Crucial foundations for this work have been laid by Bruce Smith and Gina Bloom, whose work has drawn on musicological accounts of occult spirit, especially in Gary Tomlinson, *Music in Renaissance Magic* (Chicago: University of Chicago Press, 1993); Penelope Gouk, *Music, Science, and Natural Magic in Seventeenth-Century England* (New Haven: Yale University Press, 1999).

9 On the case for the transhistorical study of audience response, see Jeremy Lopez, *Theatrical Convention and Audience Response in Early Modern Drama* (Cambridge: Cambridge University Press, 2002): "It is essential to historicize audience response in … making claims about what playwrights expected of dramatic action and their audiences; but it is then equally important to dehistoricize audience response in order to argue for the continuing vitality of theatrical tradition" (14).

10 The dusty origin of human life is emphasized etymologically in the Hebrew phrase *ha'adam aphar min ha'adamah*, "man of the dust of the ground," into whose nostrils God blew the breath of life: *vayipach b'apho nishmat hayyim* (KJV 2:7).

11 *Ruach, neshama, and nephesh* are cognate with the Arabic *rouh* روح, *nasma* نَسمة, *and nafas* نَفَس. See *A Hebrew and English Lexicon of the Old Testament*, eds. Francis Brown, S. R. Driver, and Charles A. Briggs (Oxford: Clarendon Press, 1906), 659, 675, 924–6. My thanks to Carol Fadda for her assistance with the Arabic.

12 See Ernest DeWitt Burton, *Spirit, Soul, and Flesh* (Chicago: University of Chicago Press, 1918).

13 Barbara Baert, "The Annunciation Revisited: Essay on the Concept of Wind and the Senses in Late Medieval and Early Modern Visual Culture," *Critica d'Arte* 47 (2013): 57–68.

14 Quintilian surmises that the word "verbum" derives from the vibration of words in the air (*Institutio Oratoria* 1.6).

15 See James Bono, "Medical Spirits and the Medieval Language of Life," *Traditio* 40 (1984): 91–130; Robert Pasnau, *Theories of Cognition in the Later Middle Ages* (Cambridge: Cambridge University Press, 1997).

16 Henricus Cornelius Agrippa, *Three Books of Occult Philosophy*, trans. John French (London, 1651), 14.

17 "...a string in a lute trembling to the vibration of another which has been similarly tuned" (Marsilio Ficino, *Three Books on Life*, eds. and trans. Carol Kaske and John Clark [New York: Medieval and Renaissance Texts and Studies in conjunction with the Renaissance Society of America, 1989], 361); Francis Bacon, *Sylva Sylvarum, Or A Naturall Historie: In Ten Centuries* (London, 1635), 61.

18 Scholarship on the species has focused largely on the critique of this system by fourteenth century writers and on the visible species, or images, but was not thus limited in classical and medieval sources. For brief overviews see Pasnau, *Theories of Cognition*, 14–17; Gary Hatfield, "The Workings of the Mind," 24–5. For a more comprehensive history, see Leen Spruit, *Species Intelligibilis* (Leiden: Brill, 1994), vol. 1.

19 Bacon, *Sylva Sylvarum*, 70.

20 Agrippa, *Three Books*, 14.

21 Agrippa, *Three Books*, 14.

22 Agrippa, *Three Books*, 15.

23 See Ernest B. Gilman, *Plague Writing in Early Modern England* (Chicago: University of Chicago Press, 2009), 129–36; Margaret Healy, *Fictions of Disease in Early Modern England* (Houndmills: Palgrave, 2001), 88–122; and "Discourses of the Plague in Early Modern London," ed. J. A. I. Champion, *Centre for Metropolitan History Working Papers Series* 1 (1993): 19–34.

24 Thomas Dekker, *The Wonderfull Yeare* (London, 1603), D1^{r}.

25 See Carole Rawcliffe, *Urban Bodies* (Woodridge: Boydell & Brewer, 2013), chaps. 2 and 3; Jessica Browner, "Wrong Side of the River: London's Disreputable South Bank in the Sixteenth and Seventeenth Century," *Essays in History* 36 (1994): 34–72. The scholarship on atmospheric pollution in early modern London has focused on sea coal smoke: Ken Hiltner, *What Else Is Pastoral?* (Ithaca: Cornell University Press, 2011), chap. 6; William M. Cavert, *The Smoke of London* (Cambridge: Cambridge University Press, 2016). Atmospheric corruption by human and animal bodies has been considered in the scholarship on olfaction. See Holly Dugan, *The Ephemeral History of Perfume* (Baltimore: Johns Hopkins Press, 2011), chap. 4; Kenny, "A Deal of Stinking Breath"; Knight, *Reading Green*, chap. 2.

26 Miasma and contagion theories coalesced in the period (and indeed, as Nutton has argued, in antiquity) to explain how pestilence was caused by both local, environmental factors (altitude, climate, geology, wind patterns) and the pathogens or "seeds of disease" that settled in stale, stagnant, and fetid "bad" air (mal-aria). See Vivian Nutton, "The Seeds of Disease: An Explanation of Contagion and Infection from the Greeks to the Renaissance," *Medical History* 27, no. 1 (1983): 1–34; Mary J. Dobson, *Contours of Death*

and Disease in Early Modern England (Cambridge: Cambridge University Press, 1997), chap. 1.

27 Lionel Gatford, *Logos Alexipharmakos* (Oxford, 1644), 14.

28 Gatford, *Logos*, 19.

29 Thomas Playfere, *The Power of Praier* (London, 1603), 9.

30 William Leigh, *The Drumme of Deuotion* (London, 1613), 60.

31 John Donne, "Sermon II, Preached on Christmas Day ... 1624" *LXXX Sermons*, 12.

32 See Naya Tsentourou, "Sighs and Groans: Attending to the Passions in Early Modern Prayer," *Literature Compass* 12, no. 6 (2015): 262–73; "Hamlet's 'Spendthrift Sigh': Emotional Breathing On and Off the Stage," in *Hamlet and Emotions*, eds. Paul Megna, Bríd Phillips, and R. S. White (Cham: Palgrave, 2019), 161–76.

33 John Donne, "Sermon LIV, Preached to the King at White-hall ... 1628" *LXXX Sermons*, 536.

34 Tsentourou, "Hamlet's 'Spendthrift Sigh,'" 165.

35 L. O. Aranye Fradenburg, "Le Sigh: Enactive and Psychoanalytic Insights into Medieval and Renaissance Paralanguage," in *Distributed Cognition in Medieval and Renaissance Culture*, eds. Miranda Anderson and Michal Wheeler (Oxford: Oxford University Press, 2019), 274.

36 Cicely Berry, *The Actor and the Text* (New York: Applause Theatre, 1987), 57.

37 "cipher | cypher, *n*.". OED Online. June 2020. Oxford University Press.

38 See recent projects and publications addressing this gap by members of the Breathe Oxford research team: www.ndcn.ox.ac.uk/research/breathe-oxford.

39 See Hannah Chapelle Wojciehowski, "Statues That Move: Vitality Effects in *The Winter's Tale*," *Literature and Theology* 28, no. 3 (2014): 299–315; Raphael Lyne, "Shakespeare's Vital Signs," in *Movement in Renaissance Literature*, eds. Kathryn Banks and Timothy Chesters (Cham: Palgrave, 2018), 189–212.

40 Ellen Spolsky, "Elaborated Knowledge: Reading in Pictures," *Poetics Today* 17, no. 2 (1996): 159–60.

41 Lyn Tribble's term, "affective practice," is useful here. See her critique of Teresa Brennan's theory of entrainment (via Margaret Wetherell on the "sociality of affective communication"): "'Entrainment' is a form of synchrony, of moving together in time, or responding to one another, or integrating tool and body into rhythmic exchange with others." Tribble, "Affective Contagion on the Early Modern Stage," in *Affect Theory and Early Modern Texts*, eds. Amanda Bailey and Mario DiGangi (New York: Palgrave, 2017), 204.

42 This phrase is associated with the vocal pedagogies (Berry, Linklater, Rodenburg, Block) that developed out of Shakespeare performance training at the RSC, RADA, LAMDA, and the Globe in the later twentieth century. Alongside related somatic techniques emphasizing "breath support" (Fitzmaurice and Alexander), they have become core elements of contemporary acting curricula. See Kristin Linklater, *Freeing Shakespeare's Voice* (New York: Theatre Communications Group, 1992); Patsy Rodenburg, *Speaking Shakespeare* (Houndmills: Palgrave, 2002); Giles Block and Mark Rylance, *Speaking the Speech* (London: Nick Hern, 2013).

43 Erwan Codrons et al., "Spontaneous Group Synchronization of Movements and Respiratory Rhythms," *PLOS ONE* 9, no. 9 (2014), www.ncbi.nlm.nih.gov/pmc/articles/PMC4162643/; Viktor Müller and Ulman Lindenberger,

"Cardiac and Respiratory Patterns Synchronize between Persons during Choir Singing," *PLOS ONE* 6, no. 9 (September 21, 2011): e24893, https://doi.org/10.1371/journal.pone.0024893.

44 On cognitive priming in Shakespeare, see Amy Cook, *Shakespearean Neuroplay* (New York: Palgrave, 2010).

45 Koutstaal, Wilma, "The Edges of Words," *Semiotica* 137 (2001), 57–97.

46 For important correctives to the older sociological view (Phillipe Aries) of the early modern family as emotionally and medically underinvested in the health of its children due to childhood mortality, see Albrecht Classen, ed. *Childhood in the Middle Ages and the Renaissance* (Berlin: Walter de Gruyter, 2005); Hannah Newton, *The Sick Child in Early Modern England, 1580–1720* (Oxford: Oxford University Press, 2012).

47 Bacon, *Sylva Sylvarum Or A Naturall Historie*, 73.

48 See Kent Cartwright's reading of audience response to the "theatrics of 'playing dead' " in *Shakespearean Tragedy and Its Double* (University Park: Penn State University Press, 2010), 3–5.

49 See Amy Cook's reading of this prosody in "If: Lear's Feather and the Staging of Science," in *The Return of Theory in Early Modern English Studies*, eds. Paul Cefalu and Bryan Reynolds (Houndsmills: Palgrave, 2016), 48–68.

50 As played in the 2007 Trevor Nunn production and in Jonathan Munby's 2018 production.

51 I would like to express profound gratitude to the editors of this volume for their encouragement and hard work in seeing this chapter and volume through to print during a season of plague and unrest. I am grateful, too, to the members of the 2017 ASTR Shakespeare Working Group and attendees of the 2018 RSA panels on Cognitive/Affective Cultures for their comments on early drafts of this project. My deepest thanks go to my family, Ryan, Alethea, Eden, and Lyra, for their love and support of these labors during this time.

Bibliography

Agrippa, Henricus Cornelius. *Three Books of Occult Philosophy*, translated by John French. London, 1651.

Anderson, Miranda. *The Renaissance Extended Mind*. Houndmills: Palgrave, 2015.

Anderson, Miranda, and Michael Wheeler, eds. *Distributed Cognition in Medieval and Renaissance Culture*. Edinburgh: Edinburgh University Press, 2019.

Bacon, Francis. *Sylva Sylvarum Or A Naturall Historie: In Ten Centuries*. London, 1627.

Baert, Barbara. "The Annunciation Revisited: Essay on the Concept of Wind and the Senses in Late Medieval and Early Modern Visual Culture." *Critica d'Arte* 47 (2013): 57–68.

Berry, Cicely. *The Actor and the Text*. New York: Applause Theatre, 1987.

Block, Giles, and Mark Rylance. *Speaking the Speech: An Actor's Guide to Shakespeare*. London: Nick Hern, 2013.

Bloom, Gina. *Voice in Motion: Staging Gender, Shaping Sound in Early Modern England*. Philadelphia: University of Pennsylvania Press, 2013.

Bono, James. "Medical Spirits and the Medieval Language of Life." *Traditio* 40 (1984): 91–130.

Brown, Francis, S. R. Driver, and Charles A. Briggs, eds. *A Hebrew and English Lexicon of the Old Testament*. Oxford: Clarendon Press, 1906.

Browner, Jessica. "Wrong Side of the River: London's Disreputable South Bank in the Sixteenth and Seventeenth Century." *Essays in History* 36 (1994): 34–72.

Burton, Ernest DeWitt. *Spirit, Soul, and Flesh: The Usage of [Pneuma], [Psyche], and [Sarx] in Greek Writings and Translated Works from the Earliest Period to 225 A.D., and of Their Equivalents … in the Hebrew Old Testament*. Chicago: University of Chicago Press, 1918.

Cartwright, Kent. *Shakespearean Tragedy and Its Double: The Rhythms of Audience Response*. University Park: Penn State University Press, 2010.

Cavert, William M. *The Smoke of London: Energy and Environment in the Early Modern City*. Cambridge: Cambridge University Press, 2016.

Classen, Albrecht, ed. *Childhood in the Middle Ages and the Renaissance: The Results of a Paradigm Shift in the History of Mentality*. Berlin: Walter de Gruyter, 2005.

Codrons, Erwan, Nicolò F. Bernardi, Matteo Vandoni, and Luciano Bernardi. "Spontaneous Group Synchronization of Movements and Respiratory Rhythms." *PLOS ONE* 9, no. 9 (2014). www.ncbi.nlm.nih.gov/pmc/articles/PMC4162643/.

Cook, Amy. "If: Lear's Feather and the Staging of Science." In *The Return of Theory in Early Modern English Studies: Tarrying with the Subjunctive*, edited by Paul Cefalu and Bryan Reynolds, 48–68. Houndmills: Palgrave, 2016.

Cook, Amy. *Shakespearean Neuroplay: Reinvigorating the Study of Dramatic Texts and Performance through Cognitive Science*. New York: Palgrave, 2010.

Crawley, Ashon T. *Blackpentecostal Breath: The Aesthetics of Possibility*. New York: Fordham University Press, 2016.

Dekker, Thomas. *The Wonderfull Yeare. 1603 Wherein Is Shewed the Picture of London, Lying Sicke of the Plague*. London, 1603.

Didi-Huberman, Georges. "The Imaginary Breeze: Remarks on the Air of the Quattrocento." *Journal of Visual Culture* 2, no. 3 (2003): 275–89.

Dobson, Mary J. *Contours of Death and Disease in Early Modern England*. Cambridge: Cambridge University Press, 1997.

Donne, John. *LXXX Sermons Preached by that Learned and Reverend Divine, Iohn Donne*. London, 1640.

Dugan, Holly. *The Ephemeral History of Perfume: Scent and Sense in Early Modern England*. Baltimore: Johns Hopkins Press, 2011.

Ficino, Marsilio. *Three Books on Life*. Edited and translated by Carol Kaske and John Clark. Medieval & Renaissance Texts & Studies in conjunction with the Renaissance Society of America, 1989.

Fradenburg, L. O. Aranye. "Le Sigh: Enactive and Psychoanalytic Insights into Medieval and Renaissance Paralanguage." In *Distributed Cognition in Medieval and Renaissance Culture*, edited by Miranda Anderson and Michael Wheeler, 269–85. Oxford: Oxford University Press, 2019.

Gatford, Lionel. *Logos Alexipharmakos, or, Hyperphysicall Directions in Time of Plague*. Oxford, 1644.

Gilman, Ernest B. *Plague Writing in Early Modern England*. Chicago: University of Chicago Press, 2009.

Gouk, Penelope. *Music, Science, and Natural Magic in Seventeenth-Century England*. New Haven: Yale University Press, 1999.

Griffero, Tonino. *Atmospheres: Aesthetics of Emotional Spaces*. Abingdon: Routledge, 2016.

Harris, Jonathan Gil. "The Smell of 'Macbeth.'" *Shakespeare Quarterly* 58, no. 4 (2007): 465–86.

Harvey, Elizabeth D. "Passionate Spirits." In *The Oxford Handbook of Shakespeare and Embodiment*, edited by Valerie Traub, 369–84. Oxford: Oxford University Press, 2016.

Hatfield, Gary. "The Workings of the Intellect: Mind and Psychology." In *Logic and the Workings of the Mind: The Logic of Ideas and Faculty Psychology in Early Modern Philosophy*, edited by Patricia Easton, 21–45. Atascadero: Ridgeview, 1997.

Healy, Margaret. "Discourses of the Plague in Early Modern London," edited by J. A. I. Champion. *Centre for Metropolitan History Working Papers Series*, 1 (1993): 19–34.

Healy, Margaret. *Fictions of Disease in Early Modern England: Bodies, Plagues and Politics*. Houndmills: Palgrave, 2001.

Hiltner, Ken. *What Else Is Pastoral?: Renaissance Literature and the Environment*. Ithaca: Cornell University Press, 2011.

Kenny, Amy. "'A Deal of Stinking Breath': The Smell of Contagion in the Early Modern Playhouse." In *Contagion and the Shakespearean Stage*, edited by Darryl Chalk and Mary Floyd-Wilson, 47–61. Cham: Palgrave, 2019.

Knight, Leah. *Reading Green in Early Modern England*. Farnham: Ashgate, 2014.

Koutstaal, Wilma. "The Edges of Words." *Semiotica* 137 (2001), 57–97.

Linklater, Kristin. *Freeing Shakespeare's Voice: The Actor's Guide to Talking the Text*. New York: Theatre Communications Group, 1992.

Leigh, William. *The Drumme of Deuotion*. London, 1613.

Lopez, Jeremy. *Theatrical Convention and Audience Response in Early Modern Drama*. Cambridge: Cambridge University Press, 2002.

Lyne, Raphael. "Shakespeare's Vital Signs." In *Movement in Renaissance Literature: Exploring Kinesic Intelligence*, edited by Kathryn Banks and Timothy Chesters, 189–212. Cham: Palgrave, 2018.

Mazzio, Carla. "The History of Air: Hamlet and the Trouble with Instruments." *South Central Review* 26, no. 1 (2009): 153–96.

Mentz, Steve. "A Poetics of Nothing: Air in the Early Modern Imagination." *Postmedieval* 4 (2013): 30–41.

Müller, Viktor, and Ulman Lindenberger. "Cardiac and Respiratory Patterns Synchronize between Persons during Choir Singing." *PLOS ONE* 6, no. 9 (September 21, 2011): e24893. https://doi.org/10.1371/journal.pone.0024893.

Newton, Hannah. *The Sick Child in Early Modern England, 1580–1720*. Oxford: Oxford University Press, 2012.

Nieuwenhuis, Marijn. "Atmospheric Governance: Gassing as Law for the Protection and Killing of Life." *Environment and Planning D: Society and Space* 36, no. 2 (2017): 78–95.

Nutton, Vivian. "The Seeds of Disease: An Explanation of Contagion and Infection from the Greeks to the Renaissance." *Medical History* 27, no. 1 (1983): 1–34.

Pasnau, Robert. *Theories of Cognition in the Later Middle Ages*. Cambridge: Cambridge University Press, 1997.

Paster, Gail Kern. *Humoring the Body: Emotions and the Shakespearean Stage.* Chicago: University of Chicago Press, 2010.

Paster, Gail Kern. *The Body Embarrassed: Drama and the Disciplines of Shame in Early Modern England.* Ithaca: Cornell University Press, 1993.

Paster, Gail Kern, Kathleen Rowe, and Mary Floyd-Wilson. *Reading the Early Modern Passions: Essays in the Cultural History of Emotion.* Philadelphia: University of Pennsylvania Press, 2004.

Playfere, Thomas. *The Power of Praier.* London, 1603.

Puar, Jasbir K. *The Right to Maim: Debility, Capacity, Disability.* Chapel Hill: Duke University Press, 2017.

Quintilian. *The Orator's Education, Volume I: Books 1–2,* edited and translated by Donald A. Russell. Loeb Classical Library 124. Cambridge, MA: Harvard University Press, 2002.

Rawcliffe, Carole. *Urban Bodies: Communal Health in Late Medieval English Towns and Cities.* Woodridge: Boydell & Brewer, 2013.

Rodenburg, Patsy. *Speaking Shakespeare.* Houndmills: Palgrave, 2002.

Roychoudhury, Suparna. *Phantasmatic Shakespeare: Imagination in the Age of Early Modern Science.* Ithaca: Cornell University Press, 2018.

Sale, Carolyn. "Eating Air, Feeling Smells: Hamlet's Theory of Performance." *Renaissance Drama* 35 (2006): 145–68.

Schoenfeldt, Michael Carl. *Bodies and Selves in Early Modern England: Physiology and Inwardness in Spenser, Shakespeare, Herbert, and Milton.* Cambridge: Cambridge University Press, 1999.

Škof, Lenart. *Breath of Proximity: Intersubjectivity, Ethics and Peace.* Dordrecht: Springer, 2015.

Škof, Lenart, and Petri Berndtson, eds. *Atmospheres of Breathing.* Albany: State University of New York Press, 2019.

Smith, Bruce R. *The Acoustic World of Early Modern England: Attending to the O-Factor.* Chicago: University of Chicago Press, 1999.

Smith, Bruce R. "Within, Without, Withinwards: The Circulation of Sound in Shakespeare's Theater." In *Shakespeare's Theaters and the Effects of Performance,* edited by Farah Karim-Cooper and Tiffany Stern, 171–94. London: Bloomsbury, 2013.

Spolsky, Ellen. "Elaborated Knowledge: Reading in Pictures." *Poetics Today* 17, no. 2 (1996): 157–80.

Spruit, Leen. *Species Intelligibilis: From Perception to Knowledge.* 2 vols. Leiden: Brill, 1994.

Swarbrick, Steven. "In the Anthropocene Air: Deleuze's Encounter with Shakespeare." *Early Modern Culture* 13, no. 1 (2018): 103–14.

Tomlinson, Gary. *Music in Renaissance Magic: Toward a Historiography of Others.* Chicago: University of Chicago Press, 1993.

Tribble, Evelyn. "Affective Contagion on the Early Modern Stage." In *Affect Theory and Early Modern Texts,* edited by Amanda Bailey and Mario DiGangi, 195–212. New York: Palgrave, 2017.

Tribble, Evelyn. *Cognition in the Globe: Attention and Memory in Shakespeare's Theatre.* New York: Palgrave, 2011.

Tsentourou, Naya. "Hamlet's 'Spendthrift Sigh': Emotional Breathing On and Off the Stage." In *Hamlet and Emotions,* edited by Paul Megna, Bríd Phillips, and R. S. White, 161–76. Cham: Palgrave, 2019.

Tsentourou, Naya. "Sighs and Groans: Attending to the Passions in Early Modern Prayer." *Literature Compass* 12, no. 6 (2015): 262–73.

Wojciehowski, Hannah Chapelle. "Statues That Move: Vitality Effects in The Winter's Tale." *Literature and Theology* 28, no. 3 (2014): 299–315.

Woods, Penelope. "The Audience of the Indoor Theater." In *Moving Shakespeare Indoors: Performance and Repertoire in the Jacobean Playhouse*, edited by Andrew Gurr and Farah Karim-Cooper, 152–67. Cambridge: Cambridge University Press, 2014.

2 Recovering the Humoral Body through Original Practice Performance

Joe Falocco

Introduction

Since the late nineteenth century, a dedicated band of theater practitioners has strived to stage the plays of Shakespeare (and other early modern dramatists) by employing some of the same theatrical conventions used during the English Renaissance. In its early years, this movement was known as the "Elizabethan Revival."[1] More recently, the term "Original Practice" (OP) has been commonly used to describe it. Proponents and practitioners of OP have argued that this production style offers greater opportunities for audience engagement than traditional twentieth-century performance methods. Andrew Gurr and Karoline Szatek contend that OP audiences "respond much more actively and collectively" than playgoers who attend conventional proscenium productions.[2] For Chris Tranchell, an actor at Shakespeare's Globe, this heightened response creates for spectators and performers a "shared experience that moves the heart."[3] Fellow Globe practitioner Belinda Davison similarly notes the "wonderful feeling that the audience is also in the play with you."[4] Some scholars, however, have been understandably reluctant to accept these subjective endorsements. At a seminar at the annual convention of the American Society for Theatre Research, I extolled OP's ability to engage audience members. A leading performance scholar who was in attendance challenged me. "What empirical evidence," he asked, "do you have for these claims?" I was stumped. This chapter is in large part a response to that question. In it, I attempt to provide an explanation for the affective advantages of OP that will stand up to objective scrutiny. My contention is that OP produces heightened audience response and engagement through a sense of interconnectedness between playgoers and performers that echoes early modern notions of the humoral body.

In the pages that follow, I will refer to the work of three OP venues: the Blackfriars Playhouse at the American Shakespeare Center (ASC); Shakespeare's Globe; and the Sam Wanamaker Playhouse (SWP). Each of these venues places some of its spectators in close proximity to the actors on stage. At the Globe, audience members in the yard stand throughout the entire performance and have the opportunity to shift position and move about. Some of these "groundlings" come to the very edge of the playing area, within reach of the performers. At the ASC, some audience members sit on the stage itself on "Gallant's Stools." Spectators in the side boxes behind these stools and in the front row of the lower level of the house are also, at times, within an arm's length of the actors. The SWP does not offer seating on stage, but playgoers in its side boxes and at the front edge of its "Pit" sit in similar proximity to the playing area as their analogues at the ASC. These three playhouses also employ, with varying degrees of consistency, "universal lighting," in which both actors and audience are bathed in equal and unwavering illumination. The ASC religiously adopts this lighting strategy for all productions.[5] The Globe has fluctuated between universal lighting and other approaches during Mark Rylance's tenure as Artistic Director as well as that of his successors.[6] The SWP has sometimes varied its level of illumination within productions, most notably during 2014's *Duchess of Malfi*,[7] but Sarah Dustagheer nevertheless describes it as a venue where "performer and spectator coexist in the shared lighting, predominantly of candlelight."[8] These two performance conditions—universal lighting and, especially, the extreme proximity of some audience members to the playing area—form the basis of my argument because these conventions stand in contrast to those of most modern productions, where audience members sit in the dark at a considerable distance from a proscenium stage.

Original Practice is not unique among contemporary theatrical styles in offering universal lighting and intimate audience configurations, or in providing the increased sense of spectator engagement that these conditions produce. As Dustagheer observes, the experience of playgoers at the SWP parallels other recent trends including "immersive theater experiences, site-specific productions, and one-on-one performance."[9] The conclusions this chapter draws are therefore applicable to any performance experience that locates spectators in close proximity to the playing area and which bathes actors and audience in shared illumination. One should therefore consider OP as "experientially closer to contemporary immersive and aurally experimental theater than we might think."[10] Recognizing that Original Practice is more progressive than antiquarian may better enable observers to evaluate this production style for its contribution to contemporary theater, rather than for its relationship to the past.

Humoral Theory and Performance

Recent advances in neuroscience enable the reconciliation of some aspects of humoral theory with post-Enlightenment rationality. Broadly construed, humoralism understood the body to be governed by four essential fluids: blood, yellow bile, black bile, and phlegm. The predominance of one of these fluids within an individual led to one of four corresponding temperaments or, as Thomas Walkington referred to them in 1631, "complexions": sanguine, choleric, melancholic, or phlegmatic. This complexion was thought to influence strongly an individual's character. For instance, while a melancholic person was "the very sponge of all sad humors," those of sanguine temperament were "enriched with a greater treasury of wit."[11] For casual students of early modern drama, this paradigm explains the presence of character "types," like the choleric Corvino in Ben Jonson's *Volpone*, who seem immutably trapped in a narrow range of behavior caused by their perpetual and consistent complexion. Actual early modern understanding, however, was more sophisticated. The humoral body was, according to James I's physician Helkia Crooke, "*Transpirable* and *Trans-fluxible*," and therefore constantly mutable.[12]

Humoralism thus offered, as Gail Kern Paster notes, "a way of thinking about bodily behavior that ... finds it much easier to account for a subject's moment-to-moment fluctuations in mood and action than to account for emotional steadiness and a high degree of psychological self-sameness." The "porous and volatile" early modern body was constantly influenced by the "six Galenic nonnaturals (air, diet, rest and exercise, sleeping and waking, fullness and emptiness, and the passions)."[13] The last of these, the passions, did not solely arise within individuals but could also be absorbed from without by what John Sutton terms a "ceaseless cosmobiological exchange of vapors between body and world."[14] What we today consider internal emotions were viewed by the sixteenth-century Dutch physician Levinus Lemnius as external "spirites" that "slyly and secretly glyde into the body of man."[15] This early modern understanding is surprisingly similar to modern scholar Teresa Brennan's notion of the "transmission of affect." Like the "spirites" that were thought by Lemnius to govern our emotions, Brennan considers affects to be "material, physiological things."[16] As was the case with the humoralists, Brennan believes that "the emotions or affects of one person, and the enhancing or depressing energies that these affects entail, can enter into another." For her, as for the early moderns, "there is no secure distinction between the 'individual' and the 'environment.'"[17]

Humoral notions of affective transmission had particular resonance in the early modern playhouse where the passions of an actor were thought to "generate a wave of physical force, rolling through the aether, powerful enough to influence the spirits of others at a distance."[18] Sixteenth-century commentator Juan Luis Vives described how "the auditor's emotions are like a lyre that vibrates in response to the cords plucked" by a skillful orator.[19] I argue that, in the twenty-first century, OP enables and facilitates a similar transfer of emotions from actor to playgoer; then from one spectator to another via emotional contagion; and finally back to the performers on stage. OP (along with other modern modes of performance that situate their audiences in close proximity to and in shared illumination with the playing space) offers advantages in reception that are not available when spectators sit, as Gurr and Szatek put it, "curled up like eavesdroppers in their comfortable seats in the dark."[20] Playgoers today remain, of course, postmodern spectators whose responses sometimes differ from those of their early modern counterparts. In his critique of OP, W. B. Worthen contends, "It is hard to imagine that we can inhabit the body in ways even approximating those of Shakespeare's era," because "our ways both of understanding the body and of mapping it into the signifying web of our culture are radically altered." Yet in this same passage Worthen acknowledges that "sight, pain, [and] cold have probably not changed."[21] Nor, I suggest, have the physiological processes discussed in this chapter. The wheels of evolutionary change turn slowly, and audiences today have the same bodily equipment Elizabethans had, which leaves them physically capable of receiving similar affects in performance.

To defend my argument, I will focus on the transmission of affect in theatrical performance via smell and touch: two of the five universally recognized senses. Sight, however, also plays a role in this process. While the reaction of fellow audience members impacts spectators at all theatrical events (and even at the cinema), the convention of universal lighting, which makes playgoers deliberately visible at many OP performances, enhances the possibility of "entrainment." Robert Shaughnessy defines this phenomenon as "when two or more individuals lock into each other's rhythms," leading it to "the development of empathy and the cultivation of rapport, affiliation, and pro-sociality."[22] Shaughnessy describes this process at work in Shakespeare's Globe and partly attributes it to that amphitheater's "visual" impact on spectators. Much of the affective power of OP, however, may in fact come from smell and touch.[23] As described below, these sensory means allow performers to affect audience members sitting or standing in close proximity to the playing area. The process of emotional contagion, a phenomenon recognized in both the early modern era and our own, then allows these spectators to pass the affects received via smell and touch to fellow playgoers situated further from the stage.[24] The audience, in turn, then shares their newly augmented emotions with the performers in a perpetual affective loop.

Smell

Strong scents were a constant presence in the early modern playhouse. Outdoors, the food and drink smells and bodily odors emanating from playgoers in the yard led Thomas Middleton to dub them an "audience of stinkards."[25] At the indoor playhouses, R. B. Graves notes, such scents mingled with the smell of candles made from "rendered meat fat," which "could never disguise the fact that burning tallow was essentially broiled suet."[26] Besides being a frequent annoyance, olfactory emanations in this era were also an important form of communication. As Paster observes, "The concoction of vapors was ... one of the basic physical activities of the humoral body." She describes these "steamy or imperceptible exhalations" as "male humors in distilled form" and links the commingling of different characters' vapors to "the production of emotion."[27] According to Ruth E. Harvey, the affective impact of "vapors and smells" was considered more "immediate" than that delivered by food and drink because such odors arrived "nearer the nature of the spirit" and therefore worked "more directly."[28] An explicit connection between aromas and the affective nature of performance can be seen in Walkington's prescription for combining "musical harmony and merriment" with "a choice of fragrant smells" to facilitate "the cherishing and stirring up of the spirits."[29] With the coming of the Enlightenment, however, the role of scent in transmitting emotions fell out of favor. As recently as 1997, Piet Vroon lamented, "The scientific world is still not very much interested in the olfactory organ."[30] But in the decades since Vroon's observation, researchers have once again championed the affective power of smell. Brennan, for instance, asserts that "chemical entrainment works mainly by smell; that is to say, unconscious olfaction."[31] To understand how smell produces affective change, and how it might enable the transmission of affect between actors and audience in OP performance, one must consider the controversial topic of human chemosignals.

Throughout many portions of the animal kingdom, communication by olfaction is essential for survival. Often this takes place via pheromones, which are the "odors with which an animal lures others of the same species to engage in a certain kind of behavior—or even forces them to."[32] Their influence in many insects is far-reaching, as with female moths who can use pheromones to summon potential mates a kilometer away.[33] Some researchers accept the presence of pheromones in mammals, and others also advocate for their existence in humans. Vroon and Christine M. Drea probably go as far as anyone in claiming that human olfactory signals produce reactions similar to those generated by pheromones in other species.[34] The existence of human pheromones, however, is hotly disputed. Richard L. Doty is the most vociferous critic of this idea, as evidenced by the title of his book, *The Great Pheromone Myth*. While Doty acknowledges that bodily "odors and fragrances" have the power to "alter mood states and physiological arousal," he disputes the assertion that "agents purported to be pheromones *uniquely* alter such states."[35] No one, in other words, doubts the affective power of smell in influencing human behavior. The question is whether any of the substances that cause these odors rise to the level of pheromones by triggering irresistible actions on the part of human receivers. In the absence of such "relatively fixed and automatic responses," Katrin T. Lubke and Bettina M. Pause argue that "the term 'pheromonal communication' should be avoided" when discussing humans. Instead of "pheromone," they therefore prefer the nomenclature "chemosensory signal" or "chemosignal" in reference to people.[36] It is my contention that in OP performances such chemosignals facilitate the transmission of affect between performers and those playgoers located on or immediately adjacent to the stage.

Making allowances for what laypeople might refer to as "free will" in human subjects, Lubke and Pause provide extensive evidence that people "have sensitive and well-developed chemosensory abilities, capable of mediating social behaviors, and moreover, that humans are well-equipped for producing chemosensory signals."[37] In an example with direct bearing on theatrical reception, Lubke and Pause claim that chemosensory signals can heighten the visual, motor, and brain systems of receivers. Under chemosensory influence, sight and hearing improve, along with "enhanced neuronal energy (P3 amplitude), originating from medial frontal brain areas." This may explain some of the thrill playgoers feel in live performance. The assertion that "humans respond with an augmented startle reflex to sudden loud tones in the context of chemosensory anx-iety signals" rings true for anyone who has sat in a crowded auditorium when a firearm is discharged on stage.[38] With their extreme proximity to performers, playgoers on and immediately adjacent to the stage at OP performances are positioned to exchange chemosensory messages that are more subtle than those produced by a gunshot.

Human chemosignals play a significant role in sexual attraction. Researchers have documented their influence in guiding women to choose mates who will improve the immune function of potential offspring.[39] Lubke and Pause also note that "depending on their sexual orientation, both men and women display specific patterns of preferences for body odors obtained from homosexual and heterosexual men and women."[40] Besides provoking sexual desire, human male chemosignals stimulate a wide range of behaviors including "adult male-male dominance" as well as "male bonding," "the release of aggression or submission," and the ability "to mark territory."[41] All of these phenomena play a role in the complex relationship between actors and audience in live performance. Dominance and aggression, for example, are always factors in stand-up comedy, where those on stage must either "die" (fail to make the audience laugh) or "kill" (receive big laughs). This is not to suggest that human performers can, like moths, project their chemosignals for a kilometer, or even to the back row of a large auditorium, but they can easily exert chemosensory influence on spectators in close proximity to the stage at OP productions or in other performances that feature similarly intimate configurations. Holly Dugan argues that the smelling of human "vapors" in the early modern playhouse was a "critical component and effect of performance."[42] Original Practice, I suggest, enables similar olfactory impact in the twenty-first century.

Touch

There are times in OP performance when actors literally "touch" audi-ence members, in the traditional sense of the term. Reviewing moments at the SWP when performers have "clambered over audience members to exit from the stage boxes," "handed a guitar" to a playgoer, and even "cheekily pinch[ed] a pit spectator on the cheek," Dustagheer concludes, "For those closest to the actors in stage boxes and in the pit, then, this theater is one of touch."[43] This notion of a "theater of touch" takes on greater significance when one considers recent advances in neuroscience that confirm that sensations normally associated with the tactile sense can be engendered without physical contact. These postmodern discoveries are in surprising agreement with early modern humoral theory. As Margaret Healy explains, during the Renaissance "the body's fleshy envelope was imagined to be so fragile and permeable that it seemed to provide very little protection against incursion."[44] It followed that "the transmission of 'evil qualitie(s)' across the protective corporeal carapace could occur by 'fascination' and without tactile contact." In other words, "you could be 'touched' in this period without being touched."[45] An analogous scientific breakthrough involves the discovery of "mirror neurons." These were first observed by scientists at the University of Parma, who found that such neurons "discharge both when [a] monkey does a particular action and when it observes another individual" performing that same action.[46] While "evidence for analogous systems in humans is largely indirect," a wide range of experimental data strongly suggests the presence of mirror neurons in humans.[47]

Some researchers believe that such neurons "enable people to understand each other's emotions."[48] Functional magnetic resonance imaging (fMRI), for instance, has shown that mirror neurons are activated both when subjects experience disgust by inhaling unpleasant odors and when they observe facial expressions of disgust in others. Giacomo Rizzolatti and Corrado Sinigaglia claim that this same process takes place with all the "primary emotions" (fear, anger, pain, surprise, joy, etc.), and not just with disgust.[49] They also connect the function of mirror neurons to the process of theatrical reception. Paraphrasing Peter Brook from an unspecified interview, Rizzolatti and Sinigaglia cite the director's view "that with the discovery of mirror neurons, neuroscience had finally started to understand what has long been common knowledge in the theatre: the actor's efforts would be in vain if he were not able to ... share his bodily sounds and movements with the spectators, who thus actively contribute to the event and become one with the players on the stage."[50] Brook asserts that this mingling of affect between performers and audience is "the basis on which the theatre evolves and revolves," and that mirror neurons "now provide this sharing with a biological explanation." The increased proximity to the playing area afforded by OP improves some spectators' opportunities to utilize mirror neurons in this manner (because they can see the stage better), and the convention of universal lighting enhances the two-way sharing of emotion between actors and playgoers that Brook extolls. While these effects also take place in more traditional modes of theatrical production, another neuron discovery may help define an audience experience that is unique to configurations in which some audience members are extremely close to the performers.

Unlike mirror neurons, which react to visual stimuli, one class of somatosensory neurons responds in a tactile fashion to the presence of beings or objects close to, but not touching, the subject's body. These are the F4 bimodal neurons, which detect stimuli that appear to subjects "within that specific space portion which ... appears to constitute an extension of their somatosensory receptive field;" these neurons register objects and people that "appear in the spatial region which includes all the objects at arm's length and which for convenience sake we call peripersonal or near space."[51] In the case of spectators situated on or adjacent to the stage of an OP performance, these somatosensory neurons periodically sense the presence of performers. As with the visual sensations relayed via mirror neurons, the tactile information received in this manner is affectively charged. The resulting exchange between actor and spectator is necessarily a two-way street, intensifying the "living link with the audience" described by Globe performer William Russell.[52]

The neuronic activity described by the Italian researchers is in harmony with early modern notions of acting grounded in humoral theory. According to Joseph Roach, it was thought that an actor's "passions," by "irradiating the bodies of spectators," could "transfer the contents of his heart to theirs, altering their moral natures."[53] As Thomas Wright observed in 1604, a performer's passion "seemeth to me to resemble the wind a trumpeter bloweth in at one end of the trumpet; and in what manner it proceedeth from him so it issueth forth at the other end of the trumpet." As a result, "the affection poureth forth itself by all means possible to discover unto the beholders and auditors how the actor is affected."[54] Francis Bacon was wary of these "effluxions from spirit to spirit, when men are in presence one with another" and likened this affective transmission to the spread of disease "from body to body (as the plague and the like)," because it "work[ed] most upon weak minds and spirits."[55] This negative interpretation was seized upon by theater's enemies. Farah Karim-Cooper notes, "within the ireful complex of anti-theatrical discourse, the theatrical performance is perceived to have the capacity to transfer spiritual contagion to the receptive sensibilities of the audience."[56] As noted in this chapter's introduction, this concept of "contagion" is key to my argument. If contemporary neuroscience reveals how smell and touch enable performers to impact the spectators through whose peripersonal space they pass (on or adjacent to the playing area of an OP production, or of another theatrical venture with a similarly intimate configuration), contagion explains how the affects thus engendered then transfer to the rest of the audience.

Contagion

In his induction to *Bartholomew Fair*, Ben Jonson admonishes "every man" in the audience to make up his own mind about the play and not to "censure by contagion" in allowing himself to be swayed by "another's voice or face that sits by him."[57] This notion of contagion as an essential aspect of performance dates back to the classical writings of Cicero and Quintilian and was embraced by Renaissance rhetoricians like Nicholas Caussin and Jaques Amyot.[58] Early modern audiences, according to Allison P. Hobgood, "understood affective contagion as a powerful possibility in theater;" playgoing was therefore "an intensely corporeal, highly emotive activity characterized by risky, even outright dangerous bodily transformation."[59] Original Practice, I assert, enhances the potential for such contagion in contemporary performance.

In recent decades, researchers have sought to establish the physiological mechanism by which emotional contagion occurs. They have struggled, however, to distinguish between the "behavioral contagion" conclusively documented by Ladd Wheeler and emotional contagion.[60] As Marco Tamietto and his colleagues frame the question, "To what extent do emotional contagion responses originate from motor mimicry or rather are induced by an emotional state in the observer?" They describe the "chicken or the egg" quandary at the center of this discussion. One hypothesis suggests that "observable (i.e., expressive) aspects of emotional contagion are based on mimicry." An alternative theory "considers emotional contagion as an initial marker of affective, instead of motor-mimetic, reactions." The findings of Tamietto's team support the latter paradigm. In an effort to isolate a "psychophysiological index of autonomic activity" that would respond to emotional input but not to "motor-mimetic" impulses, these scientists tracked pupil dilation in patients rendered blind by striate cortex lesions, but who nevertheless possess "blindsight."[61] Such individuals have the "remarkable" ability to determine "the location or identity of stimuli presented in their blind field," despite being unable to see.[62] The results of the Tamietto group were "consistent with the notion that detection of emotional signals activates affect programs of old evolutionary origin." This contradicts "the processing sequence envisaged by motor theories of emotional contagion." The researchers conclude that their subjects "did not simply imitate the motor pattern observed in the stimuli"—a motor pattern that, after all, they could not actually "see." Instead, these patients "resonated to th[e] affective meaning" of the behavior to which they were exposed. Emotional contagion therefore "represents an instance of truly affective reaction."[63] Lubke and Pause also find evidence for this phenomenon in their work on olfactory chemosignals, as do fellow scientists I. Wallrabenstein and colleagues.[64]

The evidence for emotional contagion as a means of affective transfer is therefore quite strong, and Robert Shaughnessy identifies it as "a cognitive phenomenon which is especially characteristic of Globe performance." Shaughnessy describes a matinee, attended primarily by students, at which young girls standing in the audience became infatuated with the performers playing Romeo and Benvolio and howled in a "synchronized performance of arousal" whenever these actors came on stage. This reaction began in one section of the yard adjacent to the playing area and then spread throughout the rest of the house. Shaughnessy notes, "In terms of its visual and acoustic environment and spatial organization, Shakespeare's Globe is an highly emotionally contagious space."[65] This is surely correct and derives from the amphitheater's excellent acoustics and frequent use of universal lighting. The affective transfer Shaughnessy describes is, however, also heightened by the Globe's olfactory and tactile environment. Given the extensive evidence linking human chemosignals to sexual attraction (even the skeptical Doty acknowledges their impact on "physiological arousal"[66]), the lustful adolescents described by Shaughnessy were influenced, at least in part, by scent. Those close enough to the stage would have also felt a tactile thrill (via their F4 bimodal neurons) whenever Romeo or Benvolio passed within their peripersonal space. Emotional contagion then allowed the received affects to pass to other members of the audience through what Sigal G. Barsade terms a "Ripple Effect."[67] Such affective transfer is heightened at the Globe due to the ability of playgoers in the yard to move about and therefore increase their proximity to fellow spectators and to the performers on stage. But emotional contagion also flourishes in other OP venues. While audience members at the SWP are stationary, spectators at the front of its pit and in its side boxes are frequently within an arm's length of the performers. Since "no one is more than around nine meters from the stage" at the SWP,[68] the contagious affects described by Shaughnessy travel a shorter total distance to impact the entire audience than they do at the Globe. This is also the case at the similarly intimate ASC, where onstage spectators on the "Gallants' Stools" find themselves within the peripersonal space of performers as frequently as do the "groundlings" at the Globe. Meanwhile, audience members in the side boxes of the ASC and in the front row of its main house are as close to the actors as their counterparts at the SWP.

Conclusion

Early modern spectators, for Hobgood, were "anything but passive recipients of dramatic emotion;" instead, "they put in further jeopardy their already vulnerable humoral natures" to satisfy "the affective demands of a fearsome Shakespearean stage."[69] Original Practice restores some of this excitement to twenty-first-century performance. In a recent volume dedicated to exploring the sensory environment of the English Renaissance, Karim-Cooper asks, "How do early modern theatres offer an alternative sensory environment to modern theatres?"[70] One answer is that these playhouses facilitated the transmission of affect through means that were understood by humoral theory and which are now being reaffirmed by modern science. The early moderns had not yet fallen prey to what Antonio R. Damasio terms "Descartes' error: the abyssal separation between body and mind."[71] Instead, they understood the inherent interconnectedness of thoughts, emotions, and bodily functions. Michael C. Schoenfeldt saw in this an explanation for humoralism's resurgence. "It is just this complex mode of connection between body and mind," he wrote in 1999, "towards which contemporary medicine, with all its mechanistic suppositions, is being driven to endorse by its own researches into the body."[72] The more recent discoveries involving olfactory chemosignals and somatosensory neurons described in this chapter bear out Schoenfeldt's prediction. Once considered antiquated, some aspects of humoral theory have thus become "new" again. Such is also the case with OP stagings of early modern drama, which enable a greater transmission of affect through universal lighting and intimate configurations that allow some audience members to share peripersonal space with performers. By utilizing affective processes understood by both humoral theory and modern neuroscience, OP, as Dustagheer observes, "fus[es] the early modern and modern," as part of a broader "trend in theatrical intimacy" that derives from "a millennial desire for human connection in a postmodern world."[73] Rather than an antiquarian exercise, Original Practice exemplifies the theater of the future.

Notes

1 As in the title of Robert Speaight's *William Poel and the Elizabethan Revival* (Cambridge, MA: Harvard University Press, 1954).
2 Andrew Gurr and Karoline Szatek, "Women and Crowds at the Theater," *Medieval and Renaissance Drama in England* 21 (2008): 161.
3 Qtd. in Stephen Purcell, *Shakespeare in the Theatre: Mark Rylance at the Globe* (London: Bloomsbury, 2017), 110.
4 Qtd. in Purcell, *Shakespeare*, 110.
5 "Mission, Staging, and Beliefs," American Shakespeare Center, accessed July 21, 2020.https://americanshakespearecenter.com/about/.
6 Joe Falocco, *Reimagining Shakespeare's Playhouse: Early Modern Staging Conventions in the Twentieth Century* (Cambridge: D. S. Brewer, 2010), 163–70; Kevin A. Quarmby, "OP PC or PAR RIP?," *Shakespeare Bulletin* 36, no. 4 (2018): 579–85.
7 Peter Kirwan, rev. of *The Duchess of Malfi*, dir. Dominic Dromgoole, *Shakespeare Bulletin* 32, no. 2 (2014): 295.
8 Sarah Dustagheer, "'Intimacy' at the Sam Wanamaker Playhouse," *Shakespeare Bulletin* 35, no. 2 (2017): 231.
9 Dustagheer, "Intimacy," 228, 233.
10 Dustagheer, "Intimacy," 234, 237.
11 Thomas Walkington, *The Optick Glasse of Humors* (1631) (Delmar: Scholars' Facsimiles and Reprints, 1981), 130, 131, 113.
12 Qtd. in Gail Kern Paster, *The Body Embarrassed: Drama and the Disciplines of Shame in Early Modern England* (Ithaca: Cornell University Press, 1993), 9.
13 Gail Kern Paster, *Humoring the Body: Emotions and the Shakespearean Stage* (Chicago: University of Chicago Press, 2004), 60, 23, 76.

14 John Sutton, *Philosophy and Memory Traces: Descartes to Connectionism* (Cambridge: Cambridge University Press, 1998), 134.

15 Levinus Lemnius, *The Touchstone of Complexions*, trans. Thomas Newton (London, 1581 [1576]), 22^r.

16 Teresa Brennan, *The Transmission of Affect* (Ithaca: Cornell University Press, 2004), 3.

17 Brennan, *The Transmission of Affect*, 6. Brennan does not specifically address theatrical reception, nor, to my knowledge, have performance scholars cited Brennan's work in connection to OP. This may be a missed opportunity. Brennan (who passed away in 2003) observed, "Research on entrainment has not (to my knowledge) been linked to the study of groups and gatherings" (52). Robert Shaughnessy (cited below) has made such a linkage in his study of Shakespeare's Globe. He does not, however, cite Brennan's work. Had Shaughnessy considered Brennan, he might have expanded his study to include the olfactory factors that are her primary focus.

18 Joseph R. Roach, *The Player's Passion: Studies in the Science of Acting* (Newark: University of Delaware Press, 1985), 45.

19 Paraphrased in Wayne A. Rebhorn, *The Emperor of Men's Minds* (Ithaca: Cornell University Press, 1995), 88.

20 Gurr and Szatek, "Women and Crowds," 162.

21 W. B. Worthen, "Staging 'Shakespeare': Acting, Authority, and the Rhetoric of Performance," in *Shakespeare, Theory, and Performance*, ed. James C. Bulman (London: Routledge, 1996), 23.

22 Robert Shaughnessy, "Connecting the Globe: Actors, Audience and Entrainment," *Shakespeare Survey* 68 (2015): 295.

23 Shaughnessy, "Connecting the Globe," 304.

24 Rebhorn, *Emperor*, surveys classical notions of emotional contagion and examines how they influenced early modern scholars; Gustave LeBon, in *The Crowd* (1895) (New Brunswick: Transaction Publishers, 1995), incorporated the idea of emotional contagion into a modern theory of mass psychology.

25 Thomas Middleton, "Father Hubburd's Tales Or, The Ant and the Nightingale," ed. Adrian Wess, in *Thomas Middleton: The Collected Works*, general editors Gary Taylor and John Lavagnino (Oxford: Clarendon Press, 2007), 279.

26 R. B. Graves, *Lighting the Shakespearean Stage* (Carbondale: Southern Illinois University Press, 1999), 14.

27 Gail Kern Paster, "*Bartholomew Fair* and the Humoral Body," in *Early Modern English Drama: A Critical Companion*, eds. Garret Sullivan et al. (New York: Oxford University Press, 2006), 266–67.

28 Ruth E. Harvey, *The Inward Wits: Psychological Theory in the Middle Ages and the Renaissance* (London: Warburg Institute, University of London, 1975), 27.

29 Walkington, *The Optick Glasse*, 100.

30 Piet Vroon with Anton van Amerongen and Hans de Vries, *Smell: The Secret Seducer*, trans. Paul Vincent (New York: Farrar, Straus and Giroux, 1997), 11. Brennan similarly notes, "After the seventeenth century the concept of transmission [which she links to "unconscious olfaction"] lost ground ... Notions of animal magnetism in the eighteenth century contributed to the subsequent decline of interest in the transmission of affect. Variants of the

idea became feminized, a sure symptom of slipping status" (*The Transmission of Affect*, 17).

31 Brennan, *The Transmission of Affect*, 9.

32 Vroon, *Smell*, 126.

33 Edward O. Wilson, *The Meaning of Human Existence* (New York: W. W. Norton, 2014), 83–4.

34 Vroon, *Smell*, 138; Christine M. Drea, "D'scent of man: A Comparative Survey of Primate Chemosignaling in Relation to Sex," *Hormones and Behavior* 68 (2015): 121–3.

35 Richard L. Doty, *The Great Pheromone Myth* (Baltimore: Johns Hopkins University Press, 2010), 125–6.

36 Katrin T. Lubke and Bettina M. Pause, "Always Follow Your Nose: The Functional Significance of Social Chemosignals in Human Reproduction and Survival," *Hormones and Behavior* 68 (2015): 141, 135.

37 Lubke and Pause, "Always Follow," 135.

38 Lubke and Pause, "Always Follow," 139, 135.

39 Drea, "D'scent," 128.

40 Lubke and Pause, "Always Follow," 139.

41 Alex Comfort, "The Likelihood of Human Pheromones," in *Pheromones*, ed. Martin C. Birch (New York: American Elsevier Publishing, 1974), 387–8.

42 Holly Dugan, "'As dirty as Smithfield and as stinking every whit': The Smell of the Hope Theatre," in *Shakespeare's Theatres and the Effects of Performance*, eds. Farah Karim-Cooper and Tiffany Stern (London: Bloomsbury, 2013), 209.

43 Dustagheer, "Intimacy," 232.

44 Margaret Healy, "Anxious and Fatal Contacts: Taming the Contagious Touch" in *Sensible Flesh: On Touch in Early Modern Culture*, ed. Elizabeth D. Harvey (Philadelphia: University of Philadelphia Press, 2003), 22.

45 Healy, "Anxious and Fatal Contacts," 22–3.

46 Paul Thagard, *The Brain and the Meaning of Life* (Princeton: Princeton University Press, 2010), 188.

47 Thagard, *The Brain*, 189.

48 Thagard, *The Brain*, 189.

49 Giacomo Rizzolatti and Corrado Sinigaglia, *Mirrors in the Brain,* trans. Frances Anderson (Oxford: Oxford University Press, 2008), 174, 187.

50 Rizzolati and Sinigaglia, *Mirrors*, ix.

51 Rizzolati and Sinigaglia, *Mirrors,* 54–5, 62.

52 Qtd. in Pauline Kiernan, *Staging Shakespeare at the New Globe* (New York: St. Martin's Press, 1999), 133.

53 Roach, *Player's Passion*, 27.

54 Thomas Wright, *The Passions of the Mind in General* [1604], ed. William Webster Newbold (New York: Garland Publishing, 1986), 212–13.

55 Francis Bacon, *The Works of Francis Bacon,* eds. James Spedding, Robert Leslie Ellis, and Douglas Denon Heath, [1887] vol. 5 (St. Clare Shores, MI: Scholarly Press, 1969), 5.135, 5.119.

56 Farah Karim-Cooper, "The Sensory Body in Shakespeare's Theatres" in *The Five Senses in Medieval and Early Modern England*, eds. Annette Kern-Stähler, Beatrix Busse, and Wietse de Boer (Boston: Brill, 2016), 273.

57 Ben Jonson, *Bartholomew Fair*, in *English Renaissance Drama: A Norton Anthology*, eds. David Bevington, Lars Engle, Katharine Eisman Maus, and Eric Rasmussen (New York: W.W. Norton, 2002), Induction 96–8.

58 Rebhorn, *The Emperor of Men's Minds*, 87, 92.
59 Allison P. Hobgood, *Passionate Playgoing in Early Modern England* (Cambridge: Cambridge University Press, 2014), 54, 10.
60 Ladd Wheeler, "Toward a Theory of Behavioral Contagion," *Psychological Review* 73, no. 2 (1966): 185.
61 Marco Tamietto, Lorys Castelli, Sergio Vighetti, Paola Perozzo, Giuliano Geminiani, Lawrence Weiskrantz, and Beatrice de Gelder, "Unseen Facial and Bodily Expressions Trigger Fast Emotional Reactions," *Proceedings of the National Academy of Sciences of the United States of America* 106, no. 42 (2009): 17664, 17661, 17662.
62 J. S. Morris, B. DeGelder, L. Weiskrantz, and R. J. Dolan, "Differential Extrageniculostriate and Amygdala Responses to Presentation of Emotional Faces in a Cortically Blind Field," *Brain* 124 (2001): 1241.
63 Tamietto et. al, "Unseen Facial and Bodily Expressions," 17665, 17661.
64 Lubke and Pause, "Always follow," 139; I. Wallrabenstein, J. Gerber, S. Rasche, I. Croy, S. Kurtenbach, T. Hummel, and H. Hatt, "The Smelling of Hedione Results in Sex-Differentiated Human Brain Activity," *NeuroImage* 113 (2015): 365.
65 Shaughnessy, "Connecting the Globe," 304.
66 Doty, *The Great Pheromone Myth*, 125–6.
67 Sigal G. Barsade, "The Ripple Effect: Emotional Contagion and its Influence on Group Behavior," *Administrative Science Quarterly* 47, no. 4 (2002): 644.
68 Dustagheer, "Intimacy," 231.
69 Hobgood, *Passionate Playgoing*, 61.
70 Karim-Cooper, "The Sensory Body," 277.
71 Antonio R. Damasio, *Descartes' Error: Emotion, Reason, and the Human Brain* (New York: Grosset/Putnam, 1994), 249.
72 Michael C. Schoenfeldt, *Bodies and Selves in Early Modern England: Physiology and Inwardness in Spenser, Shakespeare, Herbert, and Milton*, (Cambridge: Cambridge University Press, 1999), 10.
73 Dustagheer, "Intimacy," 234, 230.

Bibliography

American Shakespeare Center. "Mission, Staging, and Beliefs." Accessed July 21, 2020. https://americanshakespearecenter.com/about/.
Bacon, Francis. *The Works of Francis Bacon,* edited by James Spedding, Robert Leslie Ellis, and Douglas Denon Heath (1887) Vol. 5. St. Clare Shores, MI: Scholarly Press, 1969.
Barsade, Sigal G. "The Ripple Effect: Emotional Contagion and its Influence on Group Behavior." *Administrative Science Quarterly* 47, no. 4 (2002): 644–75.
Brennan, Teresa. *The Transmission of Affect.* Ithaca: Cornell University Press, 2004.
Comfort, Alex. "The Likelihood of Human Pheromones." In *Pheromones*, edited by Martin C. Birch, 386–96. New York: American Elsevier Publishing, 1974.
Damasio, Antonio R. *Descartes' Error: Emotion, Reason, and the Human Brain.* New York: Grosset/Putnam, 1994.
Doty, Richard L. *The Great Pheromone Myth.* Baltimore: Johns Hopkins University Press, 2010.

Drea, Christine M. "D'scent of Man: A Comparative Survey of Primate Chemo-signaling in Relation to Sex." *Hormones and Behavior* 68 (2015): 11–33.

Dugan, Holly. "'As dirty as Smithfield and as stinking every whit': The Smell of the Hope Theatre." In *Shakespeare's Theatres and the Effects of Performance*, edited by Farah Karim-Cooper and Tiffany Stern (London: Bloomsbury, 2013), 195–213.

Dustagheer, Sarah. "'Intimacy' at the Sam Wanamaker Playhouse." *Shakespeare Bulletin* 35, no. 2 (2017): 227–46.

Falocco, Joe. *Reimagining Shakespeare's Playhouse: Early Modern Staging Conventions in the Twentieth Century*. Cambridge: D. S. Brewer, 2010.

Graves, R. B. *Lighting the Shakespearean Stage*. Carbondale: Southern Illinois University Press, 1999.

Gurr, Andrew, and Karoline Szatek. "Women and Crowds at the Theater." *Medieval and Renaissance Drama in England* 21 (2008): 157–69.

Harvey, Ruth E. *The Inward Wits: Psychological Theory in the Middle Ages and the Renaissance*. London: Warburg Institute, University of London, 1975.

Healy, Margaret. "Anxious and Fatal Contacts: Taming the Contagious Touch." In *Sensible Flesh: On Touch in Early Modern Culture*, edited by Elizabeth D. Harvey, 22–38. Philadelphia: University of Philadelphia Press, 2003.

Hobgood, Allison P. *Passionate Playgoing in Early Modern England*. Cambridge: Cambridge University Press, 2014.

Jonson, Ben. *Bartholomew Fair*. In *English Renaissance Drama: A Norton Anthology*, edited by David Bevington, Lars Engle, Katharine Eisman Maus, and Eric Rasmussen, 961–1065. New York and London: W. W. Norton, 2002.

Karim-Cooper, Farah. "The Sensory Body in Shakespeare's Theatres." In *The Five Senses in Medieval and Early Modern England*, edited by Annette Kern-Stähler, Beatrix Busse, and Wietse de Boer, 269–85. Boston: Brill, 2016.

Kiernan, Pauline. *Staging Shakespeare at the New Globe*. New York: St. Martin's Press, 1999.

Kirwan, Peter. Rev. of *The Duchess of Malfi*. Dir. Dominic Dromgoole. *Shakespeare Bulletin* 32, no. 2 (2014): 294–97.

LeBon, Gustave. *The Crowd* (1895). New Brunswick: Transaction Publishers, 1995.

Lemnius, Levinus. *The Touchstone of Complexions*, translated by Thomas Newton. London, 1581 [1576].

Lubke, Katrin T., and Bettina M. Pause. "Always Follow Your Nose: The Functional Significance of Social Chemosignals in Human Reproduction and Survival." *Hormones and Behavior* 68 (2015): 134–44.

Middleton, Thomas. "Father Hubburd's Tales Or, The Ant and the Nightingale." iIn *Thomas Middleton: The Collected Works* (general editors Gary Taylor and John Lavagnino), edited by Adrian Weiss. Oxford: Clarendon Press, 2007, 164–82.

Morris, J. S., B. DeGelder, L. Weiskrantz, and R. J. Dolan. "Differential Extrageniculostriate and Amygdala Responses to Presentation of Emotional Faces in a Cortically Blind Field." *Brain* 124 (2001): 1241–52.

Paster, Gail Kern. *The Body Embarrassed: Drama and the Disciplines of Shame in Early Modern England*. Ithaca: Cornell University Press, 1993.

Paster, Gail Kern. *Humoring the Body: Emotions and the Shakespearean Stage*. Chicago: University of Chicago Press, 2004.

Paster, Gail Kern. "*Bartholomew Fair* and the Humoral Body." In *Early Modern English Drama: A Critical Companion*, edited by Garret Sullivan, Patrick Cheney, and Andrew Hadfield, 260–71. New York: Oxford University Press, 2006.

Purcell, Stephen. *Shakespeare in the Theatre: Mark Rylance at the Globe*. London: Bloomsbury, 2017.

Quarmby, Kevin, A. "OP PC or PAR RIP?" *Shakespeare Bulletin* 36, no. 4 (2018): 567–98.

Rebhorn, Wayne A. *The Emperor of Men's Minds: Literature and the Renaissance Discourse of Rhetoric*. Ithaca: Cornell University Press, 1995.

Rizzolatti, Giacomo and Corrado Sinigaglia. *Mirrors in the Brain: How Our Minds Share Actions and Emotions*, translated by Frances Anderson. Oxford: Oxford University Press, 2008.

Roach, Joseph R. *The Player's Passion: Studies in the Science of Acting*. Newark: University of Delaware Press, 1985.

Schoenfeldt, Michael C. *Bodies and Selves in Early Modern England: Physiology and Inwardness in Spenser, Shakespeare, Herbert, and Milton*. Cambridge: Cambridge University Press, 1999.

Shaughnessy, Robert. "Connecting the Globe: Actors, Audience and Entrainment." *Shakespeare Survey* 68 (2015): 294–305.

Speaight, Robert. *William Poel and the Elizabethan Revival*. Cambridge, MA: Harvard University Press, 1954.

Sutton, John. *Philosophy and Memory Traces: Descartes to Connectionism*. Cambridge: Cambridge University Press, 1998.

Tamietto, Marco, Lorys Castelli, Sergio Vighetti, Paola Perozzo, Giuliano Geminiani, Lawrence Weiskrantz, and Beatrice de Gelder. "Unseen Facial and Bodily Expressions Trigger Fast Emotional Reactions." *Proceedings of the National Academy of Sciences of the United States of America* 16, no. 42 (2009): 17661–6.

Thagard, Paul. *The Brain and the Meaning of Life*. Princeton: Princeton University Press, 2010.

Vroon, Piet, with Anton van Amerongen and Hans de Vries. *Smell: The Secret Seducer*. Translated by Paul Vincent. New York: Farrar, Straus and Giroux, 1997.

Walkington, Thomas. *The Optick Glasse of Humors* (1631). Delmar: Scholars' Facsimiles and Reprints, 1981.

Wallrabenstein, I., J. Gerber, S. Rasche, I. Croy, S. Kurtenbach, T. Hummel, and H. Hatt. "The Smelling of Hedione Results in Sex-Differentiated Human Brain Activity." *NeuroImage* 113 (2015): 365–73.

Wheeler, Ladd. "Toward a Theory of Behavioral Contagion." *Psychological Review* 73, no. 2 (1966): 179–92.

Wilson, Edward O. *The Meaning of Human Existence*. New York: W. W. Norton, 2014.

Worthen, W. B. "Staging 'Shakespeare': Acting, Authority, and the Rhetoric of Performance." In *Shakespeare, Theory, and Performance*, edited by James C. Bulman, 12–28. London: Routledge, 1996.

Wright, Thomas. *The Passions of the Mind in General* (1604), edited by William Webster Newbold. New York: Garland Publishing, 1986.

3 Haptic Experience and Fluid Boundaries

Macbeth and Czech Nationalism at Český Krumlov's Revolving Theater

Jennifer A. Low

A stage may be framed by a proscenium or by a ring of spectators—so says theater scholar Arnold Aronson. Environmental theater is achieved when the spectator "is somehow incorporated within the frame, surrounded by the frame, or surrounded by several distinct frames."[1] The design of Joan Brehms's outdoor theater, located in the town of Český Krumlov (about 110 miles from Prague), which takes advantage of its lovely setting in the grounds of the state castle, would seem to fulfill Aronson's criteria. Brehms created a revolving auditorium, initially just forty seats resting on a wooden disk, turned by a host of stagehands who rotated the disk to follow the action that took place around it. The original 1958 model was superseded by three updated versions: now the auditorium has a seating capacity of 644, and rows of seats rest on risers to create a steep gradient rising toward the back.[2] The area surrounding the auditorium serves as the playing area, and while the boundary of one segment is clearly demarcated by the façade of the Bellarie summer house, the remaining circumference of the circle (about 270 degrees) represents a playing area that extends outward indefinitely.[3]

Brehms's design challenges the playgoer's expectations of the relation between the seating area and the performer's area and violates common assumptions about topographic stability. With the rotation of the auditorium, the designation of the stage area is altered as well: its boundaries are no longer clear. If the audience, rather than the performance area, is the designated center of the theater, then performing can take place anywhere that is not the auditorium itself.

This challenge to received sensibilities was, in fact, the goal of the design. According to Vladimír Semrád:

> The purpose of the revolving theatre is completely serious: to disrupt, to destroy deliberately and functionally the convention of a proscenium stage, to use inversely the principle and functions of the stage turntable, therefore to try kinetics in the theatre by the movement of the auditorium, to search for a new stage design ... modes and means, ... specific directional procedures and means of actors' expressions.[4]

The conception of this theater seems inspired by many mid-twentieth-century theater practitioners' interest in breaking down the division between performers and spectators, characterized by Josette Féral as "framed theatrical space ... a cleft that divides space into the 'outside' and the 'inside' of theatricality ... the space that defines both alterity and theatricality."[5] While the auditorium's movement might be perceived as summarily dividing the bodies present into active performers and passive spectators, other factors come into play. The radical reorientation of the seating area that Brehms designed changes the audience's relation to the stage. With the space of the stage extending indefinitely outward, the auditorium is not necessarily excluded from the performance area either. While the spectator's ability to move about may be limited by the mechanical movement that rotates the seating area, kinetic experience may be more significant than the audience members' motility.

Although early scholars of the postwar avant-garde such as Richard Schechner (1973), Arnold Aronson (1977), and Josette Féral (1988) did not consider physiological aspects of the senses, Stephen Di Benedetto, writing in 2010, points out that because touch and the perception of position and motion (the haptic sense) are proximal senses, they are "ten times stronger than verbal or emotional contact" and provide a means for theatergoers "to experience the work in a more direct fashion."[6] When the director Martin Glaser staged Shakespeare's *Macbeth* at the revolving auditorium theater as part of the 2011 South Bohemia Theatre Festival, he used Brehms's design as both a performance space and an implied environment in which the audience was included in the "illusionistic time and place of the play."[7] The momentum and instability of the moving auditorium inflected the audience's experience of *Macbeth*'s Scottish setting, as did the unstable and inchoate boundaries of the performance space. Insofar as *Macbeth* is a play about nationalism and nation-building, this motif was enhanced by the theatrical setting, functioning one way for Czech nationals in attendance and another way for those spectators more familiar with *Macbeth* in English.

The Performance Experience

For attendees at *Macbeth* in 2011, the show began, after a long wait while twilight fell, with a jerk. The seating area began to turn fast, and then faster; audience members watched as the surrounding area slipped away to the left. Dusk had fallen; they could see clouds of smoke and hear heavy breathing, then women's cries and unrecognizable sounds. Many people seated on the auditorium platform felt dizzy, and some were nauseated. Environmental theater can achieve a variety of effects. What kind of a *Macbeth* could this be?

The seating area is what defines this space as a theater—it is ringed by a worn path bare of grass—but all the area surrounding the auditorium serves as a playing area, most of it extending outward indefinitely.

Opposite the Bellarie summer house is a narrow, grassy clearing; the trees of the densely wooded area beyond it seem to encroach upon the empty space. Midway between the summer house and the clearing is a place where the path widens. Trees stand nearby, but just a few.[8]

Director Martin Glaser used blocking that worked with this design as well as with the movement of the auditorium to disrupt the audience's usual experience of space. The domestic spaces of *Macbeth* were represented in parts of the performance area: Macbeth's closet and his banquet hall were clearly delineated and experienced as parts of a home. Many scenes in the play, however, were never experienced as occurring *in* a place because they took place, so to speak, *on the move*: they occurred as actors kept pace with the slowly revolving auditorium. As a result, the battlefield scenes and some of the encounters with the witches occurred in an indeterminate space that altered the audience's experience of Shakespeare's Scotland, rendering it a dynamic area that one moves through rather than inhabiting. The actors' walking delineated a shifting space in which things happened and actions were carried out. Their "Scotland" may be said to be grounded only by the tread of feet.

The Stage as Surround

Schechner argues in *Environmental Theater* that

> [t]he first scenic principle of environmental theater is to create and use whole spaces. Literally spheres of spaces, spaces within spaces, spaces which contain, or envelop, or relate, or touch all the areas where the audience is and/or the performers perform.[9]

What happens, though, in an open-air theater? Andy Lavender points out that placement within the playing area

> betokens an effect of presence as much as an act of organization. ... To that end, *mise en scène* is an arrangement of space, presence, and appearance that produces an effective figuration for the spectator. ... [M]ise en scène is an aesthetic system that engages the viewer in the act of viewing. ... A *mise en scène* can feature various elements of the medium, including the rhythmic and spatial dynamics of exits, entrances and movement within scenes; the architectonic nature of space—more or less open, confining, sweeping, shadowy and so forth.[10]

Brehms's turntable doesn't merely dictate spectators' behaviors, it redefines space and generates a new experience of spatiality. By rendering it necessary that all the action must be performed around the seating area, the turntable defines the performance space in the most literal terms: grass is worn away by the tread of the actors' shoes. But this path defines only one side of the performance area—what would be the lip of the stage in a proscenium theater. Most open-air theaters have a platform stage; this one does not. This stage is centered on and around the audience. Significantly, it is the *outer* edges of the stage—the borders of the *up*stage area—that are undefined. For 270 degrees around the turntable, there are no walls, no structures. How far out (or back) does the performance area extend? The open-air aspect of this theater is particularly significant in a play like *Macbeth*, whose climax occurs when the protagonist is told that the natural world has become animated and is coming to engulf him. Does the staging area extend only five feet from the perimeter of the turntable? Ten? Does the staging area extend farther out on some parts of the circle than others? Can it extend indefinitely, or do the actors need a space beyond which they are understood to disappear? While the audience cannot walk among the actors, as in so many of Schechner's productions, their perceptions necessarily shape their understanding of the performance and the performance area.

Schechner asserts that "there is an actual, living relationship between the spaces of the body and the spaces the body moves through ... people communicate with space and with each other through space; [there are] ways of locating centers of energies and boundaries ... 'auras' and 'lines of energy.'"[11] The actors in Glaser's *Macbeth* structured the space equally by their numerousness and by their small numbers. Shakespeare makes his spectators assume that the small crowd of supernumeraries playing unnamed characters represents a much larger number. How many soldiers did Glaser's soldiers represent? Behind the tree that couldn't be seen because of the other trees, beside the fallen log obscured by the shadows, a mass of unseen supernumeraries loomed, ghosting the visible men who tramped and shouted and fell.[12] The space extended to an unknown degree into the darkness; anything there could have been an actor, or actors.

Just as Brehms's turntable shapes the performance space, it also defines the space belonging to playgoers. In contrast to the freedom to wander provided in immersive theater (also known as promenade theater), this theater design requires spectators to remain seated. The turntable's revolutions create a shared experience that melds the seated onlookers into a collective audience, in stark contrast to the individuals who wander through immersive environments. Schechner's point about bodies and lines of energy can also be applied to the audience, "one of the agents of theatre," as W. B. Worthen notes.[13] There is no appropriate term for "playgoer" that truly characterizes the experience of attending a play in this venue: neither hearing the play (as "audience") nor watching it (as "spectator") is germane to experiencing the push of air, the sense of one's body impeding the flow of air created by the spinning. Perhaps "witness" signifies the weight of one's own physical presence; but what, then, is implied about the necessity for judgment? The initial spin of the turntable was so unexpected that every person seated on the structure had to develop their own interpretation of it. Was the experience of vertigo what the director intended? Perhaps the revolutions were intended as a metaphor for going into a fictive space or for going back in time, perhaps as a challenge to the solidity of judgment. These are all possible ways that the playgoers may have experienced the use of the mechanism; what is sure is that physical experience shaped the impressions people brought to the initial action. With the seating area constantly moving, the kinetic experience of Glaser's *Macbeth* was something like an amusement park ride—perhaps like a grittier, more complex "Pirates of the Caribbean." But the haptic experience was much more powerful than what Disney engineers could provide with a series of animatronic panoramas slipping by during a slow-moving river ride. Macbeth's revolt against "fair sequence and succession," his disruption of the natural order, was something we experienced through our bodies. Schechner contrasts appearance and function: "The stage designer is often concerned with effect: how does it *look* from the house? The environmentalist is concerned with structure and use: how does it *work?*"[14] The night I was present at Glaser's *Macbeth*, the job of the rotation was accomplished successfully: its effect was visceral, making the playgoers not merely auditors or watchers but people who experienced the performance in their guts.

Glaser's use of the mechanism throughout the play both challenged and expanded upon one of Schechner's central dicta: "The environmentalist is not trying to create the illusion of a place; he wants to create a functioning space."[15] The space of the performance was vitalized by the director's control of audience movement. An audience that is *told* to shift its location shambles about, herded by the directive. Compare this audience's experience with that of the playgoers at Luca Ronconi's immersive production of *Orlando Furioso*: shoved this way and that by actors and moving platforms, Ronconi's playgoers were bombarded by sensation as they experienced the performance.[16] The playgoers at Glaser's *Macbeth* were not crowded or shoved by hands or other bodies, but they were pushed through space, moved toward specific sightlines. This was no revolving restaurant, rotating staidly at the rate of one revolution per hour, so gently that you barely feel it: on Brehms's platform, the earth moves under people's feet (or under their seats) as their orientation is manipulated in unexpected and unpredictable ways.

"History is now and England"?[17] Standing in Place

A corollary to the experience of the seating is the experience of the performance space. Let us consider Schechner's statement again: "The environmentalist is not trying to create the illusion of a place."[18] In *Staging Place*, Schechner's colleague Una Chaudhuri examines how, in naturalistic drama, theater responds to the understanding of place—meaning setting—"as a factor of knowledge and a code of representation."[19] She challenges "the habitual ... opposition between naturalism and the experimental stage practice known as environmental theatre."[20] Chaudhuri asserts, "The relationship between naturalism and environmentalism is, in fact, a continuum that has been disguised as a rupture."[21] Place, commonly structured in the early modern public theaters of London by pictorial language, deictics, and the design of the thrust stage, is reconfigured here by theatrical practice that seems to conform to the standards of environmentalism.

Chaudhuri avers that the "fully iconic, single-set, middle-class living room of realism produced so closed and so *complete* a stage world that it supported the new and powerful fantasy of the stage not as a place to pretend in or to perform on but a place to *be*."[22] In contrast, the bare stage of early modern public theaters in London was understood as evocative: Marlowe furnished it in *Tamburlaine*, Shakespeare tested its power with the choruses of *Henry V*, and Jonson satirized it with Sir Epicure Mammon's bombastic entrance speech in *The Alchemist*. Words defined the place, and platial conventions of past theatrical traditions often shaped understanding as well. Action tended to orient actors and spectators alike, and gestures could designate platial signifiers. In the final analysis, the design of the theater could also delineate place: the heavens were painted above, hell was in the cellarage. Place was outlined by the boundary of the stage.

Glaser took a different approach. In his production, scenes not clearly located in an interior were hardly "staged" at all. In this production, the mimetic space of the action in *Macbeth* was in flux unless set firmly within domestic or feudal locations. Scenes within the castle were staged within fixed locations: at the top of the stairs fronting the building façade, at the foot of the stairs, or at a banquet table placed upon the grass. Scenes occurring outdoors were often anchored by a prop around which the actors clustered. More often, however, they emphasized the occasional nature of the theater setting, as the actors remained in motion, walking steadily to keep up with the slowly rotating turntable. The effect of this action was to weaken the grounding of the play in Scotland—in fact, to derail the production of any clearly designated place. In his essay "Building Dwelling Thinking," Martin Heidegger says, "[O]nly something *that is itself a location* can make space for a site. The location is not already there before the bridge is."[23] Similarly, Henri Lefebvre's statement, "(Social) space is a (social) product," suggests that some sort of structure may be necessary to create a sense of place.[24] Place felt elusive in this production: characters never seemed to get anywhere, as scenes tended to conclude with darkening lights rather than the characters' arrival at a destination. Randomness was staged, though probably not enacted; characters who were killed seemed to fall along the path wherever their death happened to occur. This indeterminate orientation in the production recalled for me the placelessness of Beckett's *Waiting for Godot*.

As Michel de Certeau asseverates, "To walk is to lack a place. It is the indefinite process of being absent and in search of a proper [sic]."[25]

Glaser's Scotland was not delimited by the edge of a stage, nor by a circle of spectators—it could be everywhere or nowhere. It could be where the actors were or where they were going. Rather than outlining a place by striding through it, the characters seemed to be traveling toward their destiny or away from it. Whether in pursuit or being pursued, the characters moved forward, motivated by the threat of attack. The staging did not draw one's attention to place; instead, exhaustion, working muscles, fear, and danger were evident.

Union of the (British) Crowns/The Lands of the Bohemian Crown

Glaser's use of his theater highlighted an issue more generally noted in Shakespeare's history plays than in *Macbeth*: the concern with nationhood and nationalism that emerged as early modern monarchs attempted to centralize their authority.[26] Prior to the sixteenth century, most people living in England could identify with a local area and a market town, and also with an international community through the Catholic Church. But by the 1590s, when Shakespeare was composing his history plays, people identified with England—they could no longer bypass their national identity.[27] By 1606, the putative date of *Macbeth*'s first performance, England and Scotland had been yoked under one ruler for three years. At the time that Shakespeare was composing the history plays, the notion of nationhood was in flux. Nonetheless, perceiving oneself as part of the English nation was as important in that generation as perceiving oneself as a member of the national religion had been just a few generations earlier.

Scholars have long viewed *Macbeth* as a play written partially in response to James VI of Scotland's ascension to the English throne as his cousin Elizabeth's heir.[28] Yet Scotland, this clearly demarcated country, was not emphasized in Glaser's production. Instead, Glaser's use of motion produced a constant sense of dis-settlement. His combination of staging, blocking, and mechanics provoked a loss of orientation that resonated with the themes of the play, calling attention to the indeterminacy of space. If, as de Certeau says, "Travel (like walking) is a substitute for the legends that used to open up space to something different," what might be said about the relation in Glaser's production between and among history, text, and performance space?[29]

This question is particularly resonant for Czechs. British and American attendees of Glaser's production were probably thinking about Scotland, but *Macbeth* is a particularly important play for Czech people. As Martin Procházka points out, *Macbeth* was the first Shakespeare play performed in Czech: in 1786, a translator worked with a German adaptation by F. J. Fischer and a Czech chapbook to produce *Makbet, aneb Proroctví carodejnic*.[30] Procházka asserts that Shakespeare's portrayal of rebellion against aristocratic tyranny made the play attractive to the Czech population at that time: "The peasants' rebellion of 1775, followed by the abolition of serfdom and the establishment of the centralized absolutist regime of Joseph II, influenced the repertory of the Patriotic Theater, which staged the first Czech translations and adaptations of Shakespeare."[31] *Macbeth* was also staged during the 1970s in private homes in Prague following the repression of the Prague Spring by the Communist regime. Dissident theater workers led by Pavel Kohout, who translated the play into Czech, held shows in their own houses despite government surveillance. Kohout adapted the play more to be read than performed; the purpose of the stagings was to strengthen "a social bond by means of the collective effort of the actors and the public" and "[reconstitute] personal identities for viewers afflicted and depressed by the harassment of the system."[32] According to Procházka, Malcolm was characterized as "the innocent victim of the tyrant's cruelty, a 'dissident' forced to emigrate and seek foreign help to overthrow the regime. ... Malcolm was able to articulate his relationship to the whole group (including the audience) in terms of mancipatio and thus to confirm the ritualized performance of the play as a source of supreme authority."[33]

Questions of boundaries, borders, and territories are part of the national history of the Czech people and the lands of the Bohemian Crown. Though the Duchy of Bohemia was established in the ninth and tenth centuries and the Kingdom of Bohemia in 1198, the kingdom was also a part of the Holy Roman Empire for hundreds of years, and in 1526 the Bohemian Crown passed to the Habsburg dynasty. With the dissolution of the Holy Roman Empire in 1806, the Bohemian Kingdom became part of the Austrian Empire, despite rising Czech nationalism and a growing desire for an independent Czech state throughout the nineteenth century. Czechoslovakia was created in 1918 but was soon carved up by Poland, Hungary, and Germany in 1938, and in 1949 it became a Communist state within the Eastern bloc. Given the constantly fluctuating borders of Czech lands and the questions about the reality of a Czech identity, the quarrels among the noble kinsmen of Scotland and its reliance on England for aid would have been familiar fare to Czechs who seek a national identity in their nation's early history.

The sense of an unformed country created by the actors' constant pacing and the ambiguity of the border, whether of the fictive Scotland or the stage area, may have resonated for some of the Czechs in attendance. For many Czech spectators, the moving auditorium is notable primarily for its novelty value, and the visceral, embodied experience would have carried less meaning. For intellectuals and specialists in theater, any production of *Macbeth* might recall the claustrophobic and fearful readings of *Macbeth* in the 1970s. The meanings of Glaser's *Macbeth* would depend on the individual: to the degree that spectators saw a parallel to their own country in Shakespeare's Scotland, the steady pace of Glaser's actors might have suggested their nation's new ability to chart its own course. With the Velvet Revolution, Czechoslovakia returned to liberal democracy in late 1989 and peacefully dissolved into the Czech Republic and Slovakia in 1993; the Czech Republic joined the European Union (EU) eleven years later. The sense of placelessness produced by the staging may have seemed like possibility or like an enactment of an endless border, where flexibility and divergent thinking enable one to stand up to the dominant culture without directly challenging its authority.[34] It would be easy to see the final scene, in which Macduff conquers the tyrant and establishes Scotland's first earls, in the vista presented to the stilled and unmoving audience, as the moment when audience and actors mutually engaged in the creation of place within the play, the moment when the performance space became the new nation, the moment of "arrival and concreteness rather than deferral and slippage," to borrow a phrase.[35] After Glaser's use of the rotating auditorium's many possibilities, his choice finally to be still, to end with stillness, could be experienced as a founding moment, the moment when place is created.

One might use the Czech Republic as an example to counter Pierre Nora's assertion, "there are no longer *milieux de mémoire*, real environments of memory."[36] Both Prague and Český Krumlov are, arguably, exactly that. Since the castle complex was designated a world heritage site by the United Nations Educational, Scientific, and Cultural Organization (UNESCO) in 1992, there has been considerable debate around the continued existence of the revolving auditorium theater. Preservationists argue that the auditorium's presence is incompatible with the maintenance of a culturally significant historical site. Yet the theater remains—for now. The Czech Republic's Ministers of Culture seem unwilling to tear it down, prolonging its use with temporary permits. Its success depends in part on the surrounding environment, to which it is alien in period and inimical in purpose.[37] But so long as it exists, it offers visitors and theatergoers a still-living environment of memory, as Glaser's unsettling production demonstrates. If the auditorium were removed or relocated, the Český Krumlov castle would be preserved like a fly in amber. Rather than a living environment, the castle would become a *lieu de mémoire*, a place "where memory crystallizes and secretes itself ... at a particular historical moment."[38] Glaser's *Macbeth* reinforces the spectator's experience not only of the layers of time but of the flux and change of state boundaries, of their lack of stability. The spectator's nausea at the constantly moving *Macbeth* is a sign that food is still in the belly, that history is still taking place among us—perhaps especially when we rotate in a Modernist structure and yet attempt to root ourselves, through the ceremonial ritual of theater, in a much more distant past.[39]

Notes

1 Arnold Aronson, *The History and Theory of Environmental Scenography*, 2nd ed. (Ann Arbor: UMI Research Press, 1981), 2.

2 This new auditorium, constructed in 1994 by the joint-stock company Skoda Plzen, has a base firmly installed in the ground, and an electric motor controls its rotation. The diameter of the base is 21.3 meters and the elevation is 7.6 meters. The movement is driven by four electric motors, which rotate the disk around a central axle on 120 wheels. "Revolving Auditorium in Český

Krumlov," Theatre Architecture, accessed July 22, 2020. www.theatre-architecture.eu/db.html?theatreId=141.

3 To some degree, this environment exemplifies what Aronson describes as "the most totally surrounding space … a sphere with the audience suspended at the center." *Environmental Scenography*, 7.

4 Quoted in "Revolving Auditorium."

5 Josette Féral, "Theatricality: The Specificity of Theatrical Language," *SubStance* 31, nos. 2–3, issue 98/9 (2002): 97.

6 Stephen Di Benedetto, *The Provocation of the Senses in Contemporary Theatre* (New York: Routledge, 2010), 69–70.

7 Aronson, *Environmental Scenography*, 7.

8 As the reviewer Jana Machalická commented:

> The scenographer Jaromír Vlček [] used simple natural materials—wood, branches, twigs, dry grass—and created incredible suggestive sets. He … enriched the scenery of the garden with features that entered it smoothly and enhanced the authentic impression. The baroque garden transformed into a raw wilderness, a moon landscape with black stubs of branches sticking out and with ruins of hollow tree trunks. Instead of the airy mansion of the Bellaria we have a wearied construction full of cracks and all-encompassing emptiness and destruction.

Jana Machalická, "O zlu, které se vkrádá do duše" ("Of evil that creeps into one's soul"), *Lidové noviny*, August 19, 2010. Translation by Pavel Drábek, private correspondence.

9 Richard Schechner, *Environmental Theater*, revised ed. (New York: Applause, 1994), 2.

10 Andy Lavender, *Performance in the Twenty-First Century* (New York: Routledge, 2016), 78–9.

11 Schechner, *Environmental Theater*, 12.

12 I borrow a phrase here, "behind the tree that cannot be seen because of the other trees," from Margaret Atwood's masterly short story "Death by Landscape," which concludes by describing a landscape painting in which the narrator imagines a girl hidden behind a tree. *Wilderness Tips* (New York: Doubleday, 1991), 118.

13 W. B. Worthen, *Shakespeare Performance Studies* (Cambridge: Cambridge University Press, 2014), 23. I have elsewhere argued that both spectators and stage design merit more examination in their role as contributors to theatrical experience (see Jennifer A. Low, *Dramatic Spaces* [London: Routledge, 2016]).

14 Schechner, *Environmental Theater*, 31.

15 Schechner, *Environmental Theater*, 31.

16 The director Luca Ronconi's "most revolutionary production" was his stage adaptation of Ariosto's *Orlando Furioso*, which premiered in Spoleto, Italy and then moved to a number of cities including Bologna, Amsterdam, Madrid, Edinburgh, and New York (John Francis Lane, "Luca Ronconi Obituary," *The Guardian*, March 1, 2015). The production was characterized as "an environmental spectacle" and was an early example of immersive theater that owed a great deal to the European tradition of pageant theater. With the production, Ronconi wished to combine "certain American principles" crystallized in Richard Schechner's writings with theatrical forms from the medieval theater that had "fallen into disuse" (Franco Quadri, trans. Helen

R. Lane, "Orlando Furioso," *TDR* 14, no. 3 [1970]: 118). As Franco Quadri explains,

> Ronconi designed the performance for a large space, measuring at least 120 feet by 45 feet... . The central space is occupied at the same time by the audience and by the actors, who for the most part act, speak, gallop, and duel on wooden floats which are either bare or embellished with metal constructions: sheet-metal horses ... a hippogriff ... cages of gauze and plywood... . The floats, propelled by actors who for the moment are not participating in the action, pass through the whole stage area. Their continuous movement—endangering the spectators and forcing them to move away suddenly—is a means of attack and a means of communication. (119)

While the theater critic Clive Barnes panned the New York production, which took place in Bryant Park under a plastic "bubble" structure, he allowed that Ronconi's creation of a "moving audience" was an important innovation: "The concept of an ambulatory audience attending a play that is taking place in various areas simultaneously, with the audience moving as if it were at an exhibition, may have future possibilities" (Clive Barnes, "Stage: 'Orlando' and MacGowran—Sight vs. Sense," *The New York Times*, November 27, 1970, 46).

17 This line is from one of the monuments of high Modernism, T. S. Eliot's *Four Quartets* (London: Faber, 1944), 58.

18 Schechner, *Environmental Theater*, 31.

19 Una Chaudhuri, *Staging Place* (Ann Arbor: University of Michigan Press, 1995), 6.

20 Chaudhuri, *Staging Place*, 17.

21 Chaudhuri, *Staging Place*, 26.

22 Chaudhuri, *Staging Place*, 10.

23 Martin Heidegger, *Poetry, Language, Thought*, trans. Albert Hofstadter (New York: Harper & Row, 1971), 154 (italics in original).

24 Henri Lefebvre, *The Production of Space*, trans. Donald Nicholson-Smith (Oxford: Blackwell, 1991), 26.

25 Michel de Certeau, *The Practice of Everyday Life*, trans. Steven Rendall (Berkeley: University of California Press, 1984), 103.

26 The emergence of nationalism in Europe and Britain in the sixteenth and seventeenth centuries has been treated in numerous studies including Perry Anderson, *Lineages of the Absolutist State* (London: New Left Books, 1974); G. R. Elton, *The Tudor Revolution in Government* (Cambridge: Cambridge University Press, 1953); Anthony Giddens, *The Nation-State and Violence* (Berkeley: University of California Press, 1987); Liah Greenfeld, *Nationalism* (Cambridge, MA: Harvard University Press, 1992); Andrew Hadfield, "The Nation in the Renaissance" in *Reading the Nation in English Literature*, eds. Elizabeth Sauer and Julia M. Wright (London: Routledge, 2010), 135–43; Philip Schwyzer, *Literature, Nationalism, and Memory in Early Modern England and Wales* (Cambridge: Cambridge University Press, 2004); and Cathy Shrank, *Writing the Nation in Reformation England, 1530–1580* (Oxford: Oxford University Press, 2004). In *Forms of Nationhood* (Chicago: University of Chicago Press, 1992), Richard Helgerson cites several early modern works as evidence of a new nationalist project in Great Britain; among these are William Camden's *Britannia* (1586), Sir Edward Coke's

Institutes of the Laws of England (1628–44), and Richard Hakluyt's *Principal Navigations of the English Nation* (1589).

27 See Greenfeld, *Nationalism*; Shrank, *Writing the Nation*; and Daniel Woolf, "Of Nations, Nationalism, and National Identity: Reflections on the Historiographic Organization of the Past," in *The Many Faces of Clio: Cross-Cultural Approaches to Historiography,* eds. Q. Edward Wang and Franz L. Fillafer (New York: Berghahn Books, 2007), 71–103.

28 See, for example, Joseph Q. Adams, ed., *The Tragedy of Macbeth* (Boston: Houghton Mifflin, 1931), 236, 248–50; Henry N. Paul, *The Royal Play of Macbeth* (New York: Octagon, 1950), 328–30; and Lily B. Campbell, "Political Ideas in *Macbeth* IV.iii," *Shakespeare Quarterly* 2, no. 4 (October 1951): 281–6. Adams was the first officially appointed director of the Folger Shakespeare Library.

29 de Certeau, *Everyday Life*, 106–7.

30 Martin Procházka, "Shakespeare and Czech Resistance," in *Shakespeare World Views*, eds. Heather Kerr, Robin Eaden, and Madge Mitton (Newark: University of Delaware Press, 1996), 46.

31 Procházka, "Czech Resistance," 45.

32 Procházka, "Czech Resistance," 62, 63.

33 Procházka, "Czech Resistance," 63–4.

34 Cf. Gloria Anzaldua, *Borderlands/La Frontera: The New Mestiza* (San Francisco: Aunt Lute Books, 1987), 78–9.

35 Lavender, *Performance*, 27.

36 Pierre Nora, "Between Memory and History: Les Lieux de Mémoire," *Representations* 26 (Spring 1989): 7.

37 See "Revolving Auditorium."

38 Nora, "Between Memory and History," 7.

39 This work was substantially improved by the feedback I received from William N. West, Louise Geddes, Martin Procházka, and Maurizio Calbi. I am fortunate to be able to count such fine readers among my friends. I'm also extremely grateful to Pavel Drábek for our email conversations and his generous help with a mass of Czech theater reviews. Warm thanks is also due to Lucie Čepcová, Head of the Information and Documentation Department at the Institut umění—Divadelní ústav (Arts and Theatre Institute in Prague), who scoured her archives to find the reviews of this production for me.

Bibliography

Adams, Joseph Q., ed. *The Tragedy of Macbeth*. Boston: Houghton Mifflin, 1931.

Anderson, Perry. *Lineages of the Absolutist State*. London: New Left Books, 1974.

Anzaldua, Gloria. *Borderlands/La Frontera: The New Mestiza*. San Francisco: Aunt Lute Books, 1987.

Aronson, Arnold. *The History and Theory of Environmental Scenography*, revised ed. Ann Arbor: UMI Research Press, 1981.

Atwood, Margaret. *Wilderness Tips*. New York: Doubleday, 1991.

Barnes, Clive. "Stage: 'Orlando' and MacGowran—Sight vs. Sense." *The New York Times*, November 27, 1970, 46. www.nytimes.com/1970/11/27/archives/stage-orlando-and-macgowran-sight-vs-sense.html.

Campbell, Lily B. "Political Ideas in *Macbeth* IV.iii." *Shakespeare Quarterly* 2, no. 4 (October 1951): 281–6.

Chaudhuri, Una. *Staging Place: The Geography of Modern Drama*. Ann Arbor: University of Michigan Press, 1995.

de Certeau, Michel. *The Practice of Everyday Life*. Translated by Steven Rendall. Berkeley: University of California Press, 1984.

Di Benedetto, Stephen. *The Provocation of the Senses in Contemporary Theatre*. New York: Routledge, 2010.

Eliot, T. S. *Four Quartets*. London: Faber, 1944.

Elton, G. R. *The Tudor Revolution in Government: Administrative Changes in the Reign of Henry VIII*. Cambridge: Cambridge University Press, 1953.

Féral, Josette. "Theatricality: The Specificity of Theatrical Language." *SubStance* 31, nos. 2–3, issue 98/9 (2002): 94–108. Originally published in French in *Poétique* Sept. (1988): 347–61.

Giddens, Anthony. *The Nation-State and Violence: Volume Two of a Contemporary Critique of Historical Materialism*. Berkeley: University of California Press, 1987.

Greenfeld, Liah. *Nationalism: Five Roads to Modernity*. Cambridge, MA: Harvard University Press, 1992.

Hadfield, Andrew. "The Nation in the Renaissance." In *Reading the Nation in English Literature*, edited by Elizabeth Sauer and Julia M. Wright, 135–43. London: Routledge, 2010.

Heidegger, Martin. *Poetry, Language, Thought*. Translated by Albert Hofstadter. New York: Harper & Row, 1971.

Helgerson, Richard. *Forms of Nationhood: The Elizabethan Writing of England*. Chicago: University of Chicago Press, 1992.

Lane, John Francis. "Luca Ronconi Obituary." *The Guardian*, March 1, 2015. www.theguardian.com/stage/2015/mar/01/luca-ronconi.

Lavender, Andy. *Performance in the Twenty-First Century: Theatres of Engagement*. New York: Routledge, 2016.

Lefebvre, Henri. *The Production of Space*. Translated by Donald Nicholson-Smith. Oxford: Blackwell, 1991.

Low, Jennifer A. *Dramatic Spaces: Scenography and Spectatorial Perceptions*. New York: Routledge, 2016.

Machalická, Jana. "O zlu, které se vkrádá do duše" ("Of evil that creeps into one's soul"). *Lidové noviny*, August 19, 2010. www.jihoceskedivadlo.cz/porad/1023-macbeth?lang=en.

Nora, Pierre. "Between Memory and History: Les Lieux de Mémoire." *Representations* 26 (Spring, 1989): 7–24.

Paul, Henry N. *The Royal Play of Macbeth: When, Why, and How It Was Written by Shakespeare*. New York: Octagon, 1950.

Procházka, Martin. "Shakespeare and Czech Resistance." In *Shakespeare World Views*, edited by Heather Kerr, Robin Eaden, and Madge Mitton, 44–69. Newark: University of Delaware Press, 1996.

Quadri, Franco, trans. Helen R. Lane. "Orlando Furioso." *TDR* 14, no. 3 (1970): 116–24.

Revolving Theatre Český Krumlov. "History." Accessed July 22, 2020. www.otacivehlediste.cz/uvod/historie.

Schechner, Richard. *Environmental Theater* [1973], revised ed. New York: Applause, 1994.

Schwyzer, Philip. *Literature, Nationalism, and Memory in Early Modern England and Wales*. Cambridge: Cambridge University Press, 2004.

Shrank, Cathy. *Writing the Nation in Reformation England, 1530–1580*. Oxford: Oxford University Press, 2004.

Theatre Architecture. "Revolving Auditorium in Český Krumlov." Accessed July 22, 2020. www.theatre-architecture.eu/db.html?theatreId=141.

Woolf, Daniel. "Of Nations, Nationalism, and National Identity: Reflections on the Historiographic Organization of the Past." In *The Many Faces of Clio: Cross-Cultural Approaches to Historiography, Essays in Honor of Georg G. Iggers*, edited by Q. Edward Wang and Franz L. Fillafer, 71–103. New York: Berghahn Books, 2007.

Worthen, W. B. *Shakespeare Performance Studies*. Cambridge: Cambridge University Press, 2014.

Constructing Audiences

4 The most lamentable Romaine Tragedie of Titus Andronicus and Audiences from the Inns of Court

Romola Nuttall

This chapter explores the influence that the population of London's Inns of Court had as members of audiences in early modern public performance spaces—open-air amphitheaters, indoor theaters, and inn yards— by tracing the movement of onstage violence from the private Senecan dramas produced by, and familiar to, Innsmen into *Titus Andronicus*, a play written for the commercial stage. The physical movement of members of the Inns out of the private performance spaces within their institutions to public venues mirrors the textual movement of themes and motifs from privately produced dramas into *Titus*. The early production and popularity of *Titus* has been explored in relation to its Ovidian subject matter and references.[1] It is the connection between *Titus* and the Senecan tragedies produced within academic institutions at Oxford, Cambridge, and in London by students and lawyers at the Inns of Court that this chapter seeks to elucidate.[2]

The Inns most closely connected to early modern literary culture were Gray's Inn, Lincoln's Inn, Inner Temple, and Middle Temple.[3] The two Temples are on the northern embankment of the Thames; Lincoln's and Gray's Inns are slightly further north, in Holborn, just outside the western edge of the old City limits. Situated between the City and Westminster, the administrative and courtly centers of London, the Inns provided an ideal location for young men interested in securing a living by official appointments at court or entering the legal profession. Students at the Inns were relatively affluent young men, eager to pursue a legal career and benefit from the leisure pursuits London offered. Some residents were not students but paying tenants who worked in the law courts; the Inns housed senior members of the legal profession, but many members did not reside in the Inns. Together, they represented a physical and conceptual community, comprising "the largest single group of literate and cultured men in London ... [totalling] around 1,040 occupants by the end of the sixteenth century, 1,703 including those in Chancery."[4]

Shakespeare must have been familiar with dramatic culture, taste, and activity at the Inns around the time of *Titus*'s composition. The *Gesta Greyorum* (1688) famously records a performance of Shakespeare's

Comedy of Errors at Gray's Inn on December 28, 1594, and critics have highlighted the influence of the Inns' institutional interests on the play's reproduction of Plautus's *Menaechmi* and its use of what Lorna Hutson calls "the evidential plot."[5] Shakespeare's *Twelfth Night*, performed at Middle Temple in 1602, gives an instance of an ongoing relationship of patronage between the Inns and the Lord Chamberlain's Men. What has not yet been attended to is the idea of Inns members as influential to drama in commercial arenas: their presence in Elizabethan and Jacobean playhouses and inn yards is only beginning to emerge in recent scholarship.[6] Students at the Inns are known to have been regular patrons of playhouses.[7] Indeed, some critics have suggested that Inns students' "finely tuned legal wit often seems to have been the ideal audience imagined by Shakespeare."[8] My argument is that the Inns of Court played a key role as centers that supplied significant sections of audiences in commercial playing spaces and so brought a specific set of tastes to public venues—tastes strongly associated with Senecan tragedy. Of course, the tastes of Innsmen cannot be said to be homogenous, or even infallibly identifiable, but institutional exposure to Senecan drama would have created a familiarity with its generic conventions that Innsmen would have brought with them to the theaters. The degree to which Senecan plays informed the work of professional dramatists certainly suggests that acting companies found value in appropriating dramatic material with which Innsmen would be familiar. *Titus Andronicus* exemplifies this trend, particularly in its presentation of violence, and paying attention to the performance cultures of the Inns of Court around the time of *Titus*'s earliest performances illustrates the ways in which that play seems to have been designed to meet the tastes of the wealthiest members of public audiences, members who could also facilitate more lucrative private performances.[9] The population of London's Inns of Court would have met these criteria.[10]

As at court, the Inns marked seasonal festivals with revels at which attendance was compulsory for all members.[11] Secular entertainments, of which staged plays formed a major part, were most common during the Christmas season, between All Saints' Day (November 1) and Shrove Tuesday (early February). At the beginning of Elizabeth's reign, the plays that formed part of Inns revels were written and staged by the gentlemen of the Inns themselves, but after 1587 adult professional companies were brought in to supply nearly all of the Inns' dramatic entertainment.[12] The Inns had a long tradition, which they shared with the two universities, of producing drama for pedagogical as well as recreational purposes. Nearly half of those admitted as students had been to university—and it appears that students at the Inns who were not university-educated emulated literary habits associated with these communities—making it important to read the drama at the Inns of Court alongside plays produced at Oxford and Cambridge.[13] Printed Senecan translations produced by writers based at, or connected to, the Inns in the 1560s demonstrate that drama circulated within these communities to complement the understanding of classical texts as morally valuable and improving. In Jasper Heywood's preface to his translation of Seneca's *Thyestes* (1560), a dreaming Heywood tells Seneca that the project of translating his tragedies into English "shall flourish" at the Inns:

> In Lincoln's Inn and Temples twain, Grays Inn and other mo,
> Thou shalt them find whose painful pen thy verse shall flourish so.
> (Preface, 81–6)[14]

Between 1560 and 1567 eight more Senecan translations were produced by Inns writers.[15] Although they appear to have gone out of fashion in the 1570s, Thomas Newton's collected edition, *Seneca: His Tenne Tragedies* (1581), signals a renewal of interest in the genre continuing into the 1580s.[16] Seneca's tragedies were hugely influential within the arena of the Inns because he was, as Jessica Winston writes, "an orator, lawyer, and counsellor: in other words, a classical version of the sort of rhetorician and politician that those at the universities and Inns of Court were trying to become."[17]

   Seneca's eight surviving tragedies take their stories and characters from Greek tragedy; they use choric songs, follow a five-act structure, and are concerned with kings, queens, and their nemeses.[18] Unlike their Greek exemplars, Seneca's plays emphasize human, rather than divine, agency as the cause of downfall. His plays make revenge a central trope and often begin with a ghost who relates the circumstances of their death and how that death must be avenged. Seneca's plays are distinctive for their references to blood, gore, and descriptions of extreme suffering, although they deal in reports, rather than performances, of violent acts.[19] These dramatic features are found in the surviving examples of plays written and performed by members of the Inns in Elizabeth's reign: *Gorboduc, the Tragedy of Ferrex and Porrex*, "played and devised by some gentlemen of the house at Inner Temple" in the 1561–2 season; *Gismond of Salerne*, written by five members of the Inner Temple and staged there in 1565–6 or 1566–7; and *The Misfortunes of Arthur*, shown at court in 1587–8. Surviving examples of early Elizabethan plays, *Cambyses* (c. 1561) and *Horestes* (c. 1567), indicate that classical elements also informed non-academic drama (*Cambyses* and *Horestes* were shown at court but would most likely have also been performed in public venues) and it is not the object of this chapter to suggest that Senecan drama was favored exclusively by academic audiences.[20] These groups, however, would have been more exposed to this kind of drama than other groups within commercial audiences and may, therefore, have been associated with them by dramatists. The ways in which *Titus* remodels aspects of university and Inns drama supports this theory, exemplifying what Sarah Knight has identified as "a two-way traffic of authorship and influence ... between the Inns and the public theatres."[21]

Elements of *Titus* adhere closely to the Philomel myth, found in book six of Ovid's *Metamorphoses*, as translated by Arthur Golding (1567).[22] The story tells of Philomel's rape by her sister's husband, Tereus, king of Thrace. In order to conceal his crime, Tereus cuts out Philomel's tongue and abandons her in a forest. Philomel's solution is to weave a tapestry illustrating her abduction, which she is eventually able to show to her sister, Progne, Tereus's wife. The Philomel story circulated widely, in forms that would have been familiar to both Inns and university communities. For example, in 1566, a now lost Philomel–Progne play by James Calfhill was performed before Elizabeth I at Christ Church College, Oxford.[23] As Helen Slaney has argued, it would be tempting to place this play among the sources for *Titus* because George Peele, who co-authored *Titus*, studied there between 1574 and 1579 and in 1583 was employed by Christ Church to assist with the revival of two neo-Senecan Latin plays by William Gager, *Meleager* and *Rivales*.[24] Calfhill's much earlier *Progne* may only have been known to Peele from college records and manuscripts, but while its direct influence on *Titus* may only be supposed, it demonstrates a precedent for dramatization of the Philomel–Progne story within an academic community.[25]

Peele's familiarity with the dramatic tastes of academic audiences, like those based at the Inns, perhaps helps to explain the extent of *Titus*'s textual borrowings from Senecan drama. It is perhaps fair to say that, where Shakespeare's contributions lean heavily on his reading of Ovid, the early sections of the play, attributed to Peele, present stronger iterations of themes and tropes from Senecan and academic drama. Indeed, several features of Gager's *Meleager*, one of the plays that Peele was paid to stage at Christ Church in 1583, are echoed in *Titus*, most notably the performance of violence. The innovation of sixteenth-century neo-Senecan plays to their Roman forerunners is the performance, rather than the recitation, of violent acts. Mariangela Tempera has argued that the distinctive display of onstage violence in *Titus* and contemporary revenge plays was inspired by the presentation of "horror Italian-style," examples of which—plays like *Orbecche* (1543) and *Mariana* (1565)—were familiar to Elizabethan scholars interested in translating Senecan drama.[26] The bloodthirsty nature of professional plays like *Titus*, *The Spanish Tragedy*, and Peele's *The Battle of Alcazar*, is generally assumed to have come from the need to satisfy the taste of nonelite, ticket-buying audiences.[27] As its presence in academic and Inns drama shows, however, theatrical violence owes as much to the tastes of private, academic, and relatively upper-class audiences.[28]

The performed violence in *Titus*, and its clear relationship to Gager's *Meleager*, heightens this chapter's argument that commercially produced plays were written, at least in part, to appeal to the specific set of dramatic tastes associated with audiences of academic drama. *Meleager* and *Titus* share thematic and verbal references to hunting and the chase and present complex models of female sexuality. More importantly, both plays stage rash honor killings of close family members by their protagonists. After the triumphant return of the hunting party, Meleager kills his two uncles, Plexippius and Toxeus, because they refuse to honor Atalanta, the huntress who was the first to wound the Calydonian boar and with whom Meleager is deeply in love, despite her vow of celibacy. When his uncles contest his donation of the boar's spoils, "this hide, rough with bristles, and this head, fierce with its ivory tusks" to Atalanta, Meleager *"suddenly stabs them both in the side with a dagger"* (Act 3).[29] In *Titus*, when Mutius, one of Titus's few surviving sons, contradicts his father's will in supporting Lavinia's engagement to Bassianus, Titus kills him (1.1.295 SD). The unpremeditated nature of both sets of killings deepens the connection between the two plays.[30] In *Meleager*, the onstage deaths occur in the middle of the play, forming the pivotal plot point, which incurs revenge against Meleager by his mother. *Titus* takes the display of violence to an even greater degree, as people are killed onstage in nearly every act: Alarbus and Mutius in 1.1; Bassianus in 2.1; the Nurse in 4.2; Chiron and Demetrius in 5.2; Tamora, Lavinia, Saturnius, and Titus in 5.3.[31] In Act 3, the audience is confronted with the heads of Quintus and Martius and the chopping off of Titus's hand by Aaron. Such actions exaggerate the gory language of Seneca's plays and the violence shown in *Meleager*. The performance of violence in these two plays indicates very little distinction between the tastes of audience members who belonged to academic groups and those who did not. More importantly, acknowledging the extent to which onstage violence derives from academic drama illustrates a way in which audiences from academic communities, represented in London by the Inns of Court, influenced Shakespeare's drama, within both their institutional halls and public venues.

The revised Inns drama *Tancred and Gismund* (1591) provides a further example of this influence. *Tancred* first appeared as *Gismond of Salerne*, performed and written by gentlemen of the Inner Temple for the revels of 1566–7 and also shown before the Queen at Greenwich. It was reworked in 1591 by Robert Wilmot, one of the five original contributors, to popularize the drama with Inns audiences and readers and can, therefore, be used as a benchmark for determining Inns dramatic taste in the early 1590s. Wilmot's revisions, which profess they are intended to meet "the Decorum of these Daies," include the addition of four dumb shows, more blank verse and rhyming speech, more onstage movement and dialogue, and breaking up passages that appear as long speeches in the earlier version.[32] *Tancred* shows that trends in commercial drama influenced private drama but also that the direction of influence was reversible, highlighting an interplay between private and public forms of drama in the late Elizabethan period, which can be attributed to the presence of Innsmen in public playhouse audiences and their institutions' importance as patrons of drama.

Tancred dramatizes a popular story from Boccaccio's *Decameron* in which King Tancred vows that his widowed daughter Gismund will never again be subjected to the pain that comes through the death of a husband. Gismund, however, soon falls in love with a visiting earl, Guiszard, and through the agency of her aunt, Lucrece, attempts to reverse Tancred's decree. When Lucrece's persuasions fail, the pair resort to telling Guiszard of a secret entrance to Gismund's chamber. Tancred happens to see him entering her chamber and witnesses the couple exchanging vows of love and, in some versions, making love. Tancred is smitten with rage and has Guiszard arrested and killed. His heart is presented to Gismund in a cup, which she fills with poison, and, after making a last request to Tancred to be buried with her lover, drinks from, killing herself. Both Inns versions adhere to conventions of Senecan drama with a five-act structure and an opening soliloquy in which the speaker (an angry Cupid) vows to seek revenge, but the revised version introduces onstage violence.[33] At the end of the revised play, Tancred stabs out his eyes and then stabs himself on stage; in the earlier version, he makes a verbal reference to suicide and plans to creep into the tomb where Gismund's body will lie with her lover.[34] Wilmot's insertion of the blinding imitates a 1576 Italian dramatization of the Gismund story, *Tancredi*, by Frederigo Asinari, reinforcing Tempera's point that onstage violence derived from Italian plays which appear to have been familiar to Elizabethan scholars and translators.[35] Wilmot is arguably making a conscious choice to appeal to his intended audiences, the gentlemen of the Inns. Similarly, Gager's departure from Senecan convention with the onstage killings in *Meleager*, published in the same year as *Tancred*, strongly suggests that performative violence would have been a point of appeal for Inns audiences, whether encountered in institutional halls, public playhouses, or the printed book.

The spectacular violence of *Tancred* and *Meleager* speaks to the tastes of Inns audiences—tastes that this chapter has argued *Titus Andronicus* catered to as the public venues sought to appeal to this key audience.[36] Highlighting the extent to which *Titus* takes from the types of drama familiar to Inns students, particularly in its presentation of onstage violence, suggests that the companies and dramatists were designing work with the specific preferences and tastes of an influential and affluent subsection of their commercial audience in mind. Innsmen consumed drama in a range of spaces, from the halls within their institutions to London's commercial theaters. Tracing patterns of physical and textual movement foregrounds important similarities between private and professional drama and sheds new light on the influence of Innsmen as members of Shakespeare's original audiences.

Notes

1 Following Eugene M. Waith's "The Metamorphosis of Violence in *Titus Andronicus*," *Shakespeare Survey* 10 (1957): 39–49, studies of *Titus* have privileged its appropriation of classical, particularly Ovidian, source material. An influential example is Jonathan Bate, *Shakespeare and Ovid* (Oxford:

Clarendon Press, 1993). For a useful survey of *Titus* scholarship see Harold G. Metz, *Shakespeare's Earliest Tragedy* (Madison: Fairleigh Dickinson University Press, 1996).

2 There are a handful of discussions of Seneca's influence on *Titus* including Jorgen Wildt Hansen, "Two Notes on Seneca and *Titus Andronicus*," *English Philology* 93 (1973): 161–65; Mihoko Suzuki, "The Dismemberment of Hippolytus: Humanist Imitation, Shakespearean Translation," *Classical and Modern Literature* 10, no. 2 (1991): 103–12; and Helen Slaney, *The Senecan Aesthetic* (Oxford: Oxford University Press, 2016).

3 Searjeants' Inn and the Court of Chancery occupied similar areas, being the home of senior barristers and solicitors. There were also other less prominent Inns, for example, Barnard's Inn, Furnival's Inn, and Staple's Inn, which was part of Gray's Inn.

4 Alan. H. Nelson and John R. Jr. Elliott, eds., *Records of Early English Drama: Inns of Court* (Cambridge: D. S. Brewer, 2010), xv.

5 See Bradin Cormak, "Locating the *Comedy of Errors*," Richard C. McCoy, "Law Sports and the Night of Errors: Shakespeare at the Inns of Court," and Lorna Hutson, "The Evidential Plot: Shakespeare and Gascoigne at Gray's Inn," in *The Intellectual and Cultural World of the Early Modern Inns of Court*, eds. Jayne Elisabeth Archer, Elizabeth Goldring, and Sarah Knight (Manchester: Manchester University Press, 2011), 264–85, 286–301, 245–63.

6 Jackie Watson, "Satirical Expectations: Shakespeare's Inns of Court audiences," *Actes des congrès de la Société francaise Shakespeare*, 33 (2015): 2–11.

7 Andrew Gurr comments that "Inns of Court students were regular playgoers from the start, and a conspicuous presence at the amphitheatres from early on." *Playgoing in Shakespeare's London*, 3rd edn, (Cambridge: Cambridge University Press, 2004), 80. See also Jane Grogan, "'Headless Rome' and Hungry Goths: Herodotus and *Titus Andronicus*," *English Literary Renaissance* 3, no. 1 (2013): 51; Sarah Knight, "Introduction to Literature and Drama at the Early Modern Inns of Court," in Archer, Goldring, and Knight, *Intellectual and Cultural World*, 217–22, 219; Nelson and Elliott, *Inns of Court*, Appendix 14.

8 Hannah Crawforth, Sarah Dustagheer, and Jennifer Young, *Shakespeare in London* (London: Bloomsbury Arden Shakespeare, 2014), 234.

9 The most prominent example of such a possibility is Henry Wriothesley, Earl of Southampton, dedicatee of Shakespeare's narrative poems, who entered Gray's Inn as a student in 1589. Studentship lasted seven years, meaning he would have been connected to the Inn in 1594. Although there are no records of Southampton attending public playhouses, he may have influenced the selection of Shakespeare's company for performance at the grand revels of 1594–5. This possibility has been raised elsewhere. See Charlotte Carmichael Stopes, *The Life of Henry 3rd Earl of Southampton, Shakespeare's Patron* (Cambridge: Cambridge University Press, 1922), 71–2.

10 The exact date of *Titus*'s composition and first performance is unknown. Carol Chillington Rutter suggests 1593 to early 1594, based on Philip Henslowe's recording of "titus & ondronicus" as a new play, performed three times by Sussex's Men in January and February 1594, during a brief seven-week season at the Rose. *Documents of the Rose Playhouse*, 2nd ed. (Manchester: Manchester University Press, 1999), 49, 79. Gary Taylor and Rory Loughnane propose an earlier date of 1589, noting the unlikelihood of a new play's being

printed as belonging to three different acting companies. Indeed, the title-page of Q1 *Titus*, which refers to performances by Sussex's, Strange's and Pembroke's Men, implies that the playtext had been in existence long enough to pass through the repertoire of three companies by 1594. "The Canon and Chronology of Shakespeare's Works," in *The New Oxford Shakespeare: Authorship Companion*, eds. Gary Taylor and Gabriel Egan (Oxford: Oxford University Press, 2017), 491. The severe plague outbreak of 1592–3 had diminished acting companies' membership and resulted in many surviving members being absorbed into new or existing companies, which means that *Titus* could have passed between the three companies referenced on its title-page by 1594. Also in favor of an earlier dating is the tendency, which Roslyn Knutson traces, to revive older plays, rather than perform repertoire carried over from the previous season, when theaters reopened following plague closures. As Knutson argues, new company membership means not all members would have acted the play together or played the same parts as before. *The Repertory of Shakespeare's Company, 1594–1613* (Fayetteville: University of Arkansas Press, 1991), 31. This reasoning could support the idea of a late 1580s date for *Titus*, which was later revived by Sussex's Men at the Rose. However, if a revived play needed to be rehearsed with parts being reassigned to accommodate new members, a new play would take a similar amount of learning and rehearsing, which would support Rutter's dating. Moreover, a new play would have made the company more money (entry prices were doubled for the first performance of a play), which would have been an urgent concern following theater closures.

11 Paul Raffield, "The Inner Temple Revels and Legal Iconography," in Archer, Goldring, and Knight, *Intellectual and Cultural World*, 36.

12 Nelson and Elliott, *Inns of Court*, xxii.

13 Forty-two percent of Inns students were university graduates. See James McBain, "'Attentive Mindes and Serious Wits': Legal Training and Early Drama," in *The Oxford Handbook of English Law and Literature*, ed. Lorna Hutson (Oxford: Oxford University Press: 2017), 94. Blessin Adams provides a clear example of the emulation of literary habits by Ralph Stawell, a student at Middle Temple, in "History, Poetry and Law: Ralph Stawell's Legal Commonplace Book (c. 1580)," conference paper, June 14–15, 2019.

14 All quotations from the play are taken from *Thyestes* in *Elizabethan Seneca Three Tragedies*, eds. James Ker and Jessica Winston (London: MHRA, 2001).

15 *Thyestes* (1560) by Jasper Heywood, *Hercules Furens* (1561), also by Heywood, *Oedipus* (1563) by Alexander Neville, *Agamemnon, Medea, Hercules Oetaeus* (1566), and *Hippolytus* (1567), all by John Studley, and *Octavia* (c. 1566) by Thomas Nuce.

16 See Jessica Winston, *Lawyers at Play* (Oxford: Oxford University Press, 2016), 231–3, which lists as Inns writers Heywood, Neville, Studley, and Newton, whose *Tenne Tragedies* includes his own translation of *Thebais*.

17 Jessica Winston, "Seneca in Early Elizabethan England," *Renaissance Quarterly* 59, no. 1 (2006), 40.

18 Seneca's tragedies, with their original titles, are: *Hercules* (known also as *Hercules Furens*), *Troades* (*Trojan Women*, or *Troas*), *Phoenissae* (also known as *Phoenician Women* and *Thebais*), *Medea*, *Phaedra* (or *Hippolytus*), *Oedipus*, *Agamemnon*, and *Thyestes*.

19 For a fuller summary of the distinctive features of Senecan tragedy and sixteenth-century perceptions of Seneca's life and work, see Ker and Winston, *Elizabethan Seneca*, 7–15, and Slaney, *Senecan Aesthetic*, 16–38.

20 Thomas Preston, who wrote *Cambyses*, was a Master of Trinity College Cambridge, adding weight to the idea that non-academic drama responded to tastes and conventions for appropriating Seneca's plays that were established by academic institutions. On *Cambyses* and *Horestes*, see W. R. Streitberger, "Adult Playing Companies to 1583," in *The Oxford Handbook of Early Modern Theatre*, ed. Richard Dutton (Oxford: Oxford University Press, 2011), 24, 27.

21 Knight, "Introduction", 218–19.

22 Waith, "The Metamorphosis of Violence."

23 This play is thought to be a translation of Gregorio Corraro's *Progne* (1558), itself a dramatization of the story in Ovid's *Metamorphoses*. Its performance is recorded by John Bereblock, a fellow of Exeter College, in an account of the theatrical entertainments prepared for the Queen during an unusually long royal visit to Oxford in 1566. See Jayne Elisabeth Archer, Elizabeth Goldring, and Sarah Knight, eds., *The Progresses, Pageants, and Entertainments of Elizabeth I* (Oxford: Oxford University Press, 2007), 15, 100–1.

24 The first two scenes of *Titus* are attributed to Peele. For dismissal of the theory that Peele also wrote 4.1 see Anna Pruitt, "Refining the LION Collocation Test: A Comparative Study for Authorship Test Results for *Titus Andronicus* Scene 6 (=4.1)," in Taylor and Egan, *Authorship Companion*, 92–106. On Peele's authorship see Martin Wiggins, *British Drama 1533–1642: A Catalogue: Volume III: 1590–1597* (Oxford: Oxford University Press, 2013), 180; Brian Vickers, *Shakespeare, Co-Author* (Oxford: Oxford University Press, 2002), 148–243; Stefan D. Keller, "Shakespeare's Rhetorical Fingerprint. New Evidence on the Authorship of *Titus Andronicus*," *English Studies* 84, no. 2 (2003): 105–18; and David Bevington, ed., *George Peele* (Farnham: Ashgate, 2011), xi. On Calfhill's *Progne* as a source for *Titus*, see Slaney, *Senecan Aesthetic*, 55–9.

25 Calfhill's *Progne* may have been revived by later generations of students, and if so, it is possible that Peele encountered this play through revival. Future studies might pursue the idea that college plays were later revived by students in a way that had a bearing on subsequent plays written for the college and the commercial stage.

26 Mariangela Tempera, "Shakespearean Outdoings: *Titus Andronicus* and Italian Renaissance Tragedy," in *Shakespeare and Renaissance Literary Theories*, ed. Michele Marrapodi (Farnham: Ashgate, 2011), 77, 80.

27 See Crawforth, Dustagheer, and Young, *Shakespeare in London*, 21–45, and Eva Griffith's revision of Gerald Eades Bentley's work on the Red Bull and its audiences in *A Jacobean Company and its Playhouse* (Cambridge: Cambridge University Press, 2013), 13–17.

28 Richard Rowland points out that *The Entertainment at Kenilworth* (1575) provides one of the most graphic extant descriptions of bear-baiting we have; it records the dismemberment of thirteen bears, which Queen Elizabeth watched with delight. "(Gentle)Men Behaving Badly: Aggression, Anxiety, and Repertory in the Playhouses of Early Playhouses of Early Modern London," *Medieval and Renaissance Drama in England* 25 (2012): 20.

29 All references to *Meleager* are taken from Dana F. Sutton's translation in *William Gager: The Complete Works*, The Philological Museum, The Shakespeare Institute, last modified December 14, 2019, www.philological. bham.ac.uk/gager/plays/meleager/act3eng.html.

30 Mutius's death has been discussed by Brian Boyd, "Mutius: An Obstacle Removed in *Titus Andronicus*," in Bevington, *George Peele*, 449–62, and Rory Loughnane, "Re-Editing Non-Shakespeare for the Modern Reader: The Murder of Mutius in *Titus Andronicus*," *The Review of English Studies*, 68, no. 284 (2017): 268–95. Loughnane contradicts Boyd's theory that the incident is a later insertion into the play by Peele, but both read the play as a co-authored work. Neither article raises the possibility that Mutius's murder could have been inspired by the similarly honor-driven killings in Gager's *Meleager*.

31 Mutius's death is not a pivotal plot point (as is the case for Meleager's killing of Plexippius and Toxeus); however, it adds to the overall sense of loss Titus experiences within the play. His filicide also creates an interesting comparison with Aaron, a father who kills to protect his son.

32 Robert Wilmot, *The tragedie of Tancred and Gismund* (London, 1591), A1^r. *Gismond of Salerne* survives in three manuscript versions: British Library Hargrave 205, British Library Lansdowne 786, and a fragment in Folger V.a.198. On differences between the manuscript and print versions see Kyoko Iriye, "A Stylistic Comparison of *Gismond of Salerne* and *Tancred and Gismund*," *Shakespeare Studies* 4 (1965–6), 1–31, and David Klein, "According to the Decorum of these Daies," *Publications of the Modern Language Association of America* 33 (1918): 244–68.

33 *Tancred* has been suggested, somewhat begrudgingly, by J. W. Cunliffe's *Early English Classical Tragedies* (Oxford: Clarendon Press, 1912), as a source text for *Romeo and Juliet* (xc). See also Jane Kingsley-Smith, "Gismond of Salerne: An Elizabethan and a Cupidean Tragedy," *Yearbook of English Studies* 38, no. 1 (2008): 200.

34 Klein has suggested that Wilmot's insertion of the stabbing borrows from a 1576 Italian dramatization of the Gismund story. See "Decorum," 256.

35 Klein, "Decorum," 256.

36 I have found no evidence to suggest that *Titus* was ever performed within the Inns, but the Clown's reference to "Saint Stephen" (4.4.42) could be taken as an allusion to the day after Christmas Day, when plays were typically performed at court and the Inns of Court.

Bibliography

Adams, Blessin. "History, Poetry and Law: Ralph Stawell's Legal Commonplace Book (c. 1580)." Conference paper, The Early Modern Inns of Court and the Circulation of Text conference, London, June, 14–15, 2019.

Archer, Elisabeth Jayne, Elizabeth Goldring, and Sarah Knight, eds. *The Progresses, Pageants, and Entertainments of Elizabeth I*. Oxford: Oxford University Press, 2007.

Bate, Jonathan. *Shakespeare and Ovid*. Oxford: Clarendon Press, 1993.

Bevington, David. ed. *George Peele*. Farnham: Ashgate, 2011.

Boyd, Brian. "Mutius: An Obstacle Removed in *Titus Andronicus*." In *George Peele*, ed. David Bevington, 449–62. Farnham: Ashgate, 2011.

Cormak, Bradin. "Locating the *Comedy of Errors*." In *The Intellectual and Cultural World of the Early Modern Inns of Court*, edited by Jayne Elizabeth Archer, Elizabeth Goldring, and Sarah Knight, 264–85. Manchester: Manchester University Press, 2011.

Crawforth, Hannah, Sarah Dustagheer, and Jennifer Young. *Shakespeare in London*. London: Bloomsbury, 2014.

Cunliffe, J. W. ed. *Early English Classical Tragedies*. Oxford: Clarendon Press, 1912.

Gager, William. *William Gager: The Complete Works*. Translated and edited by Dana F. Sutton. The Philological Museum, The Shakespeare Institute. Last modified December 14, 2019. www.philological.bham.ac.uk/gager/.

Griffith, Eva. *A Jacobean Company and its Playhouse: The Queen's Servants at the Red Bull Theatre (c.1605–1619)*. Cambridge: Cambridge University Press, 2013.

Grogan, Jane. "'Headless Rome' and Hungry Goths: Herodotus and *Titus Andronicus*." *English Literary Renaissance* 3, no. 1 (2013): 30–61.

Gurr, Andrew. *Playgoing in Shakespeare's London*, 3rd edn. Cambridge: Cambridge University Press, 2004.

Hansen, Jorgen Wildt. "Two Notes on Seneca and *Titus Andronicus*." *English Philology* 93 (1973): 161–5.

Hutson, Lorna. "The Evidential Plot: Shakespeare and Gascoigne at Gray's Inn." In *The Intellectual and Cultural World of the Early Modern Inns of Court*, edited by Jayne Elisabeth Archer, Elizabeth Goldring, and Sarah Knight, 245–63. Manchester: Manchester University Press, 2011.

Iriye, Kyoko. "A Stylistic Comparison of *Gismond of Salerne* and *Tancred and Gismund*." *Shakespeare Studies* 4 (1965–66): 1–31.

Keller, Stefan D. "Shakespeare's Rhetorical Fingerprint. New Evidence on the Authorship of *Titus Andronicus*." *English Studies* 84, no. 2 (2003): 105–18.

Ker, James, and Jessica Winston, eds. *Thyestes* in *Elizabethan Seneca Three Tragedies*. London: MHRA, 2001.

Kingsley-Smith, Jane. "Gismond of Salerne: An Elizabethan and a Cupidean Tragedy." *Yearbook of English Studies* 38, no. 1 (2008): 199–215.

Klein, David. "According to the Decorum of these Daies." *Publications of the Modern Language Association of America* 33 (1918): 244–68.

Knight, Sarah. "Introduction to Literature and Drama at the Early Modern Inns of Court." In *The Intellectual and Cultural World of the Early Modern Inns of Court*, edited by Jayne Elisabeth Archer, Elizabeth Goldring, and Sarah Knight, 217–22. Manchester: Manchester University Press, 2011.

Knutson, Roslyn Lander. *The Repertory of Shakespeare's Company, 1594–1613*. Fayetteville: University of Arkansas Press, 1991.

Loughnane, Rory. "Re-Editing Non-Shakespeare for the Modern Reader: The Murder of Mutius in *Titus Andronicus*." *The Review of English Studies* 68, no. 284 (2017): 268–95.

McBain, James. "'Attentive Mindes and Serious Wits': Legal Training and Early Drama." In *The Oxford Handbook of English Law and Literature, 1500–1700*, edited by Lorna Hutson, 80–96. Oxford: Oxford University Press, 2017.

McCoy, Richard C. "Law Sports and the Night of Errors: Shakespeare at the Inns of Court." In *The Intellectual and Cultural World of the Early Modern Inns of Court*, edited by Jayne Elisabeth Archer, Elizabeth Goldring, and Sarah Knight, 286–301. Manchester: Manchester University Press, 2011.

Metz, Harold G. *Shakespeare's Earliest Tragedy: Studies in* Titus Andronicus. Madison: Fairleigh Dickinson University Press, 1996.

Nelson Alan. H., and John R. Jr. Elliott. eds. *Records of Early English Drama: Inns of Court.* Cambridge: D. S. Brewer, 2010.

Pruitt, Anna. "Refining the LION Collocation Test: A Comparative Study for Authorship Test Results for *Titus Andronicus* Scene 6 (=4.1)." In *The New Oxford Shakespeare: Authorship Companion*, edited by Gary Taylor and Gabriel Egan, 92–106. Oxford: Oxford University Press, 2017.

Raffield, Paul. "The Inner Temple Revels and Legal Iconography." In *The Intellectual and Cultural World of the Early Modern Inns of Court*, edited by Jayne Elisabeth Archer, Elizabeth Goldring, and Sarah Knight, 32–50. Manchester: Manchester University Press, 2011.

Rowland, Richard. "(Gentle)Men Behaving Badly: Aggression, Anxiety, and Repertory in the Playhouses of Early Modern London." *Medieval and Renaissance Drama in England* 25 (2012): 17–41.

Rutter, Carol Chillington, ed. *Documents of the Rose Playhouse*, 2nd edn. Manchester: Manchester University Press, 1999.

Slaney, Helen. *The Senecan Aesthetic.* Oxford: Oxford University Press, 2016.

Stopes, Charlotte Carmichael. *The Life of Henry 3rd Earl of Southampton, Shakespeare's Patron.* Cambridge: Cambridge University Press, 1922.

Streitberger, W. R. "Adult Playing Companies to 1583." In *The Oxford Handbook of Early Modern Theatre*, edited by Richard Dutton, 19–38. Oxford: Oxford University Press, 2011.

Suzuki, Mihoko. "The Dismemberment of Hippolytus: Humanist Imitation, Shakespearean Translation." *Classical and Modern Literature* 10, no. 2 (1991): 103–12.

Taylor, Gary, and Rory Loughnane. "The Canon and Chronology of Shakespeare's Works." In *The New Oxford Shakespeare: Authorship Companion*, edited by Gary Taylor and Gabriel Egan, 417–602. Oxford: Oxford University Press, 2017.

Tempera, Mariangela. "Shakespearean Outdoings: Titus Andronicus and Italian Renaissance Tragedy." In *Shakespeare and Renaissance Literary Theories*, edited by Michele Marrapodi, 75–88. Farnham: Ashgate, 2011.

Vickers, Brian. *Shakespeare, Co-Author: A Historical Study of Five Collaborative Plays.* Oxford: Oxford University Press, 2002.

Waith, Eugene M. "The Metamorphosis of Violence in *Titus Andronicus*." *Shakespeare Survey* 10 (1957): 39–49.

Watson, Jackie. "Satirical Expectations: Shakespeare's Inns of Court Audiences." *Actes des congrès de la Sociétè francaise Shakespeare* 33 (2015): 2–11.

Wiggins, Martin. *British Drama 1533–1642: A Catalogue, Volume III: 1590–1597.* Oxford: Oxford University Press, 2013.

W[ilmot], R[obert]. *The tragedie of Tancred and Gismund Compiled by the gentlemen of the Inner Temple* … London: Thomas Scarlet for R. Robinson, 1591.

Winston, Jessica. *Lawyers at Play: Literature, Law, and Politics at the Early Modern Inns of Court, 1558–1581.* Oxford: Oxford University Press, 2016.

Winston, Jessica. "Seneca in Early Elizabethan England." *Renaissance Quarterly* 59, no. 1 (2006): 29–58.

5 "Cleave the General Ear"

Shakespeare and the Cultural Bias of Early American Radio

Miles Drawdy

He came, a household ghost we could not ban.[1]

Bayard Taylor (1872)

"Is Shakespeare too highbrow for radio"?[2] This question—raised by Orrin Dunlap, Jr. to the readers of the *New York Times*—was certainly timely.[3] It was July 1937 and the feud between the Columbia Broadcasting System (CBS) and the National Broadcasting Corporation (NBC) had taken an odd, if inevitable, turn. For eleven weeks that summer, both networks broadcast condensed versions of Shakespeare's best-loved plays at the same time on the same day.

Quickly termed "The Battle of the Bard," these rival festivals—"The Columbia Shakespeare Cycle" and NBC's "Streamlined Shakespeare"—seemed specially designed to resolve Dunlap's question. Elaborating upon a favorite observation of contemporary reviewers, Andrew Bretz describes the cultural inflections of each program: "the 'Streamlined Shakespeare' series turned back to the high art of the New York theatre for its primary star, while 'Shakespeare Cycle' took its cast from the populist world of Hollywood film."[4] Though I agree with Bretz that "The Battle of the Bard" aggravated a cultural rift that, by 1937, had seemed to divide the American theater, I resist as inaccurate the implication that these broadcasts are essentially reducible to the politics and aesthetics of either Hollywood or Broadway. Rather, in this essay, I argue that the distinctions between these two dramatic forms—as important as those distinctions were and are—collapsed under the need to imagine an audience for Shakespeare on the air. Further, the character of that imagined audience foreclosed on the promise of radio drama by conceding to the antitheatrical prejudices established and perpetuated by nineteenth-century readers of Shakespeare.

Theaters of the Mind

As James Shapiro concisely puts it, "The history of Shakespeare in America is the history of America itself."[5] That history has been tormented by questions of belonging, participation, and agency—questions likewise central to definitions of audience. Lawrence Levine has documented how, beginning in the latter half of the nineteenth century, Shakespeare "was *transformed* from a playwright for the general public into one for a specific audience."[6] Once integrated into American popular culture through modes of burlesque, parody, and travesty, Shakespeare—"the great author of America"[7] and "the land's first citizen"[8]—was gentrified, and both his work and reputation became the property of a particular class of American intellectual.

The attempt to rescue Shakespeare from his reputation began in earnest with two films: Max Reinhardt and William Dieterle's *A Midsummer Night's Dream* (1935) and George Cukor's *Romeo and Juliet* (1936), each in its own way a reminder that "[i]t was not for the intellectuals alone that [Shakespeare] wrote."[9] In the politically resonant language of P. W. Wilson, "Broadway is outvoted by Main Street, and … [i]t is only through the screen that Main Street can be reached."[10] Writing at the end of the 1930s, scenic designer Tom Adrian Cracraft reflected on the closing decade and happily reported that the "time has passed when Broadway is any true barometer of the drama feeling of the country."[11] Producer William A. Brady was more succinct: "Broadway is not the nation."[12] And, it followed, if Broadway was not representative of the American theater then its audiences were not representative of the American public.

In the midst of this cultural struggle, and in order to claim Shakespeare as the natural birthright of the American people, critics frequently characterized cinematic audiences as the modern equivalent of early modern playgoers, all but ignoring the relevant historical and phenomenological differences. In something of a postscript to his 1941 book, *Shakespeare's Audience*, Alfred Harbage repudiates those critics who caricature Shakespeare's "literally popular" audiences as morally and intellectually inferior, demanding rather that this audience "be given much of the credit for the greatness of Shakespeare's plays."[13] Celebrating diversity as a positive condition of dramatic art, Harbage argues that the character of the audience has historically determined the development of western theater: "The drama reached its peak when the audience formed a great amalgam, and it began its decline when the amalgam was split in two."[14] As a demonstration of this theory, he gestures toward the schismatic quality of the American theater, noting that Broadway audiences "are by no means a cross section of humanity" while the "moving-picture clientele is truly universal."[15] In other words, by the summer of 1937, there were essentially *two* audiences for Shakespeare in America. For many critics, "The Battle of the Bard" perpetuated this divide.

CBS hired an impressive roster of actors—Orson Welles, Burgess Meredith, and Tallulah Bankhead, among others—each of whom would play only a single role in only a single broadcast. Meanwhile, John Barrymore was to adapt, direct, and star in all six installments of NBC's "Streamlined Shakespeare." Vice President of CBS Radio, Paul

W. Keston—in an adversarial memo sent to affiliated stations across the nation and, subsequently, to the press—confidently predicted that "our Shakespeare presentations will have far wider public appeal due to constant succession of superlative stars, each creating [a] new Shakespearian role for the air, rather than expecting one actor to play different parts from week to week."[16] While the sheer difference in cast size was obvious—"a phalanx of high-priced voices against the lone knight of NBC"[17]—many critics saw a different difference, hinted at in Keston's opposition of Columbian innovation to the tradition embodied by NBC's "one actor." These critics flippantly dismissed Welles, Meredith, and Bankhead as "actors now living temporarily in Hollywood"[18] and mocked CBS for "giving Shakespeare the benefit of the best actors it can find—well, anyways, the best known, even if some of them never have had much to do with classics before."[19] These critics insisted on an unflattering and unfair contrast: "John Barrymore is streamlining away on the Bard on NBC, while CBS is continuing its self-imposed task of corralling every actor in Hollywood and turning him into a Shakespearean declaimer."[20] These juxtapositions—albeit purged of condescension—have persisted. Scholars continue to summarize the competition as essentially a contest between "film star casts" and a "celebrated stage actor."[21] Associating "The Columbia Shakespeare Cycle" with West Coast cinematic liberalism and NBC's "Streamlined Shakespeare" with a conservative stage tradition recasts "The Battle of the Bard" as a proxy war in the ongoing cultural conflict between Hollywood and Broadway. This narrative is undeniably attractive. It is also inexact.

By imagining these actors as avatars of the cultural ideologies of either institution, this narrative simplifies their careers. From a young age, Welles was internationally recognized as an auteur working in film, stage, and radio. Lauded by critics as the "Hamlet of 1940," Meredith was frequently praised for his commitment to the stage and his refusal to succumb permanently to the temptations of Hollywood.[22] Indeed, the adapter and director of Columbia's "Shakespeare Cycle," Brewster Morgan, helpfully explained the rationale behind the program's casting: "[a]n ability to give a fresh and striking interpretation of the rôle on the air, rather than merely adapting traditional stage performances, is the principal basis upon which each of the players is being selected."[23] Though illuminating in and of itself, this comment also distinguishes Morgan's direction from Barrymore's by the pointed, if subtle, insinuation that the first two installments of NBC's "Streamlined Shakespeare" effectively recycle Barrymore's Broadway productions of *Hamlet* and *Richard III* from the previous decade. This antagonism, however, was certainly not institutional. "Leslie Howard," Morgan continues,

> who appeared as Hamlet on Broadway last season, has been selected to play Benedick, an entirely different type of part, but one in which it is felt he will appear to great advantage because of special voice and

acting qualities which qualify him uniquely for the radio performance of the witty but determined lover.[24]

Though Hollywood and Broadway were culturally, aesthetically, and politically opposed, the working reality was that actors—for reasons of ego
and economics—were only rarely committed to a single institution.

Even Barrymore, who earned his Shakespearean laurels in the early
and mid-1920s, spent most of the following decade in Hollywood
performing in films that, with increasing candor, parodied his reputation
as a celebrated stage actor. As Douglas Lanier explains, "Barrymore's later
career had had the effect of overlaying his Shakespearean credentials—
which Barrymore exploited throughout his career—with his drunken
theatrical ham persona, creating of the two a caricature of the has-
been Shakespearean."[25] Barrymore's involvement in these films further
complicates any convenient categorical distinction that would identify
each cast with either Hollywood or Broadway.

This fetishization of cast also assumes that the radio audience for each
program was derivative of either cinematic or theatrical audiences. This
theory of the two audiences is ultimately descriptive. "The Battle of the
Bard" was designed to split the listening public by forcing a choice. And
yet, insisting too fastidiously on this point risks overlooking the strange
but important fact that the very idea of a fractured audience was not only
resisted by the networks and dismissed by contemporary critics but was
also anathema to the mythology of American radio.

Radio drama is predicated on the dual separations of the actors from
the audience and of the audience from itself. It is fundamentally ironic that,
despite these separations, radio has been celebrated since its invention as
a uniquely inclusive medium. Even the commercialism of American radio
could qualify but never dispel the romantic idea that, more than either
cinema or the legitimate theater, radio provides a form of "social cohesion
to be achieved and sustained by sharing in the same imaginary."[26] As Neil
Verma has persuasively argued, "the aesthetic system that we call the theater of the mind could not have been conceptualized without inventing a
national audience to which radio could speak."[27] The radio audience was
always theoretically—if only theoretically—everyone.

Both CBS and NBC adopted this idea of radio as mandate and adver-
tisement, hoping to transform a group of listeners into an audience by
virtue of a compelling act of corporate imagination. The president of
CBS, William S. Paley, enlisted this audience in his claim that

> Columbia is offering this Shakespearian series because of the
> heightened interest of the listening public in the broadcast of fine
> drama and to further its development along the high standards
> now enjoyed in music and increasingly demanded by the American
> audience[28]

and in his offering of the series to "listeners of every level."[29] Barrymore likewise emphasized in promotional interviews his conviction that Shakespeare's plays were written "to appeal to the general public."[30] These pretensions, however, were all too easy to deflate as critics cynically wondered whether the cultural aspirations of each program could be reconciled with the public mission of each network: "neither Columbia nor NBC is thinking of listeners but of that vague value known as prestige."[31]

Even less cynical critics were clear-eyed about who exactly was likely to tune in, predicting that "a strong, somewhat select audience will be the bulk attendance at the show, with occasional sightseers dropping in on intellectual tours."[32] Making in other words the same prediction, one critic comfortably "[a]dmitted that most listeners to this type of program know the story."[33] Tellingly, one sympathetic listener lamented, "each production is worthy of a large audience, and one that is not split each Monday evening by competition."[34] This complaint registers a fact shockingly easy to overlook: as cultural events, "The Columbia Shakespeare Cycle" and NBC's "Streamlined Shakespeare" were virtually indistinguishable. This is not to say that listeners and critics did not have and express preferences. Yet, even those critics who distinguished Meredith's intelligence from Barrymore's intensity refused the network fantasy of a literally popular audience made up of listeners of every level. They likewise refused the premise of parallel audiences. Rather, these critics understood both programs as having—indeed, as sharing—a single audience.

Radio, Reading, and Anti-theater

Writing in gleeful anticipation of "The Summer of Shakespeare" and "with a good deal of enthusiasm," Burns Mantle encouraged his readers

> to start right now getting out the old Shakespeare and organize a few weeks' rereading of the plays. Or, if the plays prove too much of an assignment, get hold of that companion of your youth, Charles and Mary Lamb's "Tales from Shakespeare," and at least catch up on the stories.[35]

This advice would prove valuable, anticipating the innumerable complaints that, having been compressed into a timeslot of an hour or less, the stories themselves were difficult to follow. Yet, however generously meant, the relationship Mantle encouraged between reading and listening to Shakespeare was not innocent. By 1937, the character of radio performance and the contested cultural role of Shakespeare in America combined to situate the listening audience uncomfortably within a tradition of antitheatricality initiated by early nineteenth-century literary critics.

Most explicitly articulated by Charles Lamb in his 1811 essay, "On the Tragedies of Shakespeare Considered with Reference to their Fitness for Stage Representation," this antitheatrical theory posited that the theater is fundamentally incapable of translating Shakespeare's essence. "It may seem a paradox," Lamb admits, "but I cannot help being of opinion that the plays of Shakespeare are less calculated for performance on a stage than those of almost any other dramatist whatever."[36] To be clear, Lamb distances himself from any devout distaste for actors. He warmly recalls "the very high degree of satisfaction which I received some years back from seeing for the first time a tragedy of Shakespeare's performed... . It seemed to embody and realize conceptions which had hitherto assumed no distinct shape."[37] This is the great promise of performance and yet it is a promise which can only disappoint for, Lamb continues, "when the novelty is past, we find to our cost that, instead of realising an idea, we have only materialised and brought down a fine vision to the standard of flesh and blood. We have let go a dream, in quest of an unattainable substance."[38] In his own words, Lamb concedes, "I am not arguing that *Hamlet* should not be acted, but how much *Hamlet* is made another thing by being acted."[39] Lamb merely sought to disabuse his readers of the thought that the materiality of performance could substitute for the ecstasy of intellectual play.

The terms of this critique were then inherited by American intellectuals who, though less hostile toward the theater, nonetheless shared many of Lamb's anxieties. Ralph Waldo Emerson, whose love for Shakespeare was thoroughly public, commended his friend Edwin P. Whipple for being "one of the happy mortals who are capable of being carried away by an actor of Shakespeare."[40] Emerson recalled for Whipple the experience of watching William Charles Macready play Hamlet when, early in the first act,

> actor, theatre, all vanished in view of that solving and dissolving imagination, which could reduce this big globe and all it inherits into mere "glimpses of the moon." The play went on, but, absorbed in this one thought of the mighty master, I paid no heed to it.[41]

Carried away by the poet, Emerson relishes the disembodied language of Shakespeare unencumbered and undistracted by the gross matter of the production. So much for a local habitation and a name.

The nineteenth-century insistence on distinguishing Shakespeare the poet from Shakespeare the dramatist stoked fears of what A. C. Wheeler provocatively termed, "The Extinction of Shakespeare." Wheeler was responding to the growing sense that Shakespeare's plays no longer worked in the theater and had become mere vehicles for the exhibition of star talent and stage technologies. In his view, the public had "outgrown Shakespeare" and it was not particularly difficult to understand why.[42]

Shakespeare wrote his plays for the theatre of his time and not for the fastidious taste of ours, and he and his collaborateurs had a keen practical dramatic or theatric sense of how to reach the somewhat coarse sensibilities of that time.[43]

Poet Laureate Robert Bridges was less polite in his denunciation of those "wretched beings who can never be forgiven for their share in preventing the greatest poet and dramatist of the world from being the best artist."[44] By the turn of the century, Shakespeare's reputation as a moral poet was secure; however, this failed to mitigate the uneasiness that attended performances of *Othello* and *The Merchant of Venice*, for example. Shakespeare's early modern audience—coarse, cruel, wretched—was invoked in order to explain (and explain away) this uneasiness. The fact that the public had outgrown Shakespeare was the welcome result of nearly three centuries of moral progress.

This hard-earned moral progress, however, required policing the reception of Shakespeare in order to check the indirect influence of his original audience on their modern counterparts who, according to Bridges, should be warned that

> the foolish things in his plays were written to please the foolish, the filthy for the filthy, and the brutal for the brutal; and that, if out of veneration for his genius we are led to admire or even tolerate such things, we may be thereby not conforming ourselves to him, but only degrading ourselves to the level of his audience.[45]

The kind of condescending reading Bridges encourages opposes the figure of the critical reader to that of the rude crowd and, in doing so, puts enormous pressure on the paradox that audiences are defined by the always incomplete incorporation of the individual. Bridges elevates Shakespeare as a literary icon at the same time that he indulges in the fantasy of a modern audience more refined and more uniform than Shakespeare's own. Nineteenth-century arguments that sought to disassociate Shakespeare from the theater came to substantiate twentieth-century defenses of elitist cultural values while the notion that Shakespeare might not be entirely compatible with performance became entangled with the notion that Shakespeare might be fundamentally incompatible with a popular audience.

These arguments were so persuasive that they were not infrequently adopted by writers, actors, and directors whose work and lives were otherwise implicit defenses of the stage. Only a few years after his celebrated performance as Hamlet on Broadway, Barrymore echoed Lamb in his memoir, writing,

> *Hamlet* to me in the theater, no matter who plays it, will never be quite the play that it is in the theater of the cerebellum... . [I]t is not

strange that the acting does not always add to or enhance the reading of Shakespeare.[46]

Morgan, too, was explicit in his appeal to the ideological descendants of Lamb and Emerson. Acknowledging that "there are those who hold such a reverence for Shakespeare that they maintain it should never be played on the stage," he argued that broadcast Shakespeare should satisfy these "academicians."[47] "Their theory," he explained,

> that Shakespeare should be read but never played is based on the contention that any actor in the rôles say of Lear, Petruchio or Shylock destroys their conception of the character as it exists in their minds. For instance, John Gielgud, Leslie Howard or John Barrymore as the Melancholy Dane might not fit their physical or mental visualization of the role. To them I say that Shakespeare on the air is the answer to their prayer for each individual listener (and I trust there are millions) may build up each of the characters in his mind's eye, without any fear of having the picture destroyed by an actor whose calves are not graceful or who has an aggravating way of throwing back his raven locks.[48]

Though he simplifies the antitheatrical prejudice to a question of style, by accentuating the immateriality of radio performance, Morgan makes available the argument that radio—the theater of the mind or, in Barrymore's formulation, the theater of the cerebellum—was not a theater at all, claiming Shakespeare the poet for radio and leaving Shakespeare the dramatist to Hollywood and Broadway.

Because of its technological and cultural character, radio was able to exaggerate its relation to the literary. As Welles noted, because

> the nature of the radio demands a form impossible to the stage ... we find that radio drama is more akin to the form of the novel, to story telling, than to anything else of which it is convenient to think.[49]

By 1937, the metaphor of reading had become the preferred means of describing radio performance. It was industry wisdom that radio required "good readers rather than actors."[50] This verbal richness— "read the text," "read the lines," "read the role"[51]—was materialized in photographs of Barrymore standing at the microphone alongside his co-star and current wife, Elaine Barrie, each with script in hand.[52] The relationship between reading and radio was complicated by the introduction of Shakespeare and the debates surrounding both his reputation and his cultural role.

In their attempt to promote broadcast Shakespeare, key players at each network—aided by critics and commentators—disregarded the history of those debates and elevated radio as an extension of early modern dramaturgy and playhouse practice. They reimagined Western theater history in order to claim, as Barrymore did, "I feel that [Shakespeare] wanted them played the way we intend to play them."[53] Without an ounce of insincerity, Barrymore promised "the millions of radio listeners of the country a dramatically 'true' Shakespearean drama."[54] If these claims were imaginative, they were also academic. Morgan, whose "Shakespeare Cycle" was similarly hailed as a "true adaptation," oversaw months of research and consulted with Shakespearean experts from across the nation.[55] These aggrandizing claims of authority and authenticity buttressed the startling argument that the phenomenology of radio drama approximated that of early modern English theater. In Morgan's estimation, radio "allows the listener almost to read the mind of the character speaking in a way which was possible heretofore only in the small Elizabethan playhouses for which such speeches originally were written."[56] These arguments silently reform Shakespeare's audience—no longer wretched, unruly, and coarse but, suddenly, intelligent, astute, refined. In other words, both the modern radio audience and early modern playgoers were made to resemble the nineteenth-century reader of Shakespeare.

The relationship between reading and radio was neither merely conceptual nor metaphorical. When, early in the summer, Paley announced his network's intention "to launch a national Shakespeare … campaign," he specifically emphasized the "participation of Shakespeare clubs, college and university dramatic classes, summer literary groups, etc."[57] The gesture of Paley's "etc." did little to undermine the critical expectation that the audience for this program would be small and select. Columbia partnered with the American Library Association "to furnish a reading course in conjunction with the Shakespeare series" and installed radios in libraries across the nation. Lecture series were developed to accompany each broadcast.[58] Posters were displayed and "bibliographical pamphlets" distributed in libraries from St. Louis to San Francisco.[59] These partnerships and programs sought to congregate an audience that would have otherwise been segregated and domesticated by the very technology of radio. They attempted to situate that audience within the public spaces of a literary tradition saturated by the prejudices of nineteenth- and early twentieth-century Shakespearean critics.

It is unsurprising that the few letters mailed to the networks in response to these programs could so easily be summarized as being "in praise of Shakespeare."[60] More telling, of the 900 questionnaires sent to libraries across the nation, the only result worth reporting was "an increased demand for Shakespeare in print."[61] In her appraisal of "The Battle of the Bard," Susanne Greenhalgh concludes that "both productions fail to grasp the possibilities for radio artistry."[62] This demand for Shakespeare in print is a testament to that failure. Both CBS and NBC were all too willing to extend, in their own way, American traditions of Shakespearean performance only to belie those ambitions by a shared inability to imagine anything other than an audience of readers.

Notes

1 Bayard Taylor, "Shakespeare, New York Central Park, May 23, 1872," *Harper's Weekly*, June 8, 1872, 446.
2 Orrin E. Dunlap, Jr. "To Be or Not To Be: Broadcasters Expect to Know By Autumn If Shakespeare Is Popular on the Air," *New York Times*, July 11, 1937, 138.
3 Dunlap's question was also belated considering that Shakespeare had been on American airwaves since at least 1922. See also Michael P. Jensen, *The Battle of the Bard: Shakespeare on U.S. Radio in 1937* (Leeds: Arc Humanities Press, 2018), 7–16; Susanne Greenhalgh, "Shakespeare and Radio," in *The Edinburgh Companion to Shakespeare and the Arts*, eds. Mark Thornton Burnett, Adrian Streete, and Ramona Wray (Edinburgh: Edinburgh University Press, 2011, 541–57).
4 Andrew Bretz, "Your Master's Voice: The Shakespearean Narrator as Intermedial Authority on 1930s American Radio," in *Outerspeares: Shakespeare, Intermedia, and the Limits of Adaptation*, ed. Daniel Fischlin (Toronto: Toronto University Press, 2014), 249.
5 James Shapiro, ed., *Shakespeare in America: An Anthology from the Revolution to Now* (New York: Library of America Publishing, 2013), 1.
6 Lawrence W. Levine, *Highbrow/Lowbrow: The Emergence of Cultural Hierarchy in America* (Cambridge, MA: Harvard University Press, 1988), 56.
7 James Fenimore Cooper, *Notions of the Americans: Picked Up by a Travelling Bachelor* (London: Henry Colburn, 1828), vol. 2, 100.
8 Taylor, "Shakespeare," 446.
9 P. W. Wilson, "Hollywood Tries Out Mr. Shakespeare," *New York Times*, October 13, 1935, SM9.
10 Wilson, "Hollywood," SM9.
11 Tom Adrian Cracraft, "We Can Take It With Us," *The Billboard*, January 1, 1938, 60.
12 Qtd. in Dunlap, "To Be or Not To Be," 138.
13 Alfred Harbage, *Shakespeare's Audience* (New York: Columbia University Press, 1941), 159.
14 Harbage, *Shakespeare's Audience*, 159.
15 Harbage, *Shakespeare's Audience*, 166.
16 Qtd. in Anonymous, "'Who Discovered Shakespeare?' Is Now Strictly NBC–CBS Bone of Contention," *Variety*, June 23, 1937, 39.
17 Qtd. in Douglas Lanier, "WSHX: Shakespeare and American Radio," in *Shakespeare After Mass Media*, ed. Richard Burt (New York: Palgrave, 2002), 203.
18 Burns Mantle, "Radio Turns from Trivial to Classical," *Chicago Daily Tribune*, July 25, 1937, C2.
19 Anonymous, "Monday, Aug. 2, 1937," *Radio Mirror*, September 1937, 47.
20 Anonymous, "Monday," 47.
21 Greenhalgh, "Shakespeare and Radio," 553.
22 Burns Mantle, "Shakespeare to Be Given Over Airwaves," *Chicago Daily Tribune*, July 4, 1937, C5.
23 Qtd. in Anonymous, "Round-Up Of Actors: Stars of Theatre and Screen Are Named To Play Shakespeare on the Air," *New York Times*, June 27, 1937, 146.
24 Qtd. in Anonymous, "Round-Up Of Actors," 146.

25 Douglas Lanier, "The Idea of a John Barrymore," *Colby* 37, no. 1 (2001): 39.
26 Kate Lacey, "Radio in The Great Depression: Promotional Culture, Public Service, and Propaganda," in *Radio Reader: Essays in The Cultural History of Radio*, eds. Michele Hilmes and Jason Loviglio (New York: Routledge, 2002), 29.
27 Neil Verma, *Theater of the Mind: Imagination, Aesthetics, and American Radio Drama* (Chicago: University of Chicago Press, 2012), 6.
28 William S. Paley, qtd. in Anonymous, "Shakespeare Plays Arranged By CBS," *Broadcasting*, June 1, 1937, 62.
29 Paley, qtd. in Charles Stofberg, "Best Works of Bard To Be Heard Weekly," *The Washington Post*, June 20, 1937, T4.
30 Qtd. in Anonymous, "Barrymore Will Present 'Modern' Shakespeare," *The Washington Post*, June 20, 1937, T4.
31 Land, "Burgess Meredith's Hamlet," *Variety*, July 14, 1937, 49.
32 Anonymous, "'Hamlet,'" *The Billboard*, July 24, 1937, 10.
33 Kauf, "'Hamlet,'" *Variety*, June 23, 1937, 40.
34 Anonymous, "As You Like It: Listeners Have a Choice of Shakespeare As Broadcasters Woo the Bard," *New York Times*, July 18, 1937, X10.
35 Mantle, "Shakespeare to Be Given," C5.
36 Charles Lamb, "On the Tragedies of Shakespeare, 1811," in *Charles Lamb on Shakespeare*, ed. Joan Coldwell (Gerrards Cross: Colin Smythe, 1978), 28.
37 Lamb, "On the Tragedies," 27.
38 Lamb, "On the Tragedies," 27.
39 Lamb, "On the Tragedies," 30.
40 Edwin P. Whipple, "Some Recollections of Ralph Waldo Emerson," *Harper's Monthly* 65, no. 388 (September 1882), 580.
41 Whipple, "Some Recollections," 580.
42 A. C. Wheeler, "The Extinction of Shakespeare," in *The Arena*, ed. B. O. Flower (Boston: The Arena Publishing Co., 1890), 424.
43 Wheeler, "The Extinction of Shakespeare," 426.
44 Robert Bridges, *The Influence of the Audience: Considerations Preliminary to the Psychological Analysis of Shakespeare's Characters* (New York: Doubleday, Page & Co., 1926), 23.
45 Bridges, *Influence of the Audience*, 22–3.
46 John Barrymore, *Confessions of An Actor* (Indianapolis, IN: The Bobbs-Merrill Company, 1926), n.p.
47 Qtd. in Anonymous, "The World's A Stage: Brewster Morgan Tells How Shakespeare Is Adapted and Broadcast," *New York Times*, August 8, 1937, 144.
48 Qtd. in Anonymous, "The World's A Stage," 144.
49 Simon Callow, *Orson Welles: The Road to Xanadu* (London: Vintage Books, 1996), 373; see also Dermot Rattigan, *Theatre of Sound: Radio and the Dramatic Imagination* (Dublin: Carysfort Press, 2002), 1–2.
50 Kauf, "'Hamlet,'" 40.
51 Mantle, "Radio Turns," C2.
52 Anonymous, "Networks Resume Battle of Bards," *Broadcasting*, July 15, 1937, 30.
53 Qtd. in Anonymous, "Barrymore Will Present," T4.
54 Qtd. in Anonymous, "Barrymore Will Present," T4.
55 Stofberg, "Best Works of Bard," T4.

56 Qtd. in Anonymous, "In June's Radio Workshop: Eight Shakespeare Plays For Summer's Air," *New York Times*, June 6, 1937, 192. This belief was widely voiced at the time. Consider, for example, Rosaline Greene's blunt claim that "Shakespeare's plays were written for the ear alone" (Rosaline Greene, "Viewpoints: Says Radio Will Do Right By Shakespearean Drama," *Radio Daily*, June 30, 1937, 8; see also Jensen, *The Battle of The Bard*, 45).
57 Qtd. in Stofberg, "Best Works," T4.
58 Anonymous, "Library Tie-Ins For Shakespeare Series on CBS," *Variety*, June 16, 1937, 32.
59 Anonymous, "Library Tie-Ins," 32.
60 Dunlap, "To Be or Not To Be," 138.
61 Dunlap, "To Be or Not To Be," 138.
62 Greenhalgh, "Shakespeare and Radio," 554.

Bibliography

Anonymous. "As You Like It: Listeners Have a Choice of Shakespeare As Broadcasters Woo the Bard." *New York Times*, July 18, 1937.

Anonymous. "Barrymore Will Present 'Modern' Shakespeare." *The Washington Post*, June 20, 1937.

Anonymous. "'Hamlet.'" *The Billboard*, July 24, 1937.

Anonymous. "In June's Radio Workshop: Eight Shakespeare Plays for Summer's Air." *New York Times*, June 6, 1937.

Anonymous. "Library Tie-Ins for Shakespeare Series on CBS." *Variety*, June 16, 1937.

Anonymous. "Monday, Aug. 2, 1937." *Radio Mirror*, September 1937.

Anonymous. "Networks Resume Battle of Bards." *Broadcasting*, July 15, 1937.

Anonymous. "Round-Up of Actors: Stars of Theatre and Screen are Named to Play Shakespeare on the Air." *New York Times*, June 27, 1937.

Anonymous. "Shakespeare Plays Arranged by CBS." *Broadcasting*, June 1, 1937.

Anonymous. "The World's A Stage: Brewster Morgan Tells How Shakespeare Is Adapted and Broadcast." *New York Times*, August 8, 1937.

Anonymous. "'Who Discovered Shakespeare?' Is Now Strictly NBC-CBS Bone of Contention." *Variety,* June 23, 1937.

Barrymore, John. *Confessions of an Actor*. Indianapolis: The Bobbs-Merrill Company, 1926.

Bretz, Andrew. "Your Master's Voice: The Shakespearean Narrator as Intermedial Authority on 1930s American Radio." In *Outerspeares: Shakespeare, Intermedia, and the Limits of Adaptation*, edited by Daniel Fischlin, 230–56. Toronto: Toronto University Press, 2014.

Bridges, Robert. *The Influence of the Audience: Considerations Preliminary to the Psychological Analysis of Shakespeare's Characters*. New York: Doubleday, Page & Co., 1926.

Callow, Simon. *Orson Welles: The Road to Xanadu*. London: Vintage Books, 1996.

Cooper, James Fenimore. *Notions of the Americans: Picked Up by a Travelling Bachelor*. 2 vols. London: Henry Colburn, 1928.

Cracraft, Tom Adrian. "We Can Take It With Us." *The Billboard*, January 1, 1938.

Dunlap, Jr., and Orrin E. "To Be or Not To Be: Broadcasters Expect to Know by Autumn if Shakespeare Is Popular on the Air." *New York Times*, July 11, 1937.

Greene, Rosaline. "Viewpoints: Says Radio Will Do Right By Shakespearean Drama." *Radio Daily*, June 30, 1937.

Greenhalgh, Susanne. "Shakespeare Overheard: Performances, Adaptations, and Citations on Radio." In *The Cambridge Companion to Shakespeare and Popular Culture*, edited by Robert Shaughnessy, 175–98. Cambridge: Cambridge University Press, 2007.

Greenhalgh, Susanne. "Shakespeare and Radio." In *The Edinburgh Companion to Shakespeare and the Arts*, edited by Mark Thornton Burnett, Adrian Streete, and Ramona Wray, 541–57. Edinburgh: Edinburgh University Press, 2011.

Harbage, Alfred. *Shakespeare's Audience.* New York: Columbia University Press, 1941.

Jensen, Michael P. *The Battle of the Bard: Shakespeare on U.S. Radio in 1937.* Leeds: Arc Humanities Press, 2018.

Kauf. "'Hamlet.'" *Variety,* June 23, 1937.

Lacey, Kate. "Radio in The Great Depression: Promotional Culture, Public Service, and Propaganda." In *Radio Reader: Essays in The Cultural History of Radio*, edited by Michele Hilmes and Jason Loviglio, 21–40. New York: Routledge, 2002.

Lamb, Charles. *Charles Lamb on Shakespeare*, edited by Joan Coldwell. Gerrards Cross: Colin Smythe Ltd., 1978.

Land. "Burgess Meredith's Hamlet." *Variety,* July 14, 1937.

Lanier, Douglas. "The Idea of a John Barrymore." *Colby* 37, no. 1 (2001): 31–53.

Lanier, Douglas. "WSHX: Shakespeare and American Radio." In *Shakespeare After Mass Media*, edited by Richard Burt, 195–219. New York: Palgrave, 2002.

Levine, Lawrence W. *Highbrow/Lowbrow: The Emergence of Cultural Hierarchy in America.* Cambridge, MA: Harvard University Press, 1988.

Mantle, Burns. "Shakespeare to Be Given Over Airwaves." *Chicago Daily Tribune*, July 4, 1937.

Mantle, Burns, "Radio Turns from Trivial to Classical." *Chicago Daily Tribune*, July 25, 1937.

Rattigan, Dermot. *Theatre of Sound: Radio and the Dramatic Imagination.* Dublin: Carysfort Press, 2002.

Shapiro, James, ed. *Shakespeare in America: An Anthology from The Revolution to Now.* New York: Library of American Publishing, 2014.

Stofberg, Charles. "Best Works of Bard To Be Heard Weekly." *The Washington Post*, June 20, 1937.

Taylor, Bayard. "Shakespeare, New York Central Park, May 23, 1872." *Harper's Weekly*, June 8, 1872.

Verma, Neil. *Theater of The Mind: Imagination, Aesthetics, and American Radio Drama.* Chicago: University of Chicago Press, 2012.

Wheeler, A. C. "The Extinction of Shakespeare." In *The Arena*, edited by B. O. Flower, 423–31. Boston: The Arena Publishing Co., 1890.

Whipple, Edwin P. "Some Recollections of Ralph Waldo Emerson." *Harper's Monthly* 65, no. 388 (September 1882): 576–88.

Wilson, P. W. "Hollywood Tries Out Mr. Shakespeare." *New York Times*, October 13, 1935.

6   Indian Shakespeare Cinema and the Active Audience

Koel Chatterjee

The vast archive of Indian Shakespeare films dating back to the 1920s surpasses cinematic adaptations of Shakespeare in any other individual non-Anglophone country, thus proving the existence of a substantial appetite for Shakespeare on film among Indian audiences.[1] Indian postcolonial literary criticism has delved into the relationship between India and Shakespeare quite exhaustively, with scholars such as Gauri Viswanathan, Jyotsna Singh, Harish Trivedi, and Ania Loomba mapping and analyzing the influence and absorption of Shakespeare within indigenous performance traditions across India.[2] Recent scholarship in adaptation and film studies has also examined the "Indianization" of Shakespeare, as well as the profound resonances between Shakespeare's craft and Indian forms of entertainment.[3] Considerations of the Indian Shakespeare film, however, frequently focus on reception as interpretation and meaning-making and on the absorption of Shakespeare within traditional forms of indigenous performance styles and genres. Christine Geraghty argues that "studying how we watch films ... is an important part of understanding what films mean within a culture."[4] According to Henry Jenkins, "the difference between audience research and other film theory is not whether or not we discuss spectatorship, but how we access and talk about audience response."[5] Thus, instead of asking how Shakespeare films affect audiences, the remit of this chapter is to investigate how audiences shape Indian films and specifically Indian Shakespeare films.

The absence of a tradition of empirical research—particularly in the case of Indian film audiences—has meant that received understandings of spectatorship are largely speculative and rest on the personal views, tastes, politics, and ideological leanings of analysts rather than on the perspectives and experiences of actual audiences and their social reality.[6] Experts, in a condescending top-down approach, speak for audiences and tell audiences what they are seeing, feeling, or thinking, or how they should be reading or interpreting films.[7] The anthropologist Sara Dickey observed that in the mid-1980s, when she began her study of popular film and its significance in South India, the idea of talking to audiences about their responses to a film was not common.[8] The emphasis in study on Indian Shakespeare film and its sources and assimilation techniques within indigenous narrative practices has meant that current studies of film reception narrowly hypothesize how film audiences interpret or respond to (or *are meant to* interpret or respond to) Indianized Shakespeare films.[9] Such understandings of reception, however, which neglect the group character of the social and interactive audience, are at odds with how audiences in India experience film. In terms of methodology, however, there are practical difficulties with regard to assessing how audiences influence a Shakespeare film. Audiences are transient, dispersed, and unstructured collectivities, and are therefore difficult to access and decode.[10] Audiences of Indian films tend to be vocal and participatory, interacting with the screening experience as a group rather than as individuals. Adapting Lakshmi Srinivas's methodology, my research will thus include my own observations of and interactions with audiences at film screenings in Kolkata and London; these experiences are supplemented by conversational interviews with moviegoers and film-business insiders as well as film reviews, social media, blogs, and online forums.

It is important to note that there is an enormous disparity between film spectatorship in the West and in India. Chris Matthews, when praising *Argo* (2012) on Hardball, wondered at the spontaneous applause at the end of the screening, given that it was a film and not a live performance.[11] The question would not arise in India, where cinema is embedded in performance culture. The generalized experience and expectation of film-viewing in public settings at Western cinema theaters is that audiences are silent and immobile; film-viewing is seen as an individual experience with audience attention directed away from one another and toward the screen, the sole source of light and sound. The culture surrounding film reception in India, however, is social and participatory, closer to the experience of outdoor theater audiences at venues such as Shakespeare's Globe in London, which invites audience participation as part of the production:

> People talk throughout the film; piercing whistles, yells and cheers from boisterous "front benchers" punctuate the screening ... . Young men shout out improvised dialogue, make "catcalls" and lewd comments, people sing and hum along with the songs, and some may even dance. Audiences are known to import ritual practices of (Hindu) worship to the cinema hall as they propitiate the stars on-screen with incense ... and throw coins and flowers at the screen in appreciation.[12]

Film culture is not restricted to within the theater but permeates outside to everyday spaces. Popular cinema is a national passion and influences every aspect of public life. Film music, designed to be appropriable, is heard in shops, restaurants, taxis, and at festival celebrations and political rallies, and *filmi* dialogue inserts itself into the vocabulary of the people. Public walls are plastered from top to bottom with colorful film posters, huge billboards dominate city skylines, and cutouts of stars garlanded by worshipful fans loom above city streets. New releases are celebrated like festivals, with bands and fireworks, and theaters are decorated like temples. Films influence fashion and trends and provide content for television, radio programs, and magazines.[13] Thus, the impact of a film is shaped by the broader ways in which the film enters everyday life and is consumed and appropriated by its audiences. For the sake of brevity, I will focus in this chapter on three areas of influence that audiences have on the creation of a Shakespeare film in India, made possible by the country's unique filmmaker–audience relationship. I will first discuss how crowd response is anticipated by and pandered to by filmmakers, and how this has affected *Romeo and Juliet* adaptations in Bollywood. I will then discuss the nature of selective or episodic viewing by audiences in India, a practice that shapes Shakespearean film adaptations, indeed, the majority of films, in India. Finally, I will examine the participatory nature of Indian film audiences by exploring the role that songs and dialogues play beyond the confines of the cinema theater and how this, in turn, influences the mainstream Indian Shakespeare film.

Most Hindi films are romantic musicals about doomed lovers and a *Romeo and Juliet*–style story is often based on the legend of Romeo and Juliet, or similar legends of star-crossed lovers, rather than on Shakespeare's play. For example, in *Josh* (2000), Mansoor Khan's adaptation of *West Side Story*, the lyrics of the song "Apun bola tu meri Laila" ("I said you are my Laila") are subtitled in English as "I said you are my Juliet," thereby indicating that the Romeo and Juliet fable is interchangeable for many Indians with the Laila–Majnu story of star-crossed lovers. The star-crossed lovers trope is used in one way or another in most Indian films, and there are several variations of it in all the different film industries in India. The twenty-fifth anniversary in 2013 of the most commercially successful adaptation of *Romeo and Juliet* in India—*Qayamat Se Qayamat Tak* (1988)—coincided with the release of a cluster of *Romeo and Juliet* adaptations: *Ishaqzaade* (2012), directed by Habib Faisal, *Arshinagar* (2012) by Aparna Sen, *Issaq* (2013) by Manish Tiwary, and *Goliyon Ki Raasleela: Ram-Leela* (2013) by Sanjay Leela Bhansali. Thus, for purposes of field research, I have focused my study on appropriations of *Romeo and Juliet* in Indian cinemas due to the opportunities available to observe audiences in cinemas.

Crowd Response

Commercial cinema in India has evolved in the context of the need to appeal to audiences differentiated by religion, class, regional cultures, caste, rural–urban tastes, and varying levels of education and literacy. According to Srinivas, "the relationship between filmmaker and audience displays shades of a patron–client relationship; filmmakers are dependent on the audiences' patronage and are willing to compromise and craft the film to appeal to audience expectations."[14] Filmmakers and critics have spoken about the demands of the public and what they would be willing to pay for. Mishra describes audiences voicing exuberance at the appearance of a favorite film star, or displeasure if the film fails to live up to expectation or if there are technical difficulties, by taking out their frustration on their surroundings and ripping the upholstery with razor blades and knives.[15] Rosie Thomas notes that filmmakers "operate with an explicit concept of their audiences' imposing constraints on their filmmaking" and that "a central preoccupation ... is whether or not the audience will accept certain representations or narrative outcomes."[16] In multiple interviews and discussions of script development with Bollywood directors in the course of my research, phrases such as "our audiences will not accept" or "they'll burn down the theaters if we show that" were common.[17] Audiences talk to each other, take on the role of narrators, applaud the resolution of dramatic tension, and hiss, boo, or shout advice, providing instant feedback. As one director put it in an interview by Srinivas: "Ultimately people have to judge. There in the auditorium only that will take place."[18] In 1995, when I attended a screening of *Hum Aapke Hain Kaun* (1994) with an extended family group of twenty-five people, the entire audience gave a standing ovation to Tuffy, the on-screen family dog who played deus ex machina at a particularly tense juncture in the film. Similarly, when audiences went to see Nana Patekar, an actor admired for his "dialogue delivery," they were disappointed to find him cast as a deaf-mute character in *Khamoshi* (1996). According to Sanjay Leela Bhansali, the director, who watched the film with the audience at the Liberty theater, Mumbai, the audience at first implored the actor to speak and then resorted to booing and shouting.[19] Shankuntala Banaji describes how, during screenings she attended of *Astitva* (2000) and *Lajja* (2001), "young women broke into spontaneous and prolonged applause during 'feminist' speeches by screen characters."[20] Moreover, dialogue writer Richard Louis claims that "the audience will slap you" if it is not happy with the story, thereby suggesting an interactive relationship between the filmmakers and the audience.[21] As a result, audiences are regarded as collaborators rather than consumers whose tastes and preferences may be manipulated—a view that parallels live theater production. Filmmakers, consequently, view a film less as a commercial product on the market and more as a performance, which may be accepted or rejected.

This is borne out by the conflicting reception of *Qayamat se Qayamat Tak* (*QSQT*) and *Arshinagar* (2012). Stage productions of Shakespeare adaptations in the colonial era were resistant to tragic endings, as evidenced by the rampant Tate-ifications of Shakespeare appropriations in the Parsi theater: Rajiva Verma describes how Agha Hashr Kashmiri had a distaste for tragic endings and "did not like the idea of the audi-ence going home in tears at the end of a show."[22] The staging of death, moreover, was considered inauspicious; *Ramavarma Lilavati* (1889) by Anandrao, a version of *Romeo and Juliet* in Kannada, ended with

Friar Lawrence praying to the gods to restore the young lovers to life whereupon Vishnu descends, revives the lovers, and the play ends in a marriage.[23] *QSQT* was scripted with a happy ending by the screenwriter Nasir Hussein, Mansoor Khan's father. However, Khan shot and screened both endings for his father because he was convinced that a formulaic happy ending would not be artistically true to the film:

> Unlike Dad, I did not want a happy ending to the story, which would have been simplistic and unconvincing. The hatred was so intense that I had to show its futility with the death of the youngsters ... I liked the beginning of my father's script, but thought that I could add my own new take on a storyline inspired by "Romeo and Juliet" and similar stories even in Hindi films of lovers from warring families.[24]

In essence, it was the decision of the young cast (representative of the young audience that decided the fate of the film) that led to the retention of the tragic ending:

> [M]y father was very sceptical and insisted that I shoot a happy ending too ... Both the endings were screened. Aamir [who played Romeo/Raj], Nuzhat [Khan's sister] and Farhat [Aamir's sister] rooted for the tragic ending whereas the elderly audience liked the happy one. Finally, the younger generation won.[25]

QSQT was a runaway commercial success and began to be termed a "cult film" when it unexpectedly turned into the biggest film of the year, with some teenagers having watched it over a hundred times by the end of 1988.[26]

On the other hand, Aparna Sen, who is popular as a filmmaker in Kolkata, struck out with audiences when she adapted *Romeo and Juliet* because she experimented with form in a way that disrupted audience collaboration at reception. *Arshinagar* got mixed reviews when it was released at the end of 2012, with some people embracing the musical genre Sen worked within while others thought it too avant-garde. Not only do the characters repeatedly break the fourth wall, they also speak in dramatic verse. The riskiest move as a mainstream filmmaker, however, was Sen's imaginative use of painted backdrops: "I have experimented a lot with form in terms of production design," Sen affirmed in a NDTV interview. "This film has borrowed heavily from theatre, which is a genre that was hitherto unknown."[27] While Indian audiences are used to creative flights of fancy, with sequences that are patently unrealistic, they are used to the approximation of reality that Indian films depict, which allows them to participate in the action. For instance, according to a news report, during the one-year run of *Hum Aapke Hain Kaun* (*HAHK*), "Women in the city of Jaipur are known to have gone back to see HAHK in the clothes and jewelry they wore when they got married."[28]

One young woman who attended the film six times explained that she liked it because it was like going to a family wedding."[29]

On the way home after watching a film, audiences interactively and retrospectively reconstruct shared experiences, and films can be buoyed or destroyed by word-of-mouth reviews. I saw *Arshinagar* at a multiplex with my mother in Kolkata in December 2015. While the rhyming dialogue led to audiences trying to anticipate what characters would say, some of the audience members loudly asked the characters on-screen to "speak like a normal person." This elicited laughter and comments from other members of the audience who loudly voiced their dislike of the theatricality and "unrealism" of the film. Srinivas observes, "movie talk often involves sharing details about the number of times one has seen a film or plans to see it and is a topic for online musings on films."[30] At the end of the screening I went to, as people were filing out, they declared the film to be too *antel* (pretentious) and there seemed to be agreement that, though *Arshinagar* certainly merited one viewing because "it is an Aparna Sen film after all," older audiences and children would not be interested and repeat viewings were not warranted. Sen is consequently often relegated to Parallel film maker status with limited appeal and shunned by mainstream pan-Indian audiences who are more likely to indulge in participatory film-viewing practices.[31]

Selective Viewing

Madhava Prasad has described film production in India as "a heterogeneous form of manufacture," a process similar to watchmaking in that it involves an "assemblage of pre-fabricated parts."[32] Rather than being delivered to audiences as a standardized and finished product with a stable set of meanings, films are reassembled in encounters with audiences and at reception. Robert Hardgrave, having studied the culture of Tamil cinema, observes that most audiences "see the film as a sequence of scenes—fights, romance, songs, cabaret."[33] At a screening for *Ram-Leela* on December 1, 2013, in Kolkata, after the *holi* song sequence, a viewer jokingly told his partner, "I've got my money's worth, now we can go home."[34] Similarly, when Jisshu Sengupta (playing the Tybalt character), who has a solid fan base among young female audiences, died in *Arshinagar*, a group of schoolgirls behind me discussed leaving for a meal now that Sengupta was dead.[35] Vivian Sobchak observes that film, though objectively presented to viewers, "may be subjectively taken up in a variety of ways, not only in its entirety, but also in its parts."[36] Accordingly, moviegoers are drawn to the cinema for various reasons, be it the fights, the spectacles, or the costumes. At a screening in Kolkata on July 20, 2002, of the lavishly produced *Devdas* (2002), a woman said she had heard the costumes were very nice, so she came to see the saris and the jewelry. Another moviegoer who had heard the film's music on the radio volunteered that his sole purpose in watching the film in the theater was to see how a song was choreographed and where it fit in the story. Realizing that audiences watch a film piecemeal and that "selective viewing" is located in a broader aesthetic of watching film as spectacle and amusement, filmmakers invest a great deal in providing the expected ingredients. As early as 1935, Phanibhushan Majumdar listed "a pretty heroine, a few thrilling and comic incidents, and a few lighthearted tunes to fill the gaps" as the ingredients for a box office success, and Shakespearean tropes, plot lines, and characters frequently fit this format.[37] People also go to the cinema to see a favorite performer, the attraction of the film's plot often being secondary. For instance, the real-life couple Ranveer Singh and Deepika Padukone proved a draw for audiences of *Goliyon Ki Raasleela Ram-Leela*, with Pinterest boards, chat groups, and entertainment news articles dedicated to moviegoers discussing their desire to watch the film in order to view the chemistry between the couple.[38]

The organization of screenings in India creates the conditions for such piecemeal viewing. The intermission, for instance, which is unusual in modern films in the west, lends itself to selective engagement by Indian audiences.

> In what appears to be a strategy that can garner a broader audience, the pre and post intermission "halves" of the popular film are often designed like two separate films. Following the break there is a shift in the story, which is frequently accompanied by a change of location, and that satisfies the expectation that the film provide travelogue.[39]

QSQT, for instance, is set in Dhanakpur for the prologue and then Delhi for the rest of the film. An outing with friends to Mount Abu in Rajasthan is the setting for the first meeting of Rashmi/Juliet and Raj/Romeo. *Dhadak* (2018), one of the newest adaptations of *Romeo and Juliet,* sets the first half of the film in Jaipur and the second half in Kolkata. Selective viewing is such a big part of the reception aesthetic that film reviews underscore audience reactions to the two halves of a film. A review of *Dhadak* describes the two halves of the film in this manner: "the fresh innocence of the first half ends with an explosive scene coming right before the intermission and then you never get to see that again in the rest of the film."[40] Similarly, another online review describes the two halves of the movie: "Before the intermission, the movie is all love, drama, romance and gives you clean family entertainment. After the intermission, if you leave for a bathroom break, the story won't move!"[41]

Moviegoers do choose breaks in action to "leave for a bathroom break" or to head out for a snack. They walk in and out of the theater in an ambulatory viewing style much like the spectators of the *Ram Lila*, performed in the open in North India. As Srinivas describes, "using their bodies to carve out routes through the film, ambulatory audiences reinvent the film; their mobility and its 'rhythms and gestures' shape film experience while making visible the ongoing process of constructing a bricolage."[42] These movements have a similar effect on audiences to hitting the fast-forward button on the remote, allowing them to avoid scenes they think of as optional, thus reshaping their reception of the film. People frequently exit the theater before a song-and-dance sequence or a dramatic scene and return ten minutes later anticipating a shift in scene. This is similar to the experience at Shakespeare's Globe, where audiences can leave the theater and return during a performance as long as they have their tickets on them. In Kolkata, ushers are equipped with flashlights to seat late arrivals, and people frequently miss the pre-interval or post-interval halves of the show. Indeed, the traditional masala film, with its introductory song-and-dance sequence, appears to accommodate late arrivals. The prologue set in Dhanakpur in *QSQT*, which introduces the feud, runs for about ten minutes before the opening credits of the film, and cast and crew members have reported repeat audiences arriving just after the opening credits, when the story resumes after fourteen years have elapsed. Srinivas also describes audiences frequently attending a movie in sections, either arriving late or exiting early to accommodate other commitments such as school timings, meals with friends, or family commitments.[43] An understanding of audience behavior, and consultation with scholars and dramaturgs familiar with local viewing cultures, is thus imperative to understanding the way Indian films are structured.

Song and Dialogues

Filmmaking in India is frequently informal and improvised; Emmanuel Grimaud observes that a film is frequently launched based on title, independent of script or theme.[44] Bollywood superstar Akshay Kumar claimed to have decided to sign onto *Chandni Chowk to China* (2009) based on a poster, and after he heard the story.[45] Thus, actors are approached and funding is secured based on a summary of the story and the people involved in the project, rather than the actual script. Then, a music company is approached to buy the song rights and market the music and the project is announced to the media once all the players are in place. It is only after the music director has been finalized that a writer, or a team of writers, construct a detailed screenplay showing how the story will unfold, including the arrangement of the film into scenes and the locations and sets, with input from the director or producer. Songs are written while the screenplay is being developed and recorded before shooting for the film begins, as the music is released several months before a film is completed in order to market it.[46] Songs are thus designed to be "appropriable" for daily life in India and have an extra-cinematic life through radio, TV, weddings, ringtones, nightclubs, and the internet.[47] Music is intrinsic to all Indian performance traditions: pre-cinema, recordings of songs from Parsi theater were made and these circulated independently of the plays.[48] In the silent film era, live musical performances accompanied screenings, attesting to the importance of song and dance as part of performance.[49] Music from films became socially important with the launch of the Hindi entertainment radio program *Vividh Bharati* in 1957; the roles of the playback singer, composer, and lyricist became significant, with films being pre-sold for distribution based on their musical appeal. This meant that the audience expected *paisa vasool* ("money's worth") from not only multitalented actors who could dance, sing, and fight, but also music directors who could produce a song for every possible storytelling device and dialogue writers (different from script writers) who specialized in *dialoguebaazi* (the art of penning/delivering dialogues that are memorable and appropriable).[50]

Audiences also frequently select a film to watch on the big screen based on its soundtrack and wish to "see the songs" ("picturized" song sequences). In the pre-digital age, audio cassettes came with songs and dialogue, which, as mentioned earlier, are designed to be appropriable in everyday contexts. Shakespeare adaptations consequently convert lines directly from the play texts to create memorable dialogues. In *QSQT*, for instance, when the lovers run away and set up house in an abandoned temple, Raj/Romeo has to go get food. As he tries to leave, Rashmi/Juliet says, "*Kal chale jaana, abhi mat jao*" ("Go tomorrow, don't go now"), in a poignant echo of Juliet's "Wilt thou be gone? It is not yet near day" (3.5.3). Growing up, Rashmi's dialogue was coded flirtation among my school friends. Similarly, the lines from *Ram-Leela* "*Marne ki sau wajah hai jeene ki sirf ek*" ("We have 100 reasons to die, and just one to live") and "*Jab Ram naam ka raag lagey, Toh paani mei bhi aag lagey*" ("when one begins to sing Ram's praise, then even water becomes flammable") were common parlance in 2013. In terms of music, unlike most films of the time, *QSQT* had only four full-length songs and a short song fragment; the songs are all unconventionally diegetic. In the 1960s and 1970s, audiences had become used to spectacular non-diegetic song and dance sequences that had the sole purpose of showcasing the dancing talents of actors like Helen or Shammi Kapoor. Each of the songs in *QSQT*, however, has a purpose in moving the plot forward and the lyrics are conversations between the lovers; in fact, lyrics and dialogue are interchangeably used throughout the film.[51] In 1988 the format of recording was transitioning from mono to stereo and *QSQT* was one of the first films with stereophonic sound. In the beginning, distributors had a lukewarm response to the film's music, but during the trial shows, audiences were appreciative of Khan's experimentation with sound. Retrospectively, critics acknowledge that *QSQT* signaled a clear transition from one era of music to the next.[52] "*Ghazab Ka Hain Din*" ("What a Wonderful Day"), with its mix of country and rock ballad reminiscent of Neil Diamond's "Play Me", introduced an arrangement that was new to Hindi music, and "*Ae Mere Humsafar*" ("Oh My Love") has a fusion feel to it with its mix of Western elements, such as the violins and electric guitar, blended into Indian percussion, such as the dholak and tabla, in a departure from familiar and established patterns. The music of *QSQT* is considered one of the factors leading to the revival of Hindi cinema and its popularity on TV film channels more than twenty-five years after its release.[53] Similarly, "Zingat," the viral song from *Sairat* (2016), the Marathi adaptation of *Romeo and Juliet*, was remade for *Dhadak*, which was an adaptation of *Sairat*. When I went to watch *Dhadak* with friends at Wembley, London, there were people dancing in the aisles during the song sequence and it appeared to be a major reason why the mostly young audience had come to watch the film on the big screen. *Bobby* (1973), *Ek Duuje Ke Liye* (1981), *1942: A Love Story* (1994), and *Goliyon Ki Raasleela Ram-Leela* (2013) all share music in common as a factor contributing to their popularity. The music from all these popular culture adaptations of *Romeo and Juliet* can still be heard on radio and on televised music shows.

Conclusion

To borrow from Susan Bennet, as a cultural commodity, film (like theater) is best understood as the result of its conditions of production and reception.[54] This chapter has sought to provide some insight into the localized film practices and audience behaviors currently missing in scholarly criticism of Indian Shakespeare on film. The overt engagement of audiences in India makes visible the collaborative "finishing" or reworking of the film in the theater; moviegoers craft entertainment out of the "raw material" of the film.[55] Embodied practices such as singing or humming along with the songs and providing "sound effects" to accompany visuals or to take on the role of narrator for companions allow audiences to move closer to the film and to amplify its "effects." Audiences even edit the film in theater, such as when repeat viewers warn companions of something horrible about to happen (as when I went to watch *Dhadak* at Wembley) or when they leave during certain sequences. *Omkara* (2006), a recent adaptation of *Othello*, was reported to have kept families away from screenings of the film at the beginning because of the non-family-friendly language modeled on Iago's lines from the original Shakespearean text.[56] The television broadcast of the film for a general audience, however, had sanitized the dialogue: "anticipating problems, Vishal [Bhardwaj, the director] had already re-dubbed potentially offensive lines, particularly Iago/Saif's dialogue, replacing obscenities with innocuous expressions."[57] Thus, rather than receiving a finished product, audiences of Indian Shakespeares participate in the filmmaking process, where film is remade and transformed through interaction. As collaborators in the entertainment, moviegoers overcome the status of being distant and passive viewers while illuminating the artificiality of the distinctions between widely held notions of production and consumption.

Notes

1 Poonam Trivedi, Paromita Chakravarti, Koel Chatterjee, and Thea Buckley, "Shakespeare Films in Indian Cinemas: An Annotated Filmography," in *Shakespeare and Indian Cinemas*, eds. Poonam Trivedi and Paromita Chakravarti (New York: Routledge, 2018), 317–27.
2 Gauri Viswanathan, "The Beginnings of English Literary Study in British India," *Oxford Literary Review* 9, no. 1/2 (1987): 2–26; Jyotsna Singh, "The Postcolonial/Postmodern Shakespeare," in *Shakespeare: World Views*, eds. Heather Kerr, Robin Eaden, and Madge Mitton (Newark: University of Delaware Press, 1996), 29–43, and *Colonial Narratives/Cultural Dialogues* (London and New York: Routledge, 1996), chapter 4; Harish Trivedi, "The Anglophone Shakespeare: The Non-Anglophone Shakespeare," in *Shakespeare without English*, eds. Sukanta Chaudhuri and Chee Seng Lim (New Delhi: Dorling Kindersley, 2006), 192–208; Ania Loomba, "'Local-manufacture made-in-India Othello fellows': Issues of Race, Hybridity, and Location in Post-Colonial Shakespeares," in *Post-Colonial Shakespeares*, eds. Ania Loomba and Martin Orkin (London and New York: Routledge, 1998), 143–63, and "Shakespeare and the Possibilities of Postcolonial Performance," in *A Companion to Shakespeare and Performance*, eds. Barbara Hodgdon and W. B. Worthen (Malden: Blackwell, 2008), 121–37.
3 See Craig Dionne and Parmita Kapadia, eds., *Bollywood Shakespeares* (Basingstoke: Palgrave Macmillan, 2014), Trivedi et al., "Shakespeare Films in Indian Cinemas," and Jonathan Gil Harris, *Masala Shakespeare* (New Delhi: Aleph, 2019).
4 Christine Geraghty, "Cinema as a Social Space: Understanding Cinema Going in Britain, 1947–63." *Framework* 42 (2000): 1.
5 Henry Jenkins, "Reception Theory and Audience Research: The Mystery of the Vampire's Kiss," in *Reinventing Film Studies*, eds. Christine Gledhill and Linda Williams (London: Arnold, 2000), 166.
6 See Jackie Stacey, *Star Gazing* (New York: Routledge, 2013), 23, on feminist theory and distaste for the messiness of "empiricist research," and Gopal Guru and Sundar Sarukkai, *The Cracked Mirror* (Oxford: Oxford University Press, 2018) for a discussion of the ethics of theorizing and representation.
7 See, for instance, Manishita Dass, *Outside the Lettered City* (Oxford: Oxford University Press, 2016), chapter 4.
8 Sara Dickey, *Cinema and the Urban Poor in South India* (Cambridge: Cambridge University Press, 1993), 416.
9 See, for instance, Bruce A. Austin, *Immediate Seating* (Belmont, CA: Wadsworth, 1989), and Annette Hill, *Shocking Entertainment* (Luton: University of Luton Press, 1997).
10 Lakshmi Srinivas, *House Full* (Chicago: University of Chicago Press, 2016), 17.
11 Srinivas, *House Full*, 225.
12 Srinivas, *House Full*, 1. While Srinivas's research was conducted in the 1990s, before the multiplex boom in India, the film culture she describes resonates with my personal experiences visiting both single screen and multiplex film theaters in Kolkata, India, and in Wembley, London. Wembley is one of the few places in London to regularly screen Indian films for a predominantly South Asian audience and I would frequent the theaters in Wembley in order

to partake of the full cinema-going experience: the shared comments with strangers before, during, and after the film, the Indian snacks, and the shared understanding of filmic codes.

13 See, for instance, Tejaswini Ganti, *Bollywood* (Abingdon: Routledge, 2013), Rachel Dwyer, *Bollywood's India* (London: Reaktion, 2014), and Ravi Vasudevan, "The Meanings of 'Bollywood,'" in *Beyond the Boundaries of Bollywood*, eds. Rachel Dwyer and Jerry Pinto (Oxford: Oxford University Press, 2011), 3–29.

14 Srinivas, *House Full*, 57.

15 Pankaj Mishra, *Butter Chicken in Ludhiana* (London: Penguin, 2006), 69. This is, of course, more difficult in multiplexes that have stricter security checks and bag-scanning facilities, but, as Srinivas describes of cinemas that cater to a larger population of male viewers belonging to the lower classes, "theatres anticipate audience's actions and have made the seats close to the screen out of hard plastic. In one Bangalore theatre, the seats are made of cement." See Marc Abrahams, "Indian Cinema—Where the Audience Joins in the Action," *The Guardian,* June 28, 2010, www.theguardian.com/education/2010/jun/28/improbable-research-indian-cinema.

16 Quoted in Robert L. Hardgrave, *When Stars Displace the Gods: The Folk Culture of Cinema in Tamil Nadu* (Austin: Center for Asian Studies, University of Texas, 1975), 101.

17 Interviews conducted by the author with Vishal Bhardwaj, Mansoor Khan, and Robin Bhatt in July 2012 and 2016, and Aparna Sen in December 2015.

18 Srinivas, *House Full*, 60.

19 Sanjay Leela Bhansali, interview with the author, March 26, 2013.

20 Shakuntala Banaji, *Reading "Bollywood"* (Basingstoke: Palgrave Macmillan, 2006), 44.

21 Srinivas, *House Full*, 61.

22 Rajiva Verma, "Shakespeare in Hindi Cinema," in *India's Shakespeares*, eds. Poonam Trivedi and Dennis Bartholomeusz (New Delhi: Pearson, 2005), 243.

23 Poonam Trivedi, "Shakespearean Tragedy in India: Politics of Genre—or How Newness Entered Indian Literary Culture," in *The Oxford Handbook of Shakespearean Tragedy*, eds. Michael Neill and David Schalkwyk (Oxford: Oxford University Press, 2016), 885.

24 R. M. Vijayakar, "25 Years of 'Qayamat Se Qayamat Taq." *India West*, April 28, 2014.

25 Shreerupa Mitra-Jha, "Mansoor Khan, the Accidental Farmer," *Governance Now*, August 4, 2014, www.governancenow.com/news/regular-story/mansoor-khan-the-accidental-farmer.

26 See Simran Bhargava, "Teenybopper Heart-Throb," *India Today*, December 15, 1988, http://indiatoday.intoday.in/story/bollywood-dreamboat-qayamat-se-qayamat-tak-makes-aamir-khan-a-teenage-sensation/1/330097.html.

27 "Filmmaker Aparna Sen: Ahead Of Her Times Or Out Of Touch?", NDTV Movies, January 2, 2016, https://movies.ndtv.com/videos/filmmaker-aparna-sen-ahead-of-her-times-or-out-of-touch-397299.

28 Quoted in Srinivas, *House Full*, 175.

29 Lakshmi Srinivas, "The Active Audience: Spectatorship, Social Relations and the Experience of Cinema in India," *Media, Culture & Society* 24, no. 2 (2002), 168.

30 Srinivas, *House Full*, 171.

31   India is primarily known for Bollywood and other regional mainstream films in the melodramatic and spectacular style, which continue to be the primary output of all film industries in India. In the immediate aftermath of Indian independence, however, filmmakers in the 1950s began to make socially conscious films portraying the average person's struggles and triumphs in newly independent India. These films are categorized as Parallel or art house cinema and cater to a niche market in India and film festival audiences abroad. Tula Goenka observes that, until recently, "Indian art-house film makers were the only ones whose work was lauded at international venues, because their realistic sensibilities hewed most closely to those of Western audiences." *Not Just Bollywood* (Delhi: Om Books International, 2014), 14.

32   Madhava Prasad, *Ideology of the Hindi Film* (Oxford: Oxford University Press, 2000), 43.

33   Hardgrave, *When Stars Displace*, 114.

34   Filmmakers incorporate song sequences set during national festivals, which will then generate more audience interest through radio and TV broadcasts of the song. Holi songs are an example of this phenomenon, and many popular films use Holi songs as romantic meet cutes in mainstream films. See, for instance, Shikha Singh, "10 Holi Songs for Your Playlist," *Book My Show*, February 25, 2019, https://in.bookmyshow.com/entertainment/music/concerts/10-holi-songs-playlist/.

35   See, for instance, "Jisshu U Sengupta Starrer 'Mahaprabhu' to have a Rerun," *Times of India,* May 12, 2020, https://timesofindia.indiatimes.com/tv/news/bengali/jisshu-u-sengupta-starrer-mahaprabhu-to-have-a-rerun/articleshow/75694595.cms.

36   Vivian Sobchak, *The Address of the Eye* (Princeton: Princeton University Press, 1992), 252.

37   Phanibhushan Majumdar, "Chalachitra O Darshak Samaj [The Cinema and its Public]." *Nachghar*, 29 (Chaitra 1341/12 April 1935), reprinted in *Chalachitra Charcha, 1934–1954*, ed. Depiprasad Ghosh (Calcutta: Pratibhash, 2011): 146. Translations from Bengali are my own.

38   See, for instance, Vedanshi Pathak, "10 Pictures of Ranveer Singh & Deepika Padukone from the Sets of Ram Leela," *Filmfare*, November 15, 2019, www.filmfare.com/features/10-pictures-of-ranveer-singh-deepika-padukone-from-the-sets-of-ram-leela-37415.html, which discusses the pair's growing relationship on set.

39   Srinivas, *House Full*, 166.

40   Bobby Sing, "Dhadak—When Just One Change Simply Ruins an Otherwise Watchable Film," *Bobby Talks Cinema,* July 20, 2018, www.bobbytalkscinema.com/recentpost/dhadak--when-just-one-chang-1956.

41   News Desk, "Dhadak Review—A Great Family Entertainer," MovieShoovy, July 23, 2018, http://movieshoovy.net/dhadak-review-a-great-family-entertainer/.

42   Srinivas, *House Full*, 170.

43   Srinivas, *House Full*, 171.

44   Emmanuel Grimaud, *Bollywood Film Studio* (Paris: CNRS, 2003), 63.

45   Srinivas, *House Full*, 36.

46   See Heather Tyrell and Rajinder Dudrah, "Music in the Bollywood Film," in *Film's Musical Moments*, eds. Ian Conrich and Estella Tincknell (Edinburgh: Edinburgh University Press, 2006), 196.

47 Anna Morcom, "Film Songs and the Cultural Synergies of Bollywood in and Beyond South Asia," in Dwyer and Pinto, *Beyond the Boundaries*, 166.

48 Mishra, *Butter Chicken*, 15.

49 For a more detailed history of the Hindi film song, see Sangita Gopal, "The Audible Past, or What Remains of the Song-Sequence in New Bollywood Cinema," *New Literary History* 46, no. 4 (2015): 805–22.

50 For a more detailed description, see Diptakirti Chaudhuri, *Written by Salim-Javed* (New Delhi: Penguin, 2015), 267–76, and Abbas Tyrewala, "Dialogues and Screenplay, Separated at Birth," *Hindustan Times,* December 12, 2014, www.hindustantimes.com/brunch/dialogues-and-screenplay-separated-at-birth-abbas-tyrewala/story-EfS1ol8YDFZ6dTv6XnyqGJ.html.

51 For a more detailed discussion of the music of *QSQT* and how it changed the way music was used in films in the Hindi film industry, see Vijayakar, "25 Years."

52 Gautam Chintamani, *Qayamat Se Qayamat Tak* (New Delhi: HarperCollins India, 2016), 83.

53 Chintamani, *Qayamat Se Qayamat Tak*, 83.

54 Susan Bennett, *Theatre Audiences*, 2nd ed. (London: Routledge, 1997), 106.

55 Srinivas, *House Full*, 177.

56 TNN, "Families Stay Away from *Omkara*," *Times of India*, August 1, 2006, http://timesofindia.indiatimes.com/entertainment/bollywood/news-interviews/Families-stay-away-from-Omkara-/articleshow/1833494.cms?referral=PM.

57 Stephen Alter, *Fantasies of a Bollywood Love Thief* (New Delhi: HarperCollins India, 2007), 239.

Bibliography

Abrahams, Marc. "Indian Cinema—Where the Audience Joins in the Action." *The Guardian,* June 28, 2010. www.theguardian.com/education/2010/jun/28/improbable-research-indian-cinema.

Alter, Stephen. *Fantasies of a Bollywood Love Thief: Inside the World of Indian Moviemaking.* New Delhi: HarperCollins India, 2007.

Austin, Bruce A. *Immediate Seating: A Look at Movie Audiences.* Belmont, CA: Wadsworth, 1989.

Banaji, Shakuntala. *Reading "Bollywood": The Young Audience and Hindi Films.* Basingstoke: Palgrave Macmillan, 2006.

Bennett, Susan. *Theatre Audiences: A Theory of Production and Reception*, 2nd ed. London: Routledge, 1997.

Bhargava, Simran. "Teenybopper Heart-Throb." *India Today,* December 15, 1988. http://indiatoday.intoday.in/story/bollywood-dreamboat-qayamat-se-qayamat-tak-makes-aamir-khan-a-teenage-sensation/1/330097.html.

Chaudhuri, Diptakirti. *Written by Salim-Javed: The Story of Hindi Cinema's Greatest Screenwriter.* New Delhi: Penguin, 2015.

Chintamani, Gautam. *Qayamat Se Qayamat Tak: The Film that Revived Hindi Cinema.* New Delhi: HarperCollins India, 2016.

Dass, Manishita, *Outside the Lettered City: Cinema, Modernity, and the Public Sphere in Late Colonial India.* Oxford: Oxford University Press, 2016.

Dickey, Sara. *Cinema and the Urban Poor in South India.* Cambridge: Cambridge University Press, 1993.

Dickey, Sara. "Still 'One Man in a Thousand'." In *Living Pictures: Perspectives on the Film Poster in India,* edited by David Blamey and Robert D'Souza, 69–78. Open Editions, 2005.

Dionne, Craig and Parmita Kapadia, eds. *Bollywood Shakespeares.* New York: Palgrave Macmillan, 2014.

Dwyer, Rachel. *Bollywood's India: Hindi Cinema as a Guide to Contemporary India.* London: Reaktion, 2014.

Ganti, Tejaswini. *Bollywood: A Guidebook to Popular Hindi Cinema.* Abingdon: Routledge, 2013.

Geraghty, Christine. "Cinema as a Social Space: Understanding Cinema Going in Britain, 1947–63." *Framework* 42 (2000): 1–8. https://8ba99043-46ef-443e-8e66-bc36ac01fd7b.filesusr.com/ugd/32cb69_dea4296d45c2450bbf7aa65cf5e35d97.pdf.

Goenka, Tula. *Not Just Bollywood: Indian Directors Speak.* Delhi: Om Books International, 2014.

Gopal, Sangita. "The Audible Past, Or what Remains of the Song-Sequence in New Bollywood Cinema." *New Literary History* 46, no. 4 (2015): 805–22.

Grimaud, Emmanuel. *Bollywood Film Studio: Ou Comment Les Films Se Font à Bombay.* Paris: CNRS, 2003.

Guru, Gopal, and Sundar Sarukkai, *The Cracked Mirror: An Indian Debate on Experience and Theory.* Oxford: Oxford University Press, 2018.

Hardgrave, Robert L. *When Stars Displace the Gods: The Folk Culture of Cinema in Tamil Nadu.* Austin, TX: Center for Asian Studies, University of Texas, 1975.

Harris, Jonathan Gil. *Masala Shakespeare: How a Firangi Writer Became Indian.* New Delhi: Aleph, 2018.

Hill, Annette. *Shocking Entertainment: Viewer Response to Violent Movies.* Luton: University of Luton Press, 1997.

Jenkins, Henry. "Reception Theory and Audience Research: The Mystery of the Vampire's Kiss." In *Reinventing Film Studies,* edited by Christine Gledhill and Linda Williams, 165–82. London: Arnold, 2000.

Josh. Directed by Mansoor Kahn. India: United Seven Combines, 2000.

Loomba, Ania. "'Local-manufacture made-in-India Othello fellows': Issues of Race, Hybridity, and Location in Post-Colonial Shakespeares." In *Post-Colonial Shakespeares,* edited by Ania Loomba and Martin Orkin, 143–63. London and New York: Routledge, 1998.

Loomba, Ania. "Shakespeare and the Possibilities of Postcolonial Performance." In *A Companion to Shakespeare and Performance,* edited by Barbara Hodgdon and W. B. Worthen, 121–37. Malden: Blackwell, 2008.

Majumdar, Panhibhushan. "Chalachitra O Darshak Samaj [The Cinema and its Public]." *Nachghar,* 29 (Chaitra 1341/12 April 1935), reprinted in Debiprasad Ghosh, ed., *Chalachitra Charcha, 1934–1954,* edited by Debiprasad Ghosh. Calcutta: Pratibhash, 2011: 146–7.

Mishra, Pankaj. *Butter Chicken in Ludhiana: Travels in Small Town India.* London: Penguin, 2006.

Mitra-Jha, Shreerupa. "Mansoor Khan, the Accidental Farmer." *Governance Now,* August 4, 2014. www.governancenow.com/news/regular-story/mansoor-khan-the-accidental-farmer.

Morcom, Anna. "Film Songs and the Cultural Synergies of Bollywood in and Beyond South Asia." In *Beyond the Boundaries of Bollywood: The Many Forms of Hindi Cinema,* edited by Rachel Dwyer and Jerry Pinto, 156–87. Oxford: Oxford University Press, 2011.

NDTV Movies. "Filmmaker Aparna Sen: Ahead Of Her Times Or Out Of Touch?" NDTV Movies, January 2, 2016, https://movies.ndtv.com/videos/filmmaker-aparna-sen-ahead-of-her-times-or-out-of-touch-397299.

News Desk. "Dhadak Review – a Great Family Entertainer." MovieShoovy, July 23, 2018. http://movieshoovy.net/dhadak-review-a-great-family-entertainer/.

Pathak, Vedanshi. "10 Pictures of Ranveer Singh and Deepika Padukone from the Sets of Ram Leela." *Filmfare*, November 15, 2019. www.filmfare.com/features/10-pictures-of-ranveer-singh-deepika-padukone-from-the-sets-of-ram-leela-37415.html.

Prasad, Madhava. *Ideology of the Hindi Film: A Historical Construction*. Oxford: Oxford University Press, 2000.

Qayamat Se Qayamat Tak. Directed by Mansoor Kahn. India: Nasir Hussain Films, 1988.

Sing, Bobby. "Dhadak—When Just One Change Simply Ruins an Otherwise Watchable Film." *Bobby Talks Cinema*, July 20, 2018. www.bobbytalkscinema.com/recentpost/dhadak--when-just-one-chang-1956.

Singh, Jyotsna. *Colonial Narratives/Cultural Dialogues: "Discoveries" of India in the Language of Colonialism*. London: Routledge, 1996.

Singh, Jyotsna. "The Postcolonial/Postmodern Shakespeare." In *Shakespeare: World Views*, edited by Heather Kerr, Robin Eaden, and Madge Mitton, 29–43. Newark: University of Delaware Press, 1996.

Singh, Shikha. "10 Holi Songs for Your Playlist." *Book My Show*, February 25, 2019. https://in.bookmyshow.com/entertainment/music/concerts/10-holi-songs-playlist/.

Sobchak, Vivian. *The Address of the Eye: A Phenomenology of Film Experience*. Princeton: Princeton University Press, 1992.

Srinivas, Lakshmi. "The Active Audience: Spectatorship, Social Relations and the Experience of Cinema in India." *Media, Culture & Society* 24, no. 2 (2002), 155–73.

Srinivas, Lakshmi. "Active Audiences and the Experience of Cinema." In *The Routledge Handbook of Indian Cinemas*, edited by K. Moti Gokulsing and Wimal Dissanayake, 377–90. New York: Routledge, 2013.

Srinivas, Lakshmi. *House Full: Indian Cinema and the Active Audience*. Chicago: University of Chicago Press, 2016.

Stacey, Jackie. *Star Gazing: Hollywood Cinema and Female Spectatorship*. New York: Routledge, 2013.

Times of India. "Jisshu U Sengupta Starrer 'Mahaprabhu' to have a Rerun." *Times of India*, May 12, 2020. https://timesofindia.indiatimes.com/tv/news/bengali/jisshu-u-sengupta-starrer-mahaprabhu-to-have-a-rerun/articleshow/75694595.cms.

Trivedi, Harish. "The Anglophone Shakespeare: The Non-Anglophone Shakespeare." in *Shakespeare without English: The Reception of Shakespeare in Non-Anglophone Countries*, edited by Sukanta Chaudhuri and Chee Seng Lim, 192–208. New Delhi: Dorling Kindersley, 2006.

Trivedi, Poonam. "Shakespearean Tragedy in India: Politics of Genre—or How Newness Entered Indian Literary Culture." In *The Oxford Handbook of Shakespearean Tragedy*, edited by Michael Neill and David Schalkwyk, 881–95. Oxford: Oxford University Press, 2016.

Trivedi, Poonam, Paromita Chakravarti, Koel Chatterjee, and Thea Buckley. "Shakespeare Films in Indian Cinemas: An Annotated Filmography." in

Shakespeare and Indian Cinemas, "Local Habitations", edited by Poonam Trivedi and Paromita Chakravarti, 317–27. New York: Routledge, 2018.

Tyrell, Heather, and Rajinder Dudrah. "Music in the Bollywood Film." In *Film's Musical Moments*, edited by Ian Conrich and Estella Tincknell, 195–208. Edinburgh: Edinburgh University Press, 2006.

Tyrewala, Abbas. "Dialogues and Screenplay, Separated at Birth." *Hindustan Times*, December 12, 2014. www.hindustantimes.com/brunch/dialogues-and-screenplay-separated-at-birth-abbas-tyrewala/story-EfS1ol8YDFZ6dTv6XnyqGJ.html.

Vasudevan, Ravi. "The Meanings of 'Bollywood'." In *Beyond the Boundaries of Bollywood: The Many Forms of Hindi Cinema*, edited by Rachel Dwyer and Jerry Pinto, 3–29. Oxford: Oxford University Press, 2011.

Verma, Rajiva. "Shakespeare in Hindi Cinema." In *India's Shakespeares: Translation, Interpretation, and Performance*, edited by Poonam Trivedi and Dennis Bartholomeusz, 240–59. New Delhi: Pearson, 2005.

Vijayakar, R. M. "25 Years of 'Qayamat Se Qayamat Taq." *India West*, April 28, 2014.

Viswanathan, Gauri. "The Beginnings of English Literary Study in British India." *Oxford Literary Review* 9, no. 1/2 (1987): 2–26.

7 Gender, Aura, and the Close-Up
Broadcasting Shakespeare for Female Audiences

Pascale Aebischer

In October 2016, the audience survey produced for the *From Live-to-Digital* report revealed that women made up 76% of audiences for English "Event Cinema" broadcasts. Of these audiences, 72% were aged between 45 and 74 years (with a concentration in the 65–74 bracket).[1] The Shakespeare productions enjoyed by these audiences, as Rachael Nicholas's research shows, were largely directed by men, both for the stage and for the screen: of the 128 single-play Shakespeare broadcasts she records between 2003 and 2017, only eighteen were directed for the stage by women and a mere nine had women screen directors.[2] Add to this that women make up fewer than 16% of characters in Shakespeare's plays and we end up with an incongruous situation in which, in the first two decades of the twenty-first century, audiences composed of a majority of white older women were watching the work of a male playwright, performed and directed, for both stage and screen, overwhelmingly by men.

These statistics form the backdrop to my examination of two broadcasts of productions set in the pressurized, predominantly, if not exclusively, male environment of army camps, and which not only sought to represent female Shakespearean characters as (in Nicholas Hytner's terms) "pretty feisty" but which, through casting decisions, increased opportunities for women performers.[3] The first is National Theatre Live and Live from Stratford-upon-Avon stalwart Robin Lough's broadcast of Nicholas Hytner's 2013 production of *Othello* for the National Theatre. In Hytner's production, re-gendering a senator added a woman to the Senate scene in Act One, while Cyprus was reimagined as a modern British army base in a foreign desert environment in which female soldiers, such as Lyndsey Marshal's Emilia, were perpetually nervous and watchful within the testosterone-laden atmosphere. The second is the broadcast, in 2017, of the all-female *Julius Caesar* for the Donmar Warehouse, which was live-camera-directed by Rhodri Huw, with Phyllida Lloyd in overall charge as director of both the stage and screen versions. Not only is the second half of Shakespeare's *Julius Caesar* concerned with the male rivalries springing up between and within opposing warring factions, but that single-sex pressure cooker was intensified by Lloyd's decision to set the entire production inside a women's prison in which Shakespeare's play was performed by the inmates. The production as a whole "asked the question, 'Who owns Shakespeare?'" and opened up the play to be owned by women inmates and women performers of different races, cultural backgrounds, and age groups.[4] In particular, it powerfully showcased performers such as Jackie Clune, Martina Laird, and Harriet Walter, whose ages correspond closely to that of the broadcast audience whom Lloyd caricatures as "like old fogies."[5] For these performers, playing male characters opens up a vast repertoire of exciting new roles at an age when finding satisfactory roles in the Shakespeare canon becomes a real challenge (who wants to be restricted to playing Queen Margaret, the Countess of Roussillon, or a witch in *Macbeth*?).

In this chapter, I want to think through the question of how the medium of theater broadcasting can generate, for its audiences, a sense of the remote performers' presence and their aura, particularly through the use of the zoom lens and the close-up. The use of these cinematographic devices, I argue, is gender-specific, so that audiences, regardless of their gender, are invited to respond to male- and female-gendered characters (but not necessarily their performers) in different ways. Analyzing how stage performances of gendered identities are reproduced and intensified through camerawork in productions that deliberately draw attention to gender norms enables me to introduce into the critical discussion of theater broadcasts an awareness of how their cinematography contributes to encoding and framing performances of gender and gendered presence for a majority female broadcast audience.

Reactivating Walter Benjamin's "Aura" in the Hybrid Medium of Theater Broadcast

The question of whether a photographic or filmic medium can reproduce the presence of the original artwork, person, or performance for viewers rooted in a different place and time has long been the subject of debate and arguably goes back to Walter Benjamin's foundational essay, "The Work of Art in the Age of Mechanical Reproduction" (1935). Reproductions, he argued, are "lacking in one element: [the artwork's] presence in time and space, its unique existence at the place where it happens to be," which guarantees its "authenticity." When it is unmoored from its original location, Benjamin finds that the "quality of [the artwork's] presence is always depreciated," leading to a "wither[ing]" of its "aura,"[6] which Erin Sullivan helpfully describes as the "ineffable substance that draws you in, that makes a work of art present, unignorable, captivating, thrilling."[7] The aura of an artwork, Benjamin explains, arises in part from "the unique phenomenon of distance" between the viewer and the artwork, a point that he develops in relation to the difference between painting or theater and the—at the time of his writing—relatively new medium of film.[8] In the theater, the viewer is "well aware of the place from which the play cannot immediately be detected as illusionary," so that theater audiences are always aware of the divide between reality and illusion. Likewise, a "painter maintains in his work a natural distance from reality." In film, by contrast, "the cameraman penetrates deeply into [the] web [of reality]," erasing from the artwork any sense of distance from the object portrayed, positionality in relation to it, and sign of the technological "equipment" used to remediate it.[9]

Despite Benjamin's broadly negative assessment of reproductive media's ability to maintain the original's aura, he also readily admits that photography and film have their positive aspects.[10] In particular, these media make it possible for artworks to reach the "masses" through an encounter between their reproduction and "the beholder or listener in his [*sic*] own particular situation" that "reactivates the object reproduced."[11] In his argument, Benjamin thus shifts from an emphasis on the "unique" work of art in a specific setting and time to a recognition that artworks designed for reproducibility may create new modes of encounter that "meet the beholder halfway" and in which the artworks are *reactivated*.[12]

This shift is key to the experience of watching theater broadcasts, which are based on productions staged and designed with an eye on their potential to be reproduced in broadcast form. In their very nature, the reception of a cinema broadcast involves the remote audience traveling to a venue in which they meet the image, which is traveling to the same destination via satellite link. But even in a home setting, for example, when watching *Julius Caesar* not via the UK-wide cinema broadcast on July 12, 2017, but on terrestrial television one year later (BBC4, June 17, 2018), there is, as Margaret Jane Kidnie explains, a mutual reaching out as the "spectator's technology-enabled body reaches out to engage in the moment with the actors' reciprocally-enabled bodies, troubling a seemingly self-evident boundary between presence and absence premised on the conjunction of body, place, and time."[13] Stephen Purcell is right to point out that theater broadcasts are "developing a set of conventions which are unique to neither film nor theatre, but specific to itself"[14]— and this means that it is worth rethinking how this medium can change the parameters of Benjamin's contention regarding the withering of the original's aura resulting from mechanical reproduction.

The mutual reaching out of audience and performer can lead to what Josette Féral refers to as "presence effects"; that is, a feeling, for the audience, "that the bodies or objects they perceive are really there within the same space and timeframe that the spectators find themselves in, when the spectators patently know that they are not there."[15] These effects arise with particular force when a performer, rather than being the object of the broadcast, takes the position of subject and appears to reach beyond the confines of the theater to touch the broadcast viewer with their aura. Such moments provoke an intensive sense of connection that belies Daniel Schulze's contention that broadcast audiences are "passive" and unable to connect with performers because "in fact they are not beyond the fourth wall but beyond the 'fifth wall' " of the screen.[16] In reviews of the two productions I consider here, it is clear that the performers were vibrantly present in the theater: Adrian Lester is described as "exuding ... charisma" as Othello, and the entire cast of *Julius Caesar* is said to have been "electrifying," especially in front of school audiences.[17] Theirs was the "transformative power, and ... life force" that Erika Fischer-Lichte explains results from stage "actors bring[ing] forth their phenomenal body and its energy" so that they "appear as *embodied minds*" to the spectators who, in response to the actors' presence, "experience both self and other as *embodied minds*."[18] This is what Fischer-Lichte terms "the radical concept of presence, written as PRESENCE": "the spectator experiences the performer and himself [*sic*] as embodied mind in a constant process of becoming—he perceives the circulating energy as a transformative and vital energy."[19]

A similar meeting of minds—one embodied, the other disembodied but nonetheless capable of bringing forth the energy of their phenomenal body—is also, I would argue, possible in a broadcast setting. When Benjamin distinguished sharply between theater and film, he did so without any sense that one day a hybrid medium would emerge that might be able to combine reproducibility and the ability to reach a mass audience with the production of a medium-specific aura and sense of positionality vis-à-vis the performance. After all, as Sullivan's analysis of broadcasts from Shakespeare's Globe reveals, one of the advantages theater broadcasts have over film is that they routinely include wide-angle shots that allow audiences to adopt "a more typically theatrical point of view, in which a close focus on individual performers is underpinned by a steady awareness of the space surrounding them," so that viewers are periodically reminded of the divide between illusion and reality and of their distance from the performance.[20]

More importantly still, given Benjamin's insistence on the viewer's distance from and positionality in relation to the artwork as the elements that preserve the artwork's aura, the camera's ability to zoom in on a performer's face in a sustained shot, thus eliminating the "sense of depth and its corresponding rules of perspectival realism," has the potential to reactivate, for the benefit of the broadcast audience, the performer's auratic presence in the here-and-now of the cinema.[21] As Alex Waldmann, fresh from performing Brutus for an RSC Live-from-Stratford-upon-Avon broadcast of *Julius Caesar*, explained to Beth Sharrock, Shakespeare's soliloquies make it possible for stage performers to calibrate their performance for the screen, allowing the "moment-to-moment process of thought" to be picked up by cameras trained on the performer "to capture minute details of emotion and expression" that may not be visible to the theater audience.[22] The camera's ability to close in on the face of a performer in long medium close-ups and close-up shots enables performers to gradually "grow" their presence so that it fills the screen with an intensity that replicates that of the early daguerreotype portrait photographs, which, for Benjamin, preserve the aura of the sitter because the slowness of the exposure "taught the models to live inside rather than outside the moment ... they grew as it were into the picture."[23] Slow exposure results in the image bearing in it the traces of "intensified temporality" as it captures "something of the subject's unfolding into the image."[24] Benjamin sees "the fleeting expression of a human face" as captured in early portraits with long exposure times as emanating the aura of "loved ones, absent or dead" with "melancholy, incomparable beauty."[25] It is at the moment when the performer is the most obviously unmoored from their location, isolated from their theatrical surroundings, that paradoxically their aura can be most powerfully communicated to the remote viewer.

At moments when the broadcast camera rests on a performer's face and the performer's thoughts unfold before the viewer as if in slow motion, the liveness of performance, which Peggy Phelan famously identified with the fact of its disappearance, becomes almost tangible for the assembled remote audience.[26] With the intensity that is particular to the close-up's ability to "[focus] on hidden details of familiar objects" so that "space expands" and "entirely new structural formations of the subject are revealed," a broadcast audience can see, frame-by-disappearing-frame, the ever-disappearing thoughts behind the performer's facial expression and eyes.[27] Like the long exposure time of early photography, the sustained focus of a broadcast camera on a face on which fleeting thoughts and emotions are always in the process of both appearing and disappearing creates, for the viewer, Fischer-Lichte's PRESENCE. Through its combination of camerawork and the live performance of the actor in the presence of an audience, in other words, the medium of theater broadcast is, in these long shots, concentrating on the unfolding of emotion and thought in a performer's face, reactivating the energy and aura of the performer's phenomenal body.

Gendering Presence: Two Case Studies

Theatrical PRESENCE and the ability to develop a sense of a performer's "aura" on the broadcast screen, however, appear to be differentially available to male and female characters in Lough and Hytner's *Othello* and Lloyd and Huw's *Julius Caesar*. That, in turn, has implications for the way the audience responds to these characters. The gendering of auratic presence is evident from the start of *Othello*'s Senate scene, which, by transferring the action from the openly theatrical set of the first scene to a much more filmic, naturalistic box set into whose space the camera penetrates deeply, "move[s] both the broadcast and the production into a different register."[28] From the start of this scene, the camerawork is at pains to articulate, for the broadcast viewer, a sense of intimacy with Othello, framing him as a charismatic performer whose energy has the power to enthrall on-stage and off-stage audiences alike. When Lester begins his first address to the senators with "Most potent, grave, and reverend signiors" (1.3.77), the camera begins to zoom in on him in a long single shot, gradually cutting out the senators who surround him until Othello is alone in a mid-shot. This shot relies on the previous scene-setting for context but effectively alters the viewer's relationship to Lester: no longer an actor on the stage, he becomes an auratic screen presence in an illusionist framework, with the slow zoom suggesting that his aura is transcending the constraints of the camera in real time.[29] That pattern is repeated for his 146-line set-piece explaining how he won Desdemona's favor, which is filmed in a very slow shot that starts from a wide angle and gradually zooms in on Othello. Almost imperceptibly, the crane-mounted camera moves sideways until it ends up placed behind the shoulder of the only woman in the scene (the re-gendered senator). This woman stands in for the broadcast viewer whose point of view she shares when Othello addresses his lines about the "Anthropophagi, and men whose heads / Do grow beneath their shoulders" specifically to her to illustrate how he can impress ladies with his exotic tales (1.2.145–6). The gradual zoom has an almost hypnotic effect that draws the viewer ever more closely into Othello's headspace and enables the aura of the actor to reach out to broadcast viewers who are just as in thrall to Lester's charismatic presence as are Desdemona and the female official in his on-stage audience.

By contrast, Desdemona is shown in a series of wide group shots and two-shots from the moment she enters this scene. The way in which Desdemona shares the frame with Othello and Brabantio to demon-strate her relationship with the two men in her life when speaking of her "divided duty" is typical (1.2.181). When a close-up shows her hurt reaction to her father's rejection, it is brief and there is no opportunity for her to grow her presence into the frame. Instead, the cameras there-after begin to exclude Desdemona. She only reappears—and shows that she has been listening intently to the men's debate throughout—when she hears that she might be kept away from Othello during his expedition to Cyprus. At that point, she springs up from her seat in a corner of the room and a camera seeks her out, framing her with the group of men in the room. The closest Desdemona gets to receiving the level of attention lavished on her husband is when Othello chimes in to support her request to accompany him to Cyprus: at that point, the camera moves sideways between her face and his, stylistically uniting the couple. But even here the camera does what it has done throughout the scene: it shows Desdemona not as an individual who attracts interest for her own sake, but as *rela-tional* and *responsive*, someone who only acquires significance through her interactions with others. That may, of course, be a result of the star casting and marketing of the production as centering on the relation-ship between Lester's Othello and Kinnear's Iago, but it is still striking to see this marketing focus on the male star translate into the minutiae of camerawork. Whereas the broadcast audience deeply feels Othello's presence and his aura is allowed to grow slowly into the frame, therefore, Desdemona remains at an emotional remove from the viewer.

Those different approaches to filming Othello and Desdemona continue throughout. As his jealousy intensifies, Lester's Othello in his big speeches consistently benefits from slow zooms that pull the viewer into his tragic emotion, giving him a vibrant presence. Purcell observes that Kinnear's Iago, too, benefits from "frequent close-ups and a tendency to close in on his soliloquizing figure."[30] Desdemona, by contrast, continues to share the screen with others. The Willow scene is representative: the most frequent camera setting frames Desdemona and Emilia together as they sing and quietly talk over a can of beer. It is only in the bedroom scenes—first, when Othello calls Desdemona "that cunning whore of Venice" (4.2.91), and second, in the murder scene—that the pattern changes. In the first of these, Othello and Desdemona get roughly equal camera time and neither benefits from a slow close-up until the very end, when Othello pushes Desdemona onto the bed and the camera rests on her; yet her agitation marks her out as the object of pity rather than a *present* subject capable of growing into the frame. In the murder scene, too, Desdemona and Othello have roughly equal amounts of screen time, with reaction shots alternating with wide shots of the pair together in a hectic edit in which the camera often rests on Desdemona's face while Othello speaks, registering her fear. The very nature of the scene precludes stillness, and the murder itself is captured in a single, distant shot of the couple on the bed, which gives the broadcast audience an almost voyeuristic view into the space as if from outside—a return to a theatrical understanding of the space that distances the viewer from both characters. Once Desdemona is dead, the camera enters the space again to focus on Othello, giving him slow zooming close-up after slow zooming close-up, thus cementing once and for all Lester's superior star appeal, aura, and presence.

Such a gendering of auratic presence in the *Othello* broadcast recurs to a remarkable degree in Lloyd's *Julius Caesar*: even with an all-female cast and a director who feels profoundly "ambivalent about stage performances on screen,"[31] the cameras' treatment of male-gendered characters differs from that of female-gendered characters; in other words, it is not only the actors who perform gender on stage, but the cameras that perform gender for the screen. What becomes clear from Lloyd's DVD commentary and an extra on "Performing Gender" is that the gendering of presence and its link to a stillness that fills the space of the theater and the broadcast screen is no accident. Both Jackie Clune (Caesar) and Lloyd speak of the improvisation exercises the cast did in order to learn to perform masculinity, which involved learning to "demand focus" and become "the biggest thing in the room" by being still, the argument being that men know they are important and entitled and therefore do not make the busy gestures women do to ingratiate themselves with their interlocutors.[32] As Lloyd put it, performing masculinity was sometimes "about taking space, sometimes … about a stillness, a directness."[33]

Figure 7.1 Auratic presence: Brutus (Harriet Walter) bidding farewell to Cassius. *Julius Caesar*, Donmar Warehouse, 2017. Screengrab.

Lloyd associates this stillness specifically with Harriet Walter, whom she describes as "one of the greatest *listening* actors there ever was. So every time I cut away to her, she is guiding the audience through this complex text... . The closer you go in, the more you see her soul."[34] Within the broadcast, this attention to masculine stillness as a way of allowing the viewer to see a performer's "soul" translates into extraordinary sequences of slowly unfolding close-ups that alternate between Martina Laird's restless Cassius and Walter's spectacularly still Brutus (Figure 7.1), whose aura seems to burn a hole into the screen as emotions fleetingly emerge and disappear again on her face. Not for nothing does Lloyd refer to Walter's "electric screen presence," and she is pleased that the in-the-round staging of the original production and its blacking out of the theater audience allows her to "get on the eyeline."[35] This allows the broadcast audience to "disappear into the action," blocking out the theater audience who, at other points (such as Caesar's murder, which happens in the midst of the appalled audience and which Lloyd herself filmed crouching behind Clune in the stalls) "really *have* to participate," acting as "400 unsuspecting extras" both in the theater and on broadcast screens.[36] Once again, male-gendered screen presence is contingent on immersion in the image and the abolition of distance and positionality.

This treatment of Brutus, Cassius, and Caesar contrasts markedly with that received by the play's few female characters: Clare Dunne's Portia, Zainab Hasan's Calpurnia, and Leah Harvey's Soothsayer. The last of these is a vulnerable prison inmate on a tricycle "who looks like she's come out of some godforsaken crack den" and who is filmed alternately in wide shots as she slowly circles the other characters on the stage or at a disconcertingly crooked angle by an upward-facing GoPro camera placed inside her bicycle basket, which conveys her "basket case" state of mind (forgive the pun).[37] Whereas this might not represent a necessarily gendered way of filming and might be more about conveying the weirdness of the character's prognostications, the same is clearly not true of Dunne's heavily pregnant Portia, whose appearance is "a first reminder that there are actual women in the production,"[38] and who is most often filmed in two-shots with either Brutus or Lucius that show her responsive and relational in much the same way as we saw with Vinall's Desdemona.

Nor is it true of Hasan's Calpurnia, who benefits from the most extreme close-up of the entire broadcast: a shot of her features set in a stony mask of dread at the thought "that Casca is going to overwhelm … Caesar" (Figure 7.2).[39] That single extreme close-up on her frozen features while Caesar talks *about* her, making her the object of discussion and the viewer's gaze, is juxtaposed with group shots which more adequately represent Lloyd's overall approach to this character: she is either left out of the frame altogether or in the foreground yet in relational positions vis-à-vis the men who "pull focus," as Clune's Caesar noticeably does in Figure 7.3. Throughout this sequence, Hasan's Calpurnia works hard "to make herself invisible" because, Lloyd explains, women are always "having to disappear when men are doing business together."[40] This deliberate seeking out of "invisibility," on Hasan's part, and its reinforcement by the way the cameras treat her, has an impact on the way the extreme close-up is read within the montage: juxtaposed with shots that stress Calpurnia's insignificance in

Figure 7.2 Extreme close-up of Calpurnia (Zainab Hasan). *Julius Caesar*, Donmar Warehouse, 2017. Screengrab.

Figure 7.3 Julius Caesar (Jackie Clune) and Calpurnia (Zainab Hasan). *Julius Caesar*, Donmar Warehouse, 2017. Screengrab.

Rome's heady political environment (and ultimately in her relationship with Caesar) and her ability to be absent to everyone around her even when she is there, the close-up seeks out her face to let it fill almost half of the frame, but without allowing her aura to reach through the frame to the broadcast viewer. As in the vast majority of theater broadcasts, in Lloyd's *Julius Caesar*, no performer looks directly into the camera, however much their aura may be reaching out to the broadcast audience—Walter's gaze in Figure 7.1, directed subtly to one side of the camera, is typical in that respect. By contrast, Hasan's Calpurnia directs her empty stare sideways out of the camera frame altogether, exhibiting what Noa Steimatsky terms "facial reticence": "the averted look implies the avoidance of face-to-face reciprocity as a basis of social interaction."[41] Even when in extreme close-up, Hasan's performance is one of absence and the audience responds to her as distant and unreachable. When, subsequently, Caesar grabs her face and pushes Calpurnia to the ground, the erasure of her facial presence and her objectification reaches its violent climax.

In both *Othello* and *Julius Caesar*, therefore, the cameras tend to treat female characters as less worthy of sustained interest in and of themselves than their male counterparts, using "theatrical" modes of filming that, while true to the positionality that marks out the original artwork, preclude them from connecting with the broadcast audience through an aura that grows into and through the screen to convey PRESENCE. That is true despite the overtly feminist agenda underpinning Lloyd's *Julius Caesar* or the paratextual features accompanying the *Othello* broadcast, which concentrate on children and middle-aged women munching popcorn, while Emma Freud's live but evidently tightly scripted pre-show interview with Hytner heavy-handedly seeks to appeal to a female audience with questions about the "really feisty" treatment of women in the production and the announcement of a forthcoming celebratory National Theatre event involving "several dames." However much these two broadcasts may have been designed with the middle-aged female audience demographic in mind, and however much Lloyd was keen to appeal to a more diverse audience, that does not translate into equal treatment of male and female characters on-screen.

The implication is quite devastating: not only do the plays themselves privilege male over female characters through sheer weight of numbers, and not only do they afford male (star) performers many more opportunities to share their character's thoughts through soliloquies, which, in turn, lend themselves to the spatiotemporal expansion of close-ups and the generation of auratic presence, but that scripted privilege is translated into a much more insidious experiential and emotional privilege in the broadcast setting. There, the majority female audience is invited, by the presence effects generated by camerawork, to experience male characters as PRESENT subjects, whereas female characters, and the women who perform them, are "absent" objects of the gaze, less charismatic and kept at an emotional remove in the remote setting of the theater. It is only when women perform men's roles, as in Lloyd's *Caesar*, that female performers, by virtue of playing male characters, are able to meet their largely female middle-aged broadcast audiences halfway as equals, reactivating the aura of the theatrical encounter in the cinema. But they only get to do that *if they play men*. Watching Lloyd's *Caesar*, middle-aged women in the audience could rejoice in the prominence and the charisma of Walters, Caird, and Clune, but they had to accept that it is only the performance of masculinity that made it possible to see their demographic counterparts in the broadcast fill the screen with the force of their PRESENCE. If theater broadcasts continue as one of the principal ways in which audiences outside metropolitan centers access productions of Shakespeare, it is worth being aware of the extent to which the medium's ability to generate presence effects continues to reinforce, in insidious ways, wider cultural prejudices that favor male performers over female ones and that train female viewers to accept their screen counterparts' invisibility and merely relational importance not just in Shakespeare's plays, but in society at large.

Notes

1 Brent Karpf Reidy, Becky Schutt, Deborah Abramson, and Antoni Durski, *From Live-to Digital: Understanding the Impact of Digital Developments in Theatre on Audiences, Production and Distribution* (Arts Council UK, October 2016), 29, 25, www.artscouncil.org.uk/sites/default/files/download-file/From_Live_to_Digital_OCT2016.pdf.

2 Rachael Nicholas, "Appendix: Digital Theatre Broadcasts of Shakespeare, 2003–17," in *Shakespeare and the 'Live' Theatre Broadcast Experience*, eds. Pascale Aebischer, Susanne Greenhalgh, and Laurie E. Osborne (London: Bloomsbury, 2018), 227–42. Nicholas's work also shows that whereas there are six women multicamera directors who have worked on Shakespeare broadcasts, there are eighteen men who have this experience, with Robin Lough, Ian Russell, and Tim van Someren directing the bulk of all Shakespeare theater broadcasts.

3 Nicholas Hytner, in Emma Freud, broadcast introduction to *Othello*, dir. stage Nicholas Hytner; dir. screen Robin Lough, NT Live, 2013 (London: National Theatre Archive).

4 Donmar Warehouse, *Julius Caesar*, dir. stage Phyllida Lloyd, dir. screen Phyllida Lloyd with live camera director Rhodri Huw (DVD, Opus Arte, 2017), DVD blurb. Nora Williams offers a fierce critique of the racial politics underpinning Harriet Walter's account of how she and Lloyd considered the cast's racial diversity plausible because it "could believably represent the racial and social mix of a prison population." As Williams puts it:

> Never mind a cast that could believably represent the population of modern London—or, for that matter, early modern London—or, for that matter, Ancient Rome. No, no—according to Walter (and, implicitly, Lloyd), it's prisons, apparently, where a multicultural group of women performing a Shakespeare play will not seem strange. How telling.

Nora Williams, "(Un-)Strangemaking Gender: Cross- and Single-Gender Productions of Shakespeare," Paper presented for the Directing and Dramaturgy Working Group at the Theatre and Performance Research Association conference, University of Exeter, September 6, 2019, http://norajwilliams.hcommons.org/tapra-2019/.

5 Phyllida Lloyd in Alex Killeen, "Screening 'Julius Caesar': In Conversation with Phyllida Lloyd," *Culturised*, July 12, 2017, https://culturised.co.uk/2017/07/screening-julius-caesar-in-conversation-with-phyllida-lloyd/. The screen release went out of its way to appeal to a younger demographic with an offer of £5 tickets for the under-25s, but while in London the audience demographic was noticeably diverse, there was no evidence of a noticeably younger demographic in attendance at screenings in the Exeter Picturehouse Cinema or Nottingham Broadway Cinema, for instance.

6 Walter Benjamin, "The Work of Art in the Age of Mechanical Reproduction," in *Illuminations*, ed. Hannah Arendt, trans. Henry Zohn (New York: Schocken Books, [1935] 1968), 220–1.

7 Erin Sullivan, "Aura, Aliveness, and Art," *Digital Shakespeares*, April 21, 2017. https://digitalshakespeares.wordpress.com/2017/04/21/aura-aliveness-and-art/.

8 Benjamin, "Work of Art," 222.

9 Benjamin, "Work of Art," 233.

10 Sullivan, "Aura," also draws attention to Benjamin's ambivalence.

11 Sullivan, "Aura," and Benjamin, "Work of Art," 223, 221.

12 Benjamin, "Work of Art," 220.

13 Margaret Jane Kidnie, "The Stratford Festival of Canada: Mental Tricks and Archival Documents in the Age of NTLive," in *Shakespeare and the "Live"*

Theatre Broadcast Experience, eds. Pascale Aebischer, Susanne Greenhalgh, and Laurie E. Osborne (London: Bloomsbury, 2018), 134.

14 Stephen Purcell, "'It's All a Bit of a Risk': Reformulating 'Liveness' in Twenty-First Century Performances of Shakespeare," in *The Oxford Handbook of Shakespeare and Performance*, ed. James C. Bulman (Oxford: Oxford University Press, 2017), 289.

15 Josette Féral, "How to Define Presence Effects: the Work of Janet Cardiff," in *Archaeologies of Presence: Art, Performance and the Persistence of Being*, eds. Gabriella Giannachi, Nick Kaye, and Michael Shanks (London: Routledge, 2012), 31.

16 Schulze, Daniel, "The Passive Gaze and Hyper-Immunised Spectators: The Politics of Theatrical Live-Broadcasting," *Journal of Contemporary Drama in English* 3, no. 2 (2015): 319. https://doi.org/10.1515/jcde-2015-0024.

17 Charles Spencer, "Othello, National Theatre, Review," *The Telegraph*, April 24, 2013, www.telegraph.co.uk/culture/theatre/william-shakespeare/10013155/Othello-National-Theatre-review.html; David Nice, "Julius Caesar, BBC Four review – electrifying TV launch of all-women Shakespeare trilogy," *The Arts Desk*, June 18, 2018, https://theartsdesk.com/theatre-tv/julius-caesar-bbc-four-review-electrifying-tv-launch-all-women-shakespeare-trilogy.

18 Erika Fischer-Lichte, *The Routledge Introduction to Theatre and Performance Studies* (London: Routledge, 2014), 34.

19 Erika Fischer-Lichte, "Appearing as Embodied Mind—Defining a Weak, a Strong and a Radical Concept of Presence," in *Archaeologies of Presence: Art, Performance and the Persistence of Being*, eds. Gabriella Giannachi, Nick Kayem, and Michael Shanks (London: Routledge, 2012), 115.

20 Erin Sullivan, "'The forms of things unknown': Shakespeare and the Rise of the Live Broadcast," *Shakespeare Bulletin* 35, no. 4 (2017): 639.

21 Mary Anne Doane, "The Close-Up: Scale and Detail in the Cinema," *differences: A Journal of Feminist Cultural Studies* 14, no. 3 (2003): 91. My reading of Benjamin runs counter to Doane's in "Close-Up," 92, where she associated the close-up with the decay of the aura, whereas my reading, taking into account Benjamin's comments on the long exposure of the daguerreotype, associates the close-up with the preservation of the aura.

22 Beth Sharrock, "A View from the Stage: Interviews with Performers," in *Shakespeare and the "Live" Theatre Broadcast Experience*, eds. Pascale Aebischer, Susanne Greenhalgh, and Laurie E. Osborne (London: Bloomsbury, 2018), 98.

23 Walter Benjamin, "A Short History of Photography," *Screen* 13, no. 1 ([1931] 1972): 17.

24 Noa Steimatsky, *The Face on Film* (Oxford: Oxford University Press, 2017), 8.

25 Benjamin, "Work of Art," 226.

26 Peggy Phelan, *Unmarked: The Politics of Performance* (London: Routledge, [1993] 2005), 146.

27 Benjamin, "Work of Art," 236.

28 Purcell, "Reformulating 'Liveness'," 289.

29 With thanks to Peter Kirwan for sharing this observation.

30 Purcell, "Reformulating 'Liveness'," 290.

31 See also Lloyd in Killeen, "Screening 'Julius Caesar.'"

32 Jackie Clune in "Performing Gender," DVD extra, Donmar Warehouse, *Julius Caesar.*
33 Phyllida Lloyd, "Director's Commentary," DVD extra, Donmar Warehouse, *Julius Caesar.*
34 Lloyd, "Director's Commentary."
35 Phyllida Lloyd, "Programme Note," *Julius Caesar*, dir. stage Phyllida Lloyd, dir. screen Phyllida Lloyd with live camera director Rhodri Huw, distributed in cinemas, 2017.
36 Lloyd, "Director's Commentary" and "Programme Note."
37 Lloyd, "Director's Commentary."
38 Lloyd, "Director's Commentary."
39 Lloyd, "Director's Commentary."
40 Lloyd, "Director's Commentary."
41 Noa Steimatsky, "On the Face, in Reticence," in *Film, Art, New Media: Museum Without Walls?* ed. Angela Delle Vacche (London: Palgrave Macmillan, 2012), 193, 196. https://doi.org/10.1057/9781137026132_9.

Bibliography

Benjamin, Walter. "A Short History of Photography." *Screen* 13, no. 1 ([1931] 1972): 5–26.

Benjamin, Walter. "The Work of Art in the Age of Mechanical Reproduction." In *Illuminations*, edited by Hannah Arendt, translated by Henry Zohn, 217–51. New York: Schocken Books, [1935] 1968.

Doane, Mary Anne. "The Close-Up: Scale and Detail in the Cinema." *differences: A Journal of Feminist Cultural Studies* 14, no. 3 (2003): 89–111.

Donmar Warehouse, *Julius Caesar*, dir. stage Phyllida Lloyd, dir. screen Phyllida Lloyd with live camera director Rhodri Huw. DVD, Opus Arte, 2017.

Féral, Josette. "How to Define Presence Effects: the Work of Janet Cardiff." In *Archaeologies of Presence: Art, Performance and the Persistence of Being*, edited by Gabriella Giannachi, Nick Kaye, and Michael Shanks, 29–49. London: Routledge, 2012.

Fischer-Lichte, Erika. "Appearing as Embodied Mind – Defining a Weak, a Strong and a Radical Concept of Presence." In *Archaeologies of Presence: Art, Performance and the Persistence of Being*, edited by Gabriella Giannachi, Nick Kaye, and Michael Shanks, 103–18. London: Routledge, 2012.

Freud, Emma. Broadcast Introduction and Interview with Nicholas Hytner. *Othello*, dir. stage Nicholas Hytner; dir. screen Robin Lough. NT Live, 2013. London: National Theatre Archive.

Kidnie, Margaret Jane. "The Stratford Festival of Canada: Mental Tricks and Archival Documents in the Age of NTLive." In *Shakespeare and the "Live" Theatre Broadcast Experience*, edited by Pascale Aebischer, Susanne Greenhalgh, and Laurie E. Osborne, 133–46. London: Bloomsbury, 2018.

Killeen, Alex. "Screening 'Julius Caesar': In Conversation with Phyllida Lloyd." *Culturised*, July 12, 2017. https://culturised.co.uk/2017/07/screening-julius-caesar-in-conversation-with-phyllida-lloyd/.

Lloyd, Phyllida. "Programme Note." *Julius Caesar*, dir. stage Phyllida Lloyd, dir. screen Phyllida Lloyd with live camera director Rhodri Huw. Distributed in cinemas, 2017.

Nice, David. "Julius Caesar, BBC Four Review—Electrifying TV Launch of All-Women Shakespeare Trilogy." *The Arts Desk*, June 18, 2018. https://theartsdesk. com/theatre-tv/julius-caesar-bbc-four-review-electrifying-tv-launch-all-women-shakespeare-trilogy.

Nicholas, Rachael. "Appendix: Digital Theatre Broadcasts of Shakespeare, 2003–17." In *Shakespeare and the "Live" Theatre Broadcast Experience*, edited by Pascale Aebischer, Susanne Greenhalgh, and Laurie E. Osborne, 227–42. London: Bloomsbury, 2018.

Phelan, Peggy. *Unmarked: The Politics of Performance*. London: Routledge [1993] 2005.

Purcell, Stephen. "'It's All a Bit of a Risk': Reformulating 'Liveness' in Twenty-First Century Performances of Shakespeare." In *The Oxford Handbook of Shakespeare and Performance*, edited by James C. Bulman, 284–301. Oxford: Oxford University Press, 2017.

Reidy, Brent Karpf, Becky Schutt, Deborah Abramson, and Antoni Durski. *From Live-to-Digital: Understanding the Impact of Digital Developments in Theatre on Audiences, Production and Distribution*. Arts Council UK, October 2016. www.artscouncil.org.uk/sites/default/files/download-file/From_Live_to_Digital_OCT2016.pdf.

Schulze, Daniel. "The Passive Gaze and Hyper-Immunised Spectators: The Politics of Theatrical Live Broadcasting." *Journal of Contemporary Drama in English* 3, no. 2 (2015): 315–26. https://doi.org/10.1515/jcde-2015-0024.

Sharrock, Beth. "A View from the Stage: Interviews with Performers." In *Shakespeare and the "Live" Theatre Broadcast Experience*, edited by Pascale Aebischer, Susanne Greenhalgh, and Laurie E. Osborne, 95–101. London: Bloomsbury, 2018.

Spencer, Charles. "Othello, National Theatre, Review." *The Telegraph*, April 24, 2013. www.telegraph.co.uk/culture/theatre/william-shakespeare/10013155/Othello-National-Theatre-review.html.

Steimatsky, Noa. *The Face on Film*. Oxford: Oxford University Press, 2017.

Steimatsky, Noa. "On the Face, in Reticence," in *Film, Art, New Media: Museum Without Walls?* edited by Angela Delle Vacche. 159–77. London: Palgrave Macmillan, 2012. https://doi.org/10.1057/9781137026132_9.

Sullivan, Erin. "Aura, Aliveness, and Art." *Digital Shakespeares*, April 21, 2017. https://digitalshakespeares.wordpress.com/2017/04/21/aura-aliveness-and-art/.

Sullivan, Erin. "'The forms of things unknown': Shakespeare and the Rise of the Live Broadcast." *Shakespeare Bulletin* 35, no. 4 (2017): 627–62.

Williams, Nora. "(Un-)Strangemaking Gender: Cross- and Single-Gender Productions of Shakespeare." Paper presented for the Directing and Dramaturgy Working Group at the Theatre and Performance Research Association conference, University of Exeter, September 6, 2019. http://norajwilliams.hcommons. org/tapra-2019/.

Performing Audiences

8 Shakespeare's Riotous Audiences

Macbeth at Astor Place, 1849

Edel Lamb

On April 5, 1849, the English actor William Charles Macready remarked in his diary "I really despise my audience, and dislike them too."[1] This opinion following a performance of *Macbeth* in Cincinnati was characteristic of his attitude toward his audiences throughout his 1848–9 American tour. His audiences regularly demonstrated disapproval by hissing, shouting, and throwing items at the stage, and the star actor's diary registered his dislike and defiance of what he termed the "barbarians."[2] Such behavior was not unusual for audiences at this time, yet this series of responses to Macready during his tour climaxed in a unique event: the Astor Place riots. On May 10, 1849, a crowd of ten to fifteen thousand gathered outside his *Macbeth* at the Astor Place Opera House, New York; at least twenty-two people were killed and over 150 injured when riots broke out and the New York State Militia opened fire.[3] While these tragic consequences to Shakespearean performance and audience response are extreme, this chapter takes the Astor Place riots, one of the most famous theater riots in history, as a case study to explore the ways in which audiences have used performances of Shakespeare to express national and social allegiances in diverse ways. It argues that Shakespearean performances, in this case *Macbeth*, provided not just a site for audiences to protest over wider issues but material for the ways in which audiences articulated discontent. Shakespeare's riotous audiences, it suggests, created a series of performances through their disruptive engagement with the play and transformed the delivery of Shakespeare on stage in unexpected ways.

The Astor Place riots have been scrutinized in scholarship on the history of theater riots, the history of New York City, and the history of American audiences' relationships with Shakespeare.[4] The large audience crammed within the Astor Place Opera House and crowding around it on May 10 had gathered in answer to a poster calling for "working men" and "free men" to "stand by" their "lawful rights" and to "express their opinions" on whether "Americans or English rule in this city."[5] The two hundred posters were printed and circulated by the "American committee," a group whose members' identities were never revealed but who seem to have been led by Isaiah Rynders, a political activist, and Ned Bluntline, a publisher and journalist.[6] This call to attend followed disruptions at Macready's performance of the same play earlier that week on the same night as another performance by homegrown star Edwin Forrest. The two Shakespearean actors—one perceived as representative of an aristocratic Englishness and the other claimed by working-class Americans—had a long history of rivalry, and their competing performances had previously provoked riotous audience responses. Shakespeare's audiences are, of course, shaped by the norms of their particular cultural moments, and in the eighteenth and nineteenth centuries riotous audience response was common and even expected.[7] In this respect, while the Astor Place riots have been cited frequently as a key moment in the broader historical shift from "active" to "passive" audiences, they occupy a place within a wider history of audience behavior that is neither distinct nor distinctly Shakespearean.[8] In spite of some scholarship that claims these riots as "Shakespearean" by focusing on the long-term rivalry between the actors to suggest that Shakespearean drama forms an important part of what riot theorists, such as Matthew Moran and David Waddington, would term the "context" of the riot, many scholars, including Joyce Green MacDonald and Frances N. Teague, have questioned if Shakespeare is even a relevant factor in the events that unfolded.[9] There is undoubtedly much more at stake in these riots than a performance of *Macbeth*. Local activists, capitalizing on the history of rivalry between two Shakespearean actors, embarked on a campaign to stir up an audience prepped to respond disruptively to the performance and to give voice to social and nationalistic concerns about the place of working-class Americans in the theater.[10]

Yet the audience was also responding to and was in part provoked by Shakespeare's play. The cause of or "explanation" for a riot, as Moran and Waddington have shown, is "rarely to be found in one single factor," with multiple flashpoints often converging in the development of unrest.[11] In his evaluation of Moran and Waddington's influential "Flashpoints" model of riot, Tim Newburn points out that, despite its useful focus on "the aetiology of disorder" and the "antecedents and context" of rioting, more attention needs to be paid to the "unfolding context of disorder" and "its aftermath."[12] Newburn proposes an extended model that evaluates riot in terms of four main sets of features: the wider social context in which disorder occurs; the dynamics of disorder; the nature of the rioting; and the "response" to disorder.[13] Focusing on the dynamics and nature of the disorder, specifically on the audience's engagement with the play, this chapter offers a new understanding of the significance of Shakespeare to audience riots. Shakespeare is not just part of the wider social context for disorder or an incidental site of violence but is a fundamental element in the evolution of disorder and its nature and dynamics. *Macbeth*, I suggest, operates not only as the site of riot but as a significant factor shaping audience behavior. In an illuminating reading of the performative nature of the Astor Place riots, Elizabeth Williamson has argued that Shakespeare's play was a crucial part of the aesthetics of the audience's behavior. The protestors, she suggests, drew on the play to become "co-creators of a series of extra-theatrical performances."[14] This chapter draws on Williamson's reading of the audience's engagement with the play and on wider performance theory, alongside riot theory, to read the riotous audience at Astor Place as, to use Susan Bennett's words, "active creator[s] of the theatrical event";[15] however, it goes further than Williamson's interpretation to read the protesting members of the audience as one of a number of audience groups participating in connected performances, all of which had a reciprocal relationship with the version of *Macbeth* delivered on stage. Macready's performance had multiple "audiences": those in the theater who supported him, those in the theater who attended with the intention of disrupting his performance, and those on the streets outside the theater who took their cues from the play delivered on stage and from each other—resulting in a series of interlinked performances. The protesting and supporting members of the audience, therefore, not only created a series of extra-theatrical performances that offered what Williamson terms "creative responses to Shakespeare's not-yet hallowed script," but also impacted the delivery of the play on stage by Macready and his company, giving rise to an artistic energy that fundamentally transformed the play's conclusion on May 10.[16] The potential of the audience to shape and transform meaning has a long history, extending back to the original performances of Shakespeare's play.[17] The multiple versions of Shakespeare's drama on and off stage at Astor Place in May 1849 operated in dialogue with each other and exemplify, in this extreme example, the ways in which Shakespearean performance can be simultaneously appropriated and creatively shaped by its audiences even in violent contexts.

Mobilizing the Audience

The ostensible trigger for the Astor Place riots was a number of performances of *Macbeth* in New York in May 1849 that constituted a theatrical battle for audiences and performative sovereignty. On Monday, May 7, William Charles Macready's performance at Astor Place was billed in direct competition to a performance of the play by Edwin Forrest at the Broadway theater, with placards placed around the city side by side.[18] Another performance of the play took place that night, with Thomas Hamblin reprising the leading role at the Bowery theater, which was, according to media reports, enthusiastically received by a full house of a primarily working-class audience.[19] Competition for the support of various audiences within New York was, it seems, being staged via performances of *Macbeth*. The media anticipated trouble before the competing performances took place, with the *Philadelphia Ledger* claiming that the "great theatrical warfare" was "the leading topic of town conversation."[20] This metaphorical "warfare" was realized when Macready's

Monday performance was met by violent protest within the theater. He subsequently canceled his performances at Astor Place but was persuaded to reprise the role on the Thursday evening, at which performance the crowd of thousands gathered and the fatal riots took place.

The protests at Macready's performances were the culmination of a long-standing rivalry between him and Forrest that had begun during the latter's 1846 UK tour, had been maintained by newspaper reports on both sides of the Atlantic, and had intensified during Macready's American tour of 1848–9. "Shakespeare" and his status as a cultural icon were at the heart of this rivalry and the subsequent riots. As many scholars have argued, Shakespeare was "normatively constitutive of British national identity" from the mid-eighteenth century, and touring actors in the eighteenth and nineteenth centuries often used Shakespearean performances to demonstrate their own artistic supremacy and to claim this icon as their own.[21] The professional rivalry between Macready and Forrest that culminated in riot was an instance of this, albeit with exceptional consequences. It was, as Nigel Cliff highlights in his foundational study of the Astor Place riots, part of wider debates about the national and social implications of ways of performing Shakespearean roles and "who controlled the national stage."[22] Audiences and reviewers in both Britain and America contrasted Macready's cultivation of an acting style that he felt resulted in a more respectable artistic experience for the middle classes with Forrest's highly charged, passionate, and physical form of acting. If Macready's style led to him being "taken up by the aristocracy" during his American tours, Forrest's hypermasculine and muscular acting style, as Lisa Merrill suggests, appealed to a "specifically working-class America version of democratic bravado."[23] National and class identity were repeatedly at stake in these actors' rivaling depictions of Shakespearean roles. The sweeping distinction of the styles of the two actors in national, cultural, and class terms was intensified by an alleged personal affront from Forrest, who hissed at one of Macready's performances in Scotland. Reports of this insult and the actors' responses circulated widely throughout Britain and America, reinforcing national distinctions and positioning Forrest's anti-British sentiment and Macready's anti-American feeling at the heart of their rivalry.[24]

Shakespearean roles and a history of Shakespearean performance and transatlantic responses were, therefore, important contextual factors that led to the riot, but they were not the only ones. As Edwin Burrows and Mike Wallace suggest, the Shakespearean actors were "stand-ins for larger and more explosive issues."[25] Irish immigrant workers formed a significant portion of the crowd that gathered outside Macready's performance of *Macbeth*, with the actor identified with England and its aristocracy at "just the moment when New York's Irish were at the height of their rage over the famine and Britain's suppression of Young Ireland's rebellion."[26] The performance also formed a focal point for protest against a range of issues. Shouts of "Three cheers for Macready, … Douglass, and

Pete Williams" by some audience members at Macready's Monday night performance also linked the English actor with abolition in implicit contrast to his theatrical rival Forrest, who had often campaigned on behalf of those in support of slavery.[27] The reference to Frederick Douglass, a former slave and powerful abolitionist, indicates the extent to which protest against the English actor's performance was more complex than American or Irish anti-English sentiment.[28] One of the ringleaders of the theater riot even brought one hundred men to disrupt a meeting of the Anti-Slavery society at which Douglass was present the following evening. The riotous energy of the audience against the performance of *Macbeth* was thus refocused and transported. The theatrical performance may have been the initial site of violent protest, but this was carried from theater space to politicized meeting. The simultaneous performances of Shakespeare's play were vehicles through which contentious questions around national and social politics could be articulated violently by a protesting crowd, with *Macbeth* focusing tensions over issues as diverse as national identity, class politics, and the abolition of slavery, and acting as the catalyst for the riot.

These performances of *Macbeth* were also co-opted to debate the economics of theatergoing and the role of theater as a public space for all.[29] The disruptive audience at Astor Place consisted largely of working-class men and boys, specifically New York's "Bowery B'hoys," for whom rowdiness and collective action were ways of affirming group identity.[30] This audience was formed on the Monday night, when Rynders and his supporters bought tickets and gave them freely to "B'hoys," and on the Thursday night by the posters calling for "working" and "free men" to "stand by their rights." Their anger was not simply directed at Macready as representative of English and aristocratic acting styles but also at the management of Astor Place Opera House itself. High ticket prices and dress codes meant that the Opera House was an aristocratic and exclusive venue, inaccessible to many.[31] The other component of the audience within the theater on both evenings consisted of regular attendees, representative of New York's elite theatergoers. Newspapers reported the cries of some protestors on May 10 that "You can't go in there without kid gloves on. I paid for a ticket, and they would not let me in, because I hadn't kid gloves and a white vest, damn 'em!"[32] These cries, combined with the fact that the crowd of between ten to fifteen thousand protestors consisted primarily of young working-class men, indicate the extent to which, beyond the choice of play by an English touring actor, the response to this particular version of *Macbeth* was concerned with the social dimensions of theatergoing in the period and of shifting class culture. The symbolic space of the theater was a primary target of the violent protest. The fatal fallout of this anger over the elite nature of Astor Place Opera House was recognized quickly as the emergence of what one newspaper bemoaned the country had previously lacked—"a high and a low class."[33] It has subsequently been interpreted as evidence of the "growing chasm between 'serious' and 'popular' culture" and as the catalyst for the ending of theater as "a shared public space" and Shakespeare as no longer being "the common property of all Americans."[34]

The Dynamics and Nature of Audience Response

The Astor Place riots, therefore, were more than a battle over Shakespeare and his tragedy. The context of theater riots, social unrest, and the long-term rivalry between actors deemed to represent distinctions between national and social states coalesced in provoking the audience to action on May 10. Yet the performance of this particular play by these actors was also part of the structural, political, and cultural contexts of mass violence within and outside the theater; because, in spite of the highly combustible social context that made Macready's two *Macbeth*s at Astor Place ripe ground for riot, the protests did not erupt spontaneously. The collective action or violence at Astor Place in 1849 was, as many instances of crowd behavior are in David Waddington and Mike King's words, "invariably restrained and well co-ordinated";[35] and both the specifics of the production at Astor Place Opera House that week and Shakespeare's play were means through which that behavior was coordinated.[36] The crowds that gathered on both the Monday and Thursday nights were prepared to stage their complaints against the performances of *Macbeth* in particular ways. Contemporary accounts were quick to recognize and characterize the audience behavior as a "drama," often superseding the production itself. William Knight Northall, for instance, begins his account of the theater on the Monday night as a "scene" that "was exceedingly curious and exciting," and notes that

> occasionally a message of some description or other was mysteriously telegraphed from the vicinity of the stage to the wings of the ampitheatre [*sic*], and vice versa, by which it was apparent that a perfect understanding existed between these two remote points, and that whatever was about to transpire, their proceedings would be in unison.[37]

In another account of the Monday night audience, Joel Headley notes that the "heterogeneous mass was orderly" and that "at short intervals telegraphic signals were made ... and answered, indicating a thoroughly arranged plan."[38] Audience members came with banners against Macready, and when these were displayed during the performance they acted as a cue for "a perfect tornado of applause, laughter, cheers and groans," as well as an incitement to throw items such as shoes and coins at the actor.[39]

Such behavior was not uncommon at eighteenth- and nineteenth-century theaters. As Marc Baer has argued, theater riots in the period were "theatrical" and "audiences were prepared to answer the stage with dramatics of their own."[40] Yet, the production itself also provided cues for a more spontaneous audience response. There were in effect two audiences within the theater: one that had come specifically armed to disrupt Macready's performances; the other comprising his supporters, who responded with their own riotous behavior. The behavior of the anti-Macready crowd, albeit over wider issues, signaled the extent to which the protest was aimed specifically at the actor. They cheered when American actor Corson Clarke came on stage as Macduff and then waited for Macready to enter as Macbeth to begin expressing their disapproval by flinging "eggs and other offensive missiles" at him and shouting "Nine cheers for Edwin Forrest!", "Down with the codfish aristocracy!", and "Huzza for native talent!" Later in the performance they shouted "Off! Off!" directly to him, while the other portion of the audience responded by screaming "Go on! Go on!"[41] The behavior of this riotous audience and the oppositional groups within it was in part planned and in part responsive, but in both cases this theatrical crowd behavior facilitated the expression of wider attitudes via the articulation of being for or against Macready. Macready interpreted the audience behavior as an attack from his professional rival, Forrest, and as demarcating the battle lines further in terms of a national as well as artistic competition, responding to the shouting crowd with an expression of "pain and shame which the intelligent and respectable must feel for their *country's* reputation."[42] The audience cries, which combined support for Macready's professional rival, protest against the aristocracy, and celebration of "native" talent, as well as Macready's response, signal the extent to which Shakespearean performance was, in this instance, a site through which contentious questions around national and social politics could be violently conveyed.

The specifics of the play of *Macbeth* also became an important part of the dynamics of riotous audience response. The multiple performances of *Macbeth* in May 1849 offered New York audiences the opportunity to express national and social allegiances in diverse ways.[43] The audience for Forrest's performance at the Broadway theater, which was apparently a "thin" one, utilized the production of *Macbeth* to negotiate these issues, responding to Forrest's delivery of "What rhubarb, senna, or what purgative drug / Would scour these English hence?" with a standing ovation and enthusiastic applause.[44] Whether or not these simultaneous stagings of *Macbeth* were deliberate, audiences were quick to seize the opportunity to claim the performances as means to express national friction. The actions at the Broadway theater illustrate that *Macbeth* not only operated as a cue for the crowd to stage opposition but also became part of this articulation. This was also the case as the play unfolded at Astor Place. For contemporary commentator Philip Hone, the riotous audience at Astor Place aligned actor and character, responding not only to the appearance of Macready onstage but to the "appearance of the 'thane of Cawdor,' " which was a cue to "salut[e]" him "with a shower of missiles," in an immersive act of participation in the world of the play.[45] Contemporary newspaper accounts also account for the audience reaction in terms of their conflation of actor and role, with one report noting that the increasing "uproar" every time Macready came on stage on the Monday evening reached "its height" when he came on as "King."[46] The crowd not only, as Bruce McConachie suggests, performed rites inspired by their experience of watching contemporary apocalyptic melodramas, but became implicated in the unfolding of the play of *Macbeth* as they reacted against the actor-character.[47] The two merged in the perspective of the crowd and they enacted their own form of battle against the usurping Macbeth and the usurping Macready. Well-known lines became cues for particular types of behavior. Macready's delivery of "So foul and fair a day I have not seen" was the moment, according to Northall, when "the business of the night," by which he means the audience's violent response, "commenced in earnest."[48] The language of the play thus initiated specific behaviors and became part of the audience response. Some audience members even went as far as appropriating lines of the play for their own impromptu performances within the theater. The witches seemed to hold a particular fascination for the protesting audience. Northall's account claims that the otherwise noisy audience watched the witches' scenes with "considerable interest" and were quiet as "long as the witches had the stage to themselves."[49] According to contemporary accounts of the Monday night's "disgraceful riots," some rioters "chanted snatches of the witches' choruses" in a staging of their riot characterized by "excellent humor."[50] This carnivalesque appropriation of the play for riotous behavior constitutes a quasi-celebratory form of protest that became part of the evening's entertainments, as the play of *Macbeth* moved from Macready's stage into his audience's arena. Yet, if the "chants" included—as Nigel Cliff has suggested they might— the ominous lines:

> When shall we three meet again?
> In thunder, lightning, or in rain?
> When the hurly-burly's done,
> When the battle's lost, and won.
>   (1.1.1–4)

then the relatively contained protest of the Monday night audience may also have formed part of the dangerous development that led to the fatal riots later that week.[51] The appropriation of the witches' lines suggests that the play's depiction of a world overturned and plunged into unnatural chaos facilitated audience behavior. In an uncanny echoing of the witches' potential role in triggering the events of the play, these audience members appropriated this energy to develop the first night of rioting into its next phase.

Macbeth On and Beyond the Stage

The audience at Macready's second performance that week, on Thursday, May 10, continued to engage with the performance in unexpected ways. According to a contemporary pamphlet, part of the audience "interrupted" Macready "with hisses and hootings" while "a large audience, who had crowded the house to sustain him," encouraged him and cheered.[52] As on the first night, some rioters had been positioned at significant points within the theater and they waited for Macready to come on stage before beginning to shout. On this occasion, Macready continued with his performance. Another "attempt was made to get up a tumult" at the lines "I will not be afraid of death and bane / Till Birnam forest comes to Dunsinane" but failed due to the actions of police positioned within the theater.[53] Nonetheless, these disorderly actions had an impact. While on the first night the shouts of the audience members had led to sections of the play going on in "dumb show," the behavior on Thursday night disrupted the aural impact of the performance in other ways.[54] When a chair was thrown, it landed in the orchestra and caused a "prestissimo movement among the musicians, not set down in the original music for 'Macbeth'."[55] One newspaper report emphasized the disruptive effect of the noise of the riotous behavior, revealing that the disruption developed through the interactions between the various groups within the theater, as

> the rioters hooting and yelling defiance whenever the audience demanded their arrest, and daring the police to arrest them. They finally sprang with threatening gestures towards the stage, Mr. Macready being there, and menaced everyone who applauded him.[56]

As lines from the play prompted reactions from the audience, the audience interactions did not simply disrupt the performance but transformed it, becoming part of the aural and visual presentation. The presence of rioters on stage as the play unfolded—"threatening" "Macbeth" and "menacing" the portion of the audience that supported this actor-character—rendered this an extreme realization of performance theorists' contention that the audience is "a tangibly active creator of the theatrical event."[57] The participation of both sides of the divided audience in Astor Place facilitated a unique presentation of the play's politics and battles as the competition for sovereignty became the struggle of an actor to maintain his performance against the onslaught of a violent crowd.

Another audience of sorts also transformed this version of *Macbeth*. Before the performance began, a "mob" had gathered "on the outside."[58] "The streets surrounding the theatre," according to one newspaper, "were crowded with the riotous, curious and the anxious, the former making desperate and almost irresistable [*sic*] efforts to enter."[59] In many contemporary accounts, this was the primary *performance* of the night, reflected in their use of the language of drama and theater to describe what many termed a "bloody tragedy."[60] Northall's recounting of the events of Thursday night claims that when police restrained the protestors in the theater "thus ended the play within" while "without the drama was approaching its terrible finale."[61] For Northall the "play" or "drama" of the night was not Macready's *Macbeth* but undoubtedly the riotous actions of those who had gathered to disrupt the events on stage, both as part of an audience within the theater and as the prospective audience, who had been refused admission, outside the theater. Nonetheless, the play on stage did not end at this point. Macready continued with his performance, even as the riotous behavior outside penetrated the building of the Opera House through noise and makeshift missiles—with "the confusion outside becoming greater every moment, and [as] stones were heard coming through the windows"—and ultimately the sound of the militia opening fire and the increasing riot outside could be heard within the theater.[62] Like the shouts from audience members that had inspired Macready to continue with his performance on Monday evening, the appearance of stones from outside the theater, the smashing of glass, and the sound of gunshots affected the actors' performances. Reflecting on his experience, Macready indicates his awareness of the moment that the "bombardment outside" began, noting that he was making his "exit with Lady Macbeth at the end of the fourth scene."[63] He recalls that the "battering at the building doors, and the windows" grew until ultimately "louder and more fierce waxed the furious noises against the building and from without."[64] This increasing violence and threat caused many audience members to leave, but it also inspired Macready's performance:

> I flung my whole soul into every word I uttered, exciting the audience to a sympathy even with the glowing words of fiction, while those dreadful deeds of real crime and outrage were roaring at intervals in our ears and rising to madness all round us.[65]

If the play had been used on the previous night to endorse "hurly-burly" and "battle," Macready consciously reclaimed it through his engagement with the riots taking place around him. His mocking delivery of lines such as "Our castle's strength / Will laugh a siege to scorn" (5.5.2–3) provoked an unusually sympathetic response from the audience, and the lines were loudly applauded.[66] Macready comments on the effect of the circumstances of this performance, claiming that "the death of Macbeth was loudly cheered, and on being lifted up and told that I was called, I went on."[67] While his dissenters took cues from the play to convey their protest, Macready responded to the experience by drawing on the heightened emotions, noise, and disruptive energy to claim an unusual empathy for the isolated, and, in this performance, victimized, Macready-Macbeth.

To a certain extent then, the riotous response of the play's multiple audiences facilitated Macready's exemplary performance of this particular role. Macbeth was the part through which he had attempted to demonstrate his superior delivery of Shakespearean character. In 1841, he claimed to "have improved Macbeth" in his aim to depict the character as "lofty, manly, or indeed as it should be heroic, that of one living to command" and portraying his "doubt" not as "that of a weak person, but of a strong mind and of a strong man."[68] In spite of this claim, Macready's Macbeth had been widely criticized, Paul Prescott points out, for its "*lack* of manliness, its passivity and moral cowardice."[69] Yet as the theater was besieged and violent protest led to real-life tragedy, Macready, it seems, achieved his aim of presenting Macbeth as a "strong" and "heroic" man under fire. The circumstances that shaped the performance enabled him to realize this desired interpretation of the character. This was endorsed by those who remained to see the final act, with many claiming that they had "never seen the fifth act of 'Macbeth' so splendidly and perfectly performed."[70] Ironically the audiences he so openly dismissed and despised became a crucial part of Macready's theatrical achievement.

This performance of *Macbeth*, therefore, was more than a coincidental site of disorderly audience behavior; it operated in dialogue with that behavior. The performance was crucial to the forms and development of the riotous behavior. It shaped the violent action of the audience—the nature of the riot. The diverse audience—gathered together by the call of political organizers and a shared sense of this theatrical event as representative of the wider exclusion of working-class New Yorkers from theaters, resulting from high admission prices and dress codes at an increasing number of venues at this time—appropriated the play to angrily, and theatrically, give expression to the concerns of a community.[71] The performance was in turn informed by and arguably benefited from the violent aural, visual, and physical effects of the riot. The protestors who set out to disrupt the performance played the "productive role" of a theater audience, and, as Alan Ackerman points out, in this example "the crowd did indeed exercise a peculiar power both over what was presented on stage and how it was presented."[72] This reciprocal engagement facilitated the performance of disorder and the articulation of national and social concerns by the crowd, and impacted on the theatrical event in unforeseen ways. While on many occasions it disrupted the running of the play, it ultimately, Macready and reviewers suggested, inspired a stronger representation of the character of Macbeth. If the riotous audience aligned itself with the play's supernatural forces of disorder and saw itself as purveyors of justice against the tyrannous behavior of Macbeth, those in the audience who supported Macready found a new empathy for the character through their alignment with the English actor and his affective performance of Macbeth as a hero overcoming unjustified violence.

Notes

1 William Toynbee, ed., *The Diaries of William Charles Macready, 1833–1851* (New York: G. P. Putnam's Sons, 1912), 2.420.
2 Toynbee, *Diaries*, 2.420.
3 For details of the Astor Place riots, including debate over the numbers killed, see Nigel Cliff, *The Shakespeare Riots* (New York: Random House, 2007); Richard Moody, *The Astor Place Riot* (Bloomington: Indiana University Press, 1958); Sean McEvoy, *Theatrical Unrest* (London: Routledge, 2016), 85–106; and Frances N. Teague, *Shakespeare and the American Popular Stage* (Cambridge: Cambridge University Press, 2006), 52–63.
4 See work listed in this chapter's bibliography by Alan Ackerman (1999), 98–109; Edwin G. Burrows and Mike Wallace (1999), 761–5; Lawrence W. Levine (1990), 60–69; Bruce A. McConachie (1985 and 1992, 119–57); Brendan P. O'Malley (2018); James Shapiro (2020), 49–82; and Teague, *Shakespeare*, 52–63.
5 Cliff, *Shakespeare Riots*, 211–12.
6 Burrows and Wallace, *Gotham* (Oxford: Oxford University Press, 1999), 763.
7 The tendency of audiences to behave disruptively has a long history. See, for example, Eric Dunnum, *Unruly Audiences and the Theater of Control in Early Modern London* (London: Routledge, 2019) and McEvoy, *Theatrical Unrest*. However, the commonplace that theater audiences in the eighteenth and early nineteenth centuries would behave riotously and disruptively is widely established in scholarship. See Marc Baer, *Theatre and Disorder in Georgian London* (Oxford: Clarendon Press, 1992), esp. 9–17; Richard Butsch, *The Making of American Audiences* (Cambridge: Cambridge University Press, 2000), 44–56; and Bruce A. McConachie, *Melodramatic Formations* (Iowa City: University of Iowa Press, 1992).
8 On the shift from an active to passive audience, see Susan Bennett, *Theatre Audiences* (London: Routledge, 1997), 3–4, and Butsch, *Making*, esp. 3–12. On the Astor Place riots as a "watershed" event in American theater, see Ackerman *The Portable Theater* (Baltimore: John Hopkins University Press, 1999), 37; John Evelev, *Tolerable Entertainment* (Amherst: University of Massachusetts Press, 2006), 82; and Levine, *Highbrow/Lowbrow* (Cambridge, MA: Harvard University Press, 1990), 56–69.
9 Matthew Moran and David Waddington, *Riots* (Basingstoke: Palgrave Macmillan, 2016), 3; Joyce Green MacDonald, "Minstrel Show Macbeth," in *Weyward Macbeth: Intersections of Race and Performance*, eds. Scott L. Newstok and Ayanna Thompson (Basingstoke: Palgrave Macmillan, 2010), 55–64; Teague, *Shakespeare*, 61.
10 This element of the riots has been well-covered in scholarship. See Cliff, *Shakespeare Riots*, esp. 208; McEvoy, *Theatrical Unrest*, 95–97; and James Shapiro, *Shakespeare in a Divided America* (London: Faber, 2020), 49–82.
11 Moran and Waddington, *Riots*, 18. According to their Flashpoints Model of Public Disorder, the flashpoints for riot are often multiple and are influenced by a variety of factors: structural, political and ideological, cultural, institutional and organizational, contextual, situational, and interactional. *Riots*, 18–24.
12 Tim Newburn, "The 2011 England Riots in Recent Historical Perspective," *British Journal of Criminology* 55 (2015): 48–9.

13 Newburn, "2011 England Riots," 49–50.

14 Elizabeth Williamson, "Fireboys and Burning Theaters: Performing the Astor Place Riots," *Journal of American Drama and Theater* 25, no. 1 (2013): 6.

15 Bennett, *Theatre Audiences*, 9.

16 Williamson, "Fireboys," 12.

17 Matteo Pangallo, *Playwriting Playgoers in Shakespeare's Theater* (Philadelphia: University of Pennsylvania Press, 2017), 7.

18 Joel T. Headley, *The Great Riots of New York, 1712–1873* (New York: E. B. Treat, 1873), 113.

19 Moody, *Astor Place*, 113.

20 Moody, *Astor Place*, 106.

21 Michael Dobson, *The Making of the National Poet* (Oxford: Clarendon Press, 1992), 7. See also Jonathan Bate, *Shakespearean Constitutions* (Oxford: Clarendon Press,1989), and Richard Foulkes, *Performing Shakespeare in the Age of Empire* (Cambridge: Cambridge University Press, 2002).

22 Cliff, *Shakespeare Riots*, 25.

23 Lisa Merrill, "Acting Like a Man: National Identity, Homoerotics, and Shakespearean Criticism in the Nineteenth-Century American Press," in *Victorian Shakespeare, Volume 1: Theatre, Drama and Performance*, eds. Gail Marshall and Adrian Poole (Basingstoke: Palgrave, 2003), 83.

24 For detailed accounts of the rivalry and its national and social contexts, see Cliff, *Shakespeare Riots*; McEvoy, *Theatrical Unrest*, 85–106; and Paul Prescott, *Reviewing Shakespeare* (Cambridge: Cambridge University Press, 2013), 47–50.

25 Burrows and Wallace, *Gotham*, 762.

26 Burrows and Wallace, *Gotham*, 762.

27 Heather S. Nathans, "'Blood Will Have Blood': Violence, Slavery and *Macbeth* in the Antebellum American Imagination," in *Weyward Macbeth: Intersections of Race and Performance*, eds. Scott L. Newstok and Ayanna Thompson (Basingstoke: Palgrave Macmillan, 2010), 29–31.

28 Dennis Berthold, "Class Acts: The Astor Place Riots and Melville's *The Two Temples*," *American Literature* 71, no. 3 (1999): 434.

29 The Astor Place riots have been read in scholarship primarily in terms of their critical position in the wider history of the social dimensions of theatergoing in the period and of shifting class culture. See esp. Levine, *Highbrow/Lowbrow*.

30 Butsch, *Making*, 48–52. On the composition of the crowds, see also Burrows and Wallace, *Gotham*, 763.

31 A contemporary report in *Home Journal* viewed the riot as a protest against "aristocratizing the pit." Levine, *Highbrow/Lowbrow*, 65. On the history of Astor Place Opera House, see Cliff, *Shakespeare Riots*, xiv–xvi.

32 Anonymous, "Dreadful Riot and Bloodshed at the Astor Place Theatre!," *The Weekly Herald*, May 12, 1849, 145.

33 Levine, *Highbrow/Lowbrow*, 60.

34 Levine, *Highbrow/Lowbrow*, 68.

35 David Waddington and Mike King, "The Disorderly Crowd: From Classical Psychological Reductionism to Socio-Contextual Theory—The Impact on Public Order Policing Strategies," *The Howard Journal* 44, no. 5 (2005): 491.

36 On the organized and coherent dimensions of riot, see Charles Tilly, Louise Tilly, and Richard Tilly, *The Rebellious Century, 1830–1930* (London: J. M. Dent, 1975), esp. 51.

37 William Knight Northall, *Behind the Curtain* (New York: W. F. Burgess, 1851), 131, 132.

38 Headley, *Great Riots*, 114.

39 Anonymous, "The New York Riot," *Boston Evening Transcript* May 9, 1849, 2.

40 Baer, *Theatre and Disorder*, 63.

41 Anonymous, "The New York Riot," 2.

42 Cliff, *Shakespeare Riots*, xvii.

43 On the appropriation of this play in this way, see MacDonald, "Minstrel Show Macbeth," and Nathans, " 'Blood Will Have Blood.' "

44 Anonymous, "Terrible Riot," *Albany Evening Journal*, May 11, 1849, 2.

45 Allan Nevins, ed., *The Diary of Philip Hone, 1828–1851* (New York: Dodd, Mead and Company, 1927), 2.360.

46 Anonymous, "The Three Macbeths," *State Gazette*, May 9, 1849, 2.

47 McConachie, *Melodramatic Formations*, 146.

48 Northall, *Behind the Curtain*, 136.

49 Northall, *Behind the Curtain*, 136.

50 Anonymous, "Terrible Riot," 2; Anonymous, "Astor Place Opera House," *New York Herald*, May 8, 1849, 4.

51 Cliff, *Shakespeare Riots*, xix.

52 Anonymous, *Account of the Terrific and Fatal Riot at the New-York Astor Place Opera House* (New York: H. M. Ranney, 1849), 5.

53 Anonymous, "Further particulars," *Albany Evening Journal*, May 12, 1849, 2.

54 Anonymous, "Astor Place," 4.

55 Anonymous, "Theatrical: The Forrest Mob in New York," *Sheffield Independent*, May 26, 1849, 6.

56 Anonymous, "The Riot of Thursday Night," *Morning Post*, May 29, 1849, 2.

57 Bennett, *Theatre Audiences*, 9.

58 Anonymous, *Account*, 5.

59 Anonymous, "Alarming Riot at the Astor Place Theatre," *New York Evening Post*, May 11, 1849, 2.

60 Anonymous, "Additional Particulars of the Terrible Riot at the Astor Place Opera House," *New York Herald*, May 12, 1849, 1.

61 Northall, *Behind the Curtain*, 145.

62 Anonymous, "The Riot of Thursday Night," *Morning Post*, May 29, 1849, 2.

63 Frederick Pollock, ed. *Macready's Reminiscences, and Selections from His Diaries and Letters* (London: Macmillan & Co, 1875), 2.617.

64 Pollock, *Macready's Reminiscences*, 2.616, 2.618.

65 Pollock, *Macready's Reminiscences*, 2.618.

66 Anonymous, "Further Particulars," 2.

67 Pollock, *Macready's Reminiscences*, 2.618.

68 Pollock, *Macready's Reminiscences*, 2.178.

69 Prescott, *Reviewing Shakespeare*, 47.

70 Anonymous, "Dreadful Riots in New York," *Lloyd's Illustrated Newspaper*, June 3, 1849.

71 On the ways in which theater gives expression to community, see Kirk W. Fuoss, *Striking Performances / Performing Strikes* (Jackson: University Press of Mississippi, 1997).

72 Bennett, *Theatre Audiences*, 1; Ackerman, *Portable Theater*, 35.

Bibliography

Ackerman, Alan. *The Portable Theater: American Literature and the Nineteenth-Century Stage*. Baltimore: John Hopkins University Press, 1999.

Anonymous. *Account of the Terrific and Fatal Riot at the New-York Astor Place Opera House, On the Night of May 10th, 1849*. New York: H. M. Ranney, 1849.

Anonymous. "Additional Particulars of the Terrible Riot at the Astor Place Opera House." *New York Herald*, May 12, 1849, 1.

Anonymous. "Alarming Riot at the Astor Place Theatre." *New York Evening Post*, May 11, 1849, 2.

Anonymous. "Astor Place Opera House." *New York Herald*, May 8, 1849, 4.

Anonymous. "Dreadful Riots in New York." *Lloyd's Illustrated Newspaper*, June 3, 1849.

Anonymous. "Dreadful Riot and Bloodshed at the Astor Place Theatre!" *The Weekly Herald*, May 12, 1849, 145.

Anonymous. "Further Particulars." *Albany Evening Journal*, May 12, 1849, 2.

Anonymous. "The New York Riot." *Boston Evening Transcript*, May 9, 1849, 2.

Anonymous. "The Riot of Thursday Night." *Morning Post*, May 29, 1849, 2.

Anonymous. "Terrible Riot." *Albany Evening Journal*, May 11, 1849, 2.

Anonymous. "Theatrical: The Forrest Mob in New York." *Sheffield Independent*, May 26, 1849, 6.

Anonymous. "The Three Macbeths." *State Gazette*, May 9, 1849, 2.

Baer, Marc. *Theatre and Disorder in Georgian London*. Oxford: Clarendon Press, 1992.

Bate, Jonathan. *Shakespearean Constitutions: Politics, Theatre, Criticism, 1730–1830*. Oxford: Clarendon Press, 1989.

Bennett, Susan. *Theatre Audiences: A Theory of Production and Reception*, 2nd ed. London: Routledge, 1997.

Berthold, Dennis. "Class Acts: The Astor Place Riots and Melville's *The Two Temples*." *American Literature* 71, no. 3 (1999): 429–61.

Burrows, Edwin G., and Mike Wallace. *Gotham: A History of New York City to 1898*. Oxford: Oxford University Press, 1999.

Butsch, Richard. *The Making of American Audiences*. Cambridge: Cambridge University Press, 2000.

Cliff, Nigel. *The Shakespeare Riots: Revenge, Drama, and Death in Nineteenth-Century America*. New York: Random House, 2007.

Dobson, Michael. *The Making of the National Poet: Shakespeare, Adaptation and Authorship 1660–1769*. Oxford: Clarendon Press, 1992.

Dunnum, Eric. *Unruly Audiences and the Theater of Control in Early Modern London*. London: Routledge, 2019.

Evelev, John. *Tolerable Entertainment: Herman Melville and Professionalism in Antebellum New York*. Amherst: University of Massachusetts Press, 2006.

Foulkes, Richard. *Performing Shakespeare in the Age of Empire*. Cambridge: Cambridge University Press, 2002.

Fuoss, Kirk W. *Striking Performances / Performing Strikes*. Jackson: University Press of Mississippi, 1997.

Headley, Joel T. *The Great Riots of New York, 1712–1873*. New York: E. B. Treat, 1873.

Levine, Lawrence W. *Highbrow/Lowbrow: The Emergence of Cultural Hierarchy in America*. Cambridge, MA: Harvard University Press, 1990.

McConachie, Bruce A. *Melodramatic Formations: American Theatre and Society, 1820–1870*. Iowa City: University of Iowa Press, 1992.

McConachie, Bruce A. "'The Theatre of the Mob': Apocalyptic Melodrama and Preindustrial Riots in Antebellum New York." In *Theatre for Working-Class Audiences in the United States, 1830–1980*, edited by Bruce A. McConachie and Daniel Friedman, 17–46. London: Greenwood Press, 1985.

MacDonald, Joyce Green. "Minstrel Show *Macbeth*." In *Weyward Macbeth: Intersections of Race and Performance*, edited by Scott L. Newstok and Ayanna Thompson, 55–64. Basingstoke: Palgrave Macmillan, 2010.

McEvoy, Sean. *Theatrical Unrest: Ten Riots in the History of the Stage, 1601–2004*. London: Routledge, 2016.

Merrill, Lisa. "Acting Like a Man: National Identity, Homoerotics, and Shakespearean Criticism in the Nineteenth-Century American Press." In *Victorian Shakespeare, Volume 1: Theatre, Drama and Performance*, edited by Gail Marshall and Adrian Poole, 82–98. Basingstoke: Palgrave, 2003.

Moody, Richard. *The Astor Place Riot*. Bloomington: Indiana University Press, 1958.

Moran, Matthew, and David Waddington. *Riots: An International Comparison*. Basingstoke: Palgrave Macmillan, 2016.

Nathans, Heather S. "'Blood Will Have Blood': Violence, Slavery and *Macbeth* in the Antebellum American Imagination." In *Weyward Macbeth: Intersections of Race and Performance*, edited by Scott L. Newstok and Ayanna Thompson, 23–34. Basingstoke: Palgrave Macmillan, 2010.

Nevins, Allan, ed. *The Diary of Philip Hone, 1828–1851*. Volume 2. New York: Dodd, Mead and Company, 1927.

Newburn, Tim. "The 2011 England Riots in Recent Historical Perspective." *British Journal of Criminology* 55 (2015): 39–64.

Northall, William Knight. *Behind the Curtain: Or, Fifteen Years' Observations Among the Theatres of New York*. New York: W. F. Burgess, 1851.

O'Malley, Brendan P. "The Astor Place Riot, 1849." In *Revolting New York: How 400 Years of Riot, Rebellion, Uprising and Revolution Shaped a City*, edited by Neil Smith and Don Mitchell, 71–82. Athens: University of Georgia Press, 2018.

Pangallo, Matteo. *Playwriting Playgoers in Shakespeare's Theater*. Philadelphia: University of Pennsylvania Press, 2017.

Pollock, Frederick, ed. *Macready's Reminiscences, and Selections from His Diaries and Letters*. Volume 2. London: Macmillan, 1875.

Prescott, Paul. *Reviewing Shakespeare: Journalism and Performance from the Eighteenth Century to the Present*. Cambridge: Cambridge University Press, 2013.

Shapiro, James. *Shakespeare in a Divided America*. London: Faber, 2020.

Teague, Frances N. *Shakespeare and the American Popular Stage*. Cambridge: Cambridge University Press, 2006.

Tilly, Charles, Louise Tilly, and Richard Tilly. *The Rebellious Century, 1830–1930*. London: J. M. Dent, 1975.

Toynbee, William, ed. *The Diaries of William Charles Macready, 1833–1851*. Volume 2. New York: G. P. Putnam's Sons, 1912.

Waddington, David, and Mike King. "The Disorderly Crowd: From Classical Psychological Reductionism to Socio-Contextual Theory—The Impact on Public Order Policing Strategies." *The Howard Journal* 44, no. 5 (2005): 490–503.

Williamson, Elizabeth. "Fireboys and Burning Theaters: Performing the Astor Place Riots." *Journal of American Drama and Theater* 25, no. 1 (2013) 5–26.

9 "How novelty may move"

Play and the Boundaries of the Play in the New York Shakespeare Festival's Mobile Theater

Adam Sheaffer

In the fall of 1963, the New York Shakespeare Festival's (NYSF) board convened after completing their second highly successful season in Central Park, in which they served over 130,000 audience members. Despite the strong association between the festival's complementary theatrical offerings and the open-air Delacorte Theater, some on the board saw the amphitheater as a limitation in meeting the festival's primary mission. The festival's founder, Joseph Papp, was especially pointed in his assessment that the festival was not reaching a "mass audience" that would never dream of patronizing the "legitimate theater."[1] This assessment would reverberate throughout the 1960s, as the festival sought myriad ways to increase the public's exposure to Shakespeare in a variety of venues, most notably the Mobile Theater (MT), launched in the summer of 1964.

The festival's interest in touring, however, began only a few months after its first outdoor performances at East River Park in 1956, when the company was known as the New York Shakespeare Workshop. In December of that year, Papp and the Parks Department developed plans to bring the company's summer productions to other spaces around the five boroughs as a "civic-cultural venture."[2] The six-site summer tour of 1957 would ultimately be curtailed because of wear and tear on the portable stage. Between 1957 and 1963, the company also explored much wider and ambitious plans, including touring the South, the Midwest, and even overseas to commemorate the 400th anniversary of Shakespeare's birth in 1964. The desire to tour further and wider was part and parcel of the NYSF's ambitions to grow the scope and reach of their operation to address and serve various audiences and publics.

The chapter that follows traces Papp and the NYSF's project to engage new audiences for Shakespeare throughout the five boroughs and unpacks some of the challenges and problems that ensued in the earliest years of this moveable theatrical project. This project was, arguably, a failure, and the NYSF did not achieve its intended aim, jettisoning Shakespeare as part of the MT after the 1968 summer touring season. Still, exploring the special dynamism of these moveable outdoor productions reveals insights about producing Shakespeare in varied and sometimes unorthodox environments. These insights would not be possible without the use of stage manager and house manager reports from the MT's first few seasons—complicated documents to be sure. Presumed in these reports are ideas about proper audience behavior in the moveable space, and this presumption must not be forgotten as both sets of artifacts reflect the desires and agenda of the NYSF. The surprise and sometimes shock of beleaguered stage managers and other practitioners trying to approximate the indoor theater experience reveals a failure to fully account for the particular circumstances and expectations of audiences/parkgoers as they used and experienced public civic spaces.

NYSF's MT operated from 1964 through 1979, at which point the company slowly phased out citywide touring from its programming.[3] In the first five years of its operation, tour sites included parks, public housing, recreational spaces, and school playgrounds, and the NYSF produced six plays by Shakespeare and his contemporaries, including *A Midsummer Night's Dream* (1964), *Henry V* and *The Taming of the Shrew* (1965), *Macbeth* (1966), *Volpone* (1967), and *Hamlet* (1968). In addition to Shakespeare and Jonson performed in English, from 1964 to 1966 the MT concluded its summer program with Spanish-language productions at selected sites. This included Lorca's *The Shoemaker's Prodigious Wife* (1964), a Pablo Neruda translation of *Romeo and Juliet* (1965), and a Spanish-language *Macbeth* (1966).

In July 1963, Papp wrote to Parks Commissioner Newbold Morris about reviving citywide touring in order to serve "culturally deprived communities" throughout the five boroughs.[4] In February 1964, the NYSF hired a young, aspiring social worker named Sophronus Mundy to guide the messaging and mission of the MT's first season.[5] Mundy drafted a proposal suggesting that the festival account for varied audience expectations of the MT's activities. He even went so far as to call the MT's productions, "Shakespeare as public event."[6] Because of the variety of neighborhoods to which the MT traveled, Mundy and the NYSF developed strategies for understanding the "character" of each neighborhood by contacting local leadership, local papers, and businesses, while collecting questionnaires from housing projects and community organizations. The festival therefore hoped to coalesce already existent "interpretive communities" with its own "horizon of expectations" in order to help constitute and shape potential audiences.[7]

The goals of such coalescence, as Mundy maintained, were "to make the Shakespeare Festival an institution for the people of greater New York," "excite a sense of civic pride," and "create numerous evenings for civic celebration throughout the neighborhoods of this great city."[8] Mundy's proposal, while idealistic, expresses something of the ambiguity of the MT's outdoor performance offerings. Encounters between the MT and its audience could be quite volatile, a fact presaged by the rhetoric used by Papp and others in advance of the citywide tour's inaugural 1964 season. Papp deployed military imagery, suggestively characterizing the

MT company and crew as "our Phalanx going out."[9] Echoing these sentiments, Mayor Robert F. Wagner proclaimed in promotional material that, "(i)n 25 local parks in all the five boroughs, a portable stage" will serve as a "battering ram breaking down the cultural walls that criss-cross our metropolis."[10] Both sentiments suggest barriers, danger, and potential unrest between the MT and the audiences it would encounter.

Framing the Outdoors, Framing the Audience

In order to analyze properly and thoroughly the dynamic of the MT's activ-ities, I will enlist various frameworks to illuminate outdoor performances and audiences. These include Erving Goffman's ideas about the loosening of involvement structures, "theatrical framing" and "keying"; Edward Casey's notion of borders and boundaries; the ecology of theater and performance explored by Baz Kershaw; and Gregory Bateson's discus-sion of danger and imbalance in play. These authors will assist in our understanding of how such varied notions of spectatorship abide in a single space, both playfully and uneasily.

Goffman characterizes "involvement structures" as rules for social engagement enforced by spaces and claims that parks encourage a *loosening* of structures.[11] So even as the MT attempted to establish what Goffman called the "theatrical frame"—with its own unique involve-ment structures—the wider topocosm of the park worked against this. The theatrical frame refers to the conventions that govern the theat-rical event and include the myriad roles audience members embodied as "onlookers," "parkgoers," and "theatergoers."[12] Because of selective inattention, distraction from other audience members, and persistent environmental shifts, the theatrical frame for the MT had to be incredibly flexible. The MT's interactions with audiences therefore embodied a sense of fluidity, which corresponds to Goffman's "central concept" of the the-atrical frame, called "the key." This key, according to Goffman is the "set of conventions by which a given activity, one already meaningful in terms of some primary framework, is transformed into something patterned on this activity but seen by participants to be something quite else."[13] Keying also resonates with Bateson's figurations of "play," and what he characterized as "meta-communication." Bateson argues that while engaged in play there is a complicated series of transmissions containing the understanding that "this is play."[14]

As supplement to the theoretical figurations of play, theatrical framing, and fluidity of role, Kershaw's "ecologies of performance" and "edge-phenomena" along with Casey's interest in edges and peripheries will prove beneficial. The former elaborates edge-phenomena as areas between ecosystems that produce dynamic and intense interactions.[15] It is also worth noting the intriguing parallel between Kershaw's use of "edge-phenomena" and Casey's use of borders and boundaries. Casey echoes Kershaw's sentiments in cartographic terms, stating that "human action intensifies" around the "peripheries" in an "arena of action."[16] This intensification helps us discern the "different ecologies" of the MT's performance space, whose edges were powerfully charged with encounters between audiences, practitioners, and MT staff.

As much as MT staff, performers, and NYSF administrators wished to entirely control the forms and functions of these ecosystems, enacting the activities and conventions of the theater often proved perilous—most especially at three notable MT sites: The Forest Houses Playground (Bronx), Morningside Park (Manhattan), and a Parks Department playground in Bedford-Stuyvesant (Brooklyn).

Shakespeare and the Bronx; or, the Case of the Forest Houses Playground

Housing projects constituted important constituencies for the MT's theatrical offerings, though by 1968 the MT did not visit any housing projects in the Bronx.[17] The elimination of these tour stops, and the reasons for this decision, hinge on the uneasy and at times volatile encounters between the NYSF's MT staff, local audiences, and the community. This was no more apparent than during the NYSF's two-night stands at the Forest Houses in the South Bronx in July 1964 and 1965. Though stage manager Nathan Caldwell, Jr. did not file any daily reports for the MT's inaugural season, he felt compelled to document the events of the July 14 and 15, 1964, performances of *A Midsummer Night's Dream* at the Forest Houses. The July 14 performance was nearly waylaid by eggs thrown toward the stage but cast and crew were able to get through the evening, in spite of the "rudeness" of those seated in the bleachers.[18] Such was the characterization of audience member Anita Fields, who along with six youngsters from her household, a half-mile from the MT site, attended the performance on July 14.

In handwritten notes following both performances, taken for the benefit of both Papp and MT personnel, Caldwell documented the challenges, incidents, and behavior of some audience members. The July 15 performance yielded even greater challenges in the form of noise, stones aimed at the stage and the bleachers on audience left, fighting in the bleachers, and police noncooperation, along with a lack of adequate fencing around the theater space. Curtain-warming remarks from Clifton James (performing the role of Bottom) at the beginning of the show as well as following intermission could not settle the audience, and the show was halted shortly after intermission. This was the first of four performances that summer canceled because of rock throwing, and Papp responded with a wire to the mayor outlining safety concerns. Caldwell insisted that the MT "cannot play in unprotected areas," and that the lack of a partition between the audience and actors resulted in fluidity between the surrounding space and the theater space, which he characterized as "conducive to disorder."[19]

The imperative to secure boundaries and borders cropped up again and again in the MT's first few seasons and underscores Casey's and Kershaw's ideas about borders and "edge-phenomena," respectively. The breaking of the "theatrical frame" occurred because of tension and slippage at the space's borders. Aisles, entrances, and even sparsely populated sections of seating became sources of anxiety, and the MT staff lamented the lack of capable ushers to police borders and allay that anxiety. Each usher, whether provided by the immediate community or community organizations, was issued a set of instructions for proper theater etiquette and comportment. According to these instructions, if the portable theater was not marked or used as such, the specter of activities such as running, standing, milling, or even wrestling haunted liminal spaces within the performance space.[20] Ushers were also expected to quiet audiences and escort disorderly spectators from the house. The rhetoric used by the NYSF in preparing ushers for encountering audiences suggests the marking of parks with practices associated with traditional theater spaces, encouraging relative passivity.

As tumultuous as the MT's 1964 visit to the Forest Houses had been, its two-night stand there in 1965 would prove even more dangerous. After struggling through a July 13 performance of *Henry V*, during which paper clips, eggs, and even "a length of steel" were hurled at the stage, the cast and crew were more than a little shaken. While they completed that performance, the following night, during a performance of *The Taming of the Shrew*, the show was stopped and canceled after a "commotion in the house." Though several prominent community members lingered after the performance to express their outrage at the "shameful disturbance," dissenting voices pleaded with the MT not to return, claiming that many in the community did not want what the festival offered.[21]

In the case of the MT's 1964 and 1965 seasons, it is not clear if the "keying" for the theatrical frame was entirely discernible to performers and audiences alike. Attempts to establish consensus between MT performers and audiences can be seen in the presence of performer Clifton James in the 1964 production operating somewhere between Bottom (who frequently addresses and commiserates with the audience), elder actor of the company, and audience curator. Confusion about James's status/identity might be partially explained by Goffman's notion of "spatial brackets," which he explains is part of the definition of keying and "commonly indicate(s) everywhere within and nowhere outside of which the keying applies on that occasion."[22] James's presence on the stage space, out of character and addressing the audience, somewhat disrupted these brackets and the "keying" necessary to uphold the theatrical frame. Additionally, the bounds of the physical stage space were fuzzy. Around the five edges of the thrust stage were stairs leading to the audience level below, creating a kind of alleyway between the audience and the stage.

This arrangement was repeated to similar effect for the 1965 and 1966 seasons.[23] The suggestion of access from the audience space to the stage space charged this boundary with an intriguing blend of fiction and reality. This blending inspired questions about the relationship between MT practitioners and the sometimes less than welcoming MT audience. The day after the canceled performance of *Taming of the Shrew* at Forest Houses, Robert Hooks, as the eponymous character in the MT's 1965 *Henry V*, performed a similarly equivocal function as James had in 1964. The show was interrupted when a woman in the audience was struck by a rock thrown from behind the control truck and had to receive medical attention. The house lights came up, and Hooks addressed the audience, most especially a group of young men heckling him from the bleachers. Questioning why anyone would want to harm the actors or the audience, Hooks stated that no one would drive him—whether as *himself* or Henry Monmouth is not entirely clear—from the stage and anyone who tried would answer to their own conscience if they injured him.[24]

Once Hooks seemed to have settled the crowd and the lights went back down, both stage manager and police thought the show could continue. Soon, however, a fight broke out among the hecklers, with conflicting reports about a brandished knife, causing audience panic. In the midst of this, one performer, out of fear or thoughtlessness, stepped off the stage toward the house with spear in hand, causing a "commotion" within the audience. Despite deploying the conventions of theatergoing, perforating the fourth wall—as in Hooks's audience address and the spear-wielding ensemble member—helped create something *other* than the theatrical fiction associated with traditional theater spaces.

These disruptions were also exacerbated by the vagaries of park and playground spaces. Assembly and setup of the portable theater posed safety risks, as it involved many large, moving pieces. Setup and break down of the space turned park and playground spaces into virtual construction sites. Photographic and video evidence from the 1964 and 1966 summer season reveals that very little differentiation was made between the spaces for the assembly and preparation of the MT's portable theater and other recreational spaces such as basketball courts, baseball diamonds, and handball courts. Setup for the MT was a massive undertaking and took nearly four hours, even with a small army of personnel. Portions of public parks and playgrounds were transformed by the presence of theater artists and technicians. And yet these spaces that the MT sought so diligently to secure proved decidedly permeable as the public congregated and played in and around the assembly site and, after setup was complete, inside the theater itself.[25]

Throughout its first two seasons, the MT explored ways to create clearer messaging about the ways its portable space was to be received and occupied by the public. With this exploration came the progressive realization that the uses and dynamics of public parks and playground spaces required more flexibility than some of the company's earlier orthodoxies about creating a certain type of order and programming. Because of how vital young people were to the dynamics of the MT's public playing spaces, the issue of how best to accommodate and/or shape their behavior toward and expectations of the touring theater took on ever-greater importance. The 1966 and 1967 MT seasons brought this issue into tighter focus after several incidents further challenged the NYSF's use of public recreational spaces and the public(s) that utilized, and in some cases vied for, that space.

Thunder in the Valley; or, the Case of Morningside Park

Following the 1964 season, the NYSF sought to address more directly the needs, tastes, and enthusiasms of young people by including after-noon performances of original works incorporating music and dance. In 1965, actor Robert Hooks, in addition to playing the title character in the MT's production of *Henry V*, helped to provide material for afternoon performances at the portable theater space. Hooks had been working with a group of young people from Harlem whom he developed into a per-formance ensemble, and they eventually developed a collection of short performance pieces called *We Real Cool*, which served as an afternoon offering at MT sites. These pieces were inspired by Gwendolyn Brook's 1959 poem of the same name and consisted of short pieces exploring con-temporary issues such as gang violence and the ongoing struggle for civil rights. The following year, the Festival created its own in-house afternoon entertainment for younger audiences. NYSF administrators crafted their own content for these performances, and the result was *Potluck!*, which included folk, rock 'n' roll music, and popular dances performed by an interracial cast of young, lithe performers.

On July 3, 1966, the MT was concluding its first week with a two-night stand at its site in Morningside Park. Near the conclusion of an hour-long afternoon performance of *Potluck!*, during what the stage man-ager described as the "squirt gun business," around 200 children rushed onto and around the stage. According to the stage manager, they had "no clear intent except noise and excitement."[26] The evening before this, the behavior of children in the audience was the subject of the MT's evolving policies toward public comportment and decorum, as the stage manager reported that there were "too many unattended, noisy children," and that he received a number of complaints that audience members could not hear above the din. Such noise and disruption—which also included the pops and whistles of exploding firecrackers from outside the theater—elicited complaints from adult audience members. For the evening performance of *Macbeth* on July 3, the MT instituted a policy that prohibited the presence of *any* children under the age of ten, even those accompanied by adults. A group of frustrated parents and chaperones voiced their dissatis-faction with this policy, one going so far as to pen a letter to Papp quoting his own program note claiming the MT served a "truly democratic audi-ence whose parallel existed at the Globe in Shakespeare's time."[27] This incident places in stark relief the challenge the MT faced in refining its purpose and practice, at once training public(s) for theatergoing while pandering to those expecting a more traditional theatergoing experience.

So children, with or without supervision, were banned from attending MT productions as the MT established generational boundaries. And yet the theatrical ecosystems encountered by the MT proved remarkably resistant to closure. The result of closure on the *evening* of July 3 was a "quiet house," and something vital and exciting—intimately wrapped up in the presence and play of children—was contained, if not entirely tamed that evening. In the examples that follow, however, the performance and the play of children blended, revealing perhaps a more vigorous, unfettered engagement with the audiences and the spaces they inhabited and imbued with life.

"Your danger's ours"; or, the Case of the Madison St. and Ralph Ave. Playground

In August 1966, during the penultimate week of the MT's tour, its production of *Macbeth* settled into a Parks Department playground at the corner of Ralph Avenue and Madison Street in the Bedford-Stuyvesant section of Brooklyn. Like other parks and playgrounds on the MT's itinerary, this space operated as a site of recreation and was bound by a large baseball diamond to the west and the school to the east. In a telling bit of reportage, a voiceover (intoned by NYSF alum George C. Scott) to a 1966 CBS news piece titled "Shakespeare in New York" claimed that the "Mobile Theater is the most complex chunk of playground equipment in use in New York, and it attracts a lot of kids."[28] For the young members of the public noted above, the boundaries—spatial, theatrical, and fictional—of conventional theater spaces did not always hold. The result was a special and sometimes chaotic atmosphere in which "the play" and the invitation "to play" blended in unexpected and exciting ways.

The MT scheduled a two-night stand at this particular space, as it had in the previous two seasons. The weather, however, did not cooperate, and the August 9, 1966, performance of *Macbeth* had to be canceled due to rain. The weather was not the only thing to prove somewhat uncooperative, as the theater manager characterized the MT's encounter with the audience: "We fought a losing battle all the way. Audience mostly kids and teenagers who came to show for want of something else to do. Lots of hostility from teenagers and kids. Cops did a good job."[29] Encountering such challenges, the MT battened down the hatches for the following evening's performance.

The August 10 performance, at the very same site, was mired by "hostility" from a handful of younger members in the portable theater's audience. At the conclusion of the presumably tense 2.2, in which Macbeth and Lady Macbeth slay Duncan, the performer playing Macbeth—identified in the stage manager's and theater manager's notes as simply "Jimmy" — was to speak the line "To know my deed, 'twere best not know myself.

/ Wake Duncan with thy knocking. I would thou couldst!" (2.2.74–5). Before exiting the stage, however, the actor remained, clutching the bloody daggers in his equally bloody hands. Irritated by the steady stream of projectiles from the audience, including paper clips and peas, the performer remained down center, "brandishing his 2 daggers," and paused for fifteen seconds before addressing a group of young people near the front of the audience, saying to them in a quiet voice "Once more." The response, surely to the chagrin of the leading player, was a "hail of peas and paper clips," at which he very sternly told them to "cut it out." Not even the grave visage and booming voice of the great James Earl Jones could immediately stem the tide of disruptions. Despite this, the fearless youngsters finally stopped, and after the next scene was performed, the house lights came up and the stage manager addressed the audience over the public address system saying the performance would not continue if members of the audience continued "harassing the actors."[30]

In contrast to earlier incidents in which performers like James and Hooks addressed the audience from the stage, the use of the PA system here shifted the frame for the audience. A disembodied voice, emanating from the same sound system that carries the voices of performers, creates a sense that the "theatrical frame" is being retuned to another "key," one in which accepted and prohibited conventions and behaviors are being respectively re-enforced and discouraged. The remainder of the performance went on without incident, and interestingly both the theater manager and stage manager insisted that the ovation and enthusiasm from the audience were the best the company had received all summer. Such enthusiasm often accompanied invitations for contact and interaction that was as suitable for a public park or playground space as for the theater space. Enforcing the rules of decorum, the Festival encountered other activities and freedoms from the audience/park-going public. If the MT, and by proxy NYSF, was to continue the strategy of pursuing the open question "What is public?" it could not afford to ignore these activities, freedoms, and the public(s) that availed themselves of both, even in the face of potential danger.

In fact, the success of this performance may be indicated by Bateson's account of "danger" and "imbalance" in the realm of play. According to Bateson, the presence of the real-life "danger" or "imbalance" to which playfulness refers—and which circulates among participants in the form of meta-communications—must be present and fictive at once for the play to work. The "presence" of danger is fundamental to the power of the fiction that circulates between audience and performer. As participants within play, meta-communication is what coheres the participants in their joint investment to play, even as they constantly acknowledge that they play. I would argue that Jones, despite clutching stage daggers, had no intention of wielding them as weapons. In this way, the *playful* dynamics of the performance potentially shuffled the *power* dynamics of the MT. In this instance, the MT went beyond merely creating docile, appreciative audiences, to crafting a dynamic and nuanced performance environment. From early on, the NYSF was aware that they were essentially playing on someone else's "turf," and so a line or series of lines needed to be drawn between recreation and leisure that might be associated with this turf and theater. Drawing this "line," claiming (always with negotiation) the "turf" of each MT space, cast and recast the NYSF's relationship to the city's neighborhoods and public(s), as at once a welcome presence, a nuisance, and, at times, a threat.[31]

While these accounts might have at first appeared to be amusing stories about disruptive audience members, I hope to have elucidated the deeper implications revolving around the ideologies reverently or irreverently embodied by audiences in highly contested spaces. The NYSF characterized MT Shakespeare productions as "public" and "civic" events. As such, even through the unruliness of projectile-hurling patrons, we can see an event that blurs the boundaries between the action onstage and action in the "house" in unexpected and instructive ways. In this spatial blurring, something crucial was happening for the NYSF as its self-appointed mission to bring Shakespeare to an idealized mass of uninitiated potential Shakespeare audiences clashed with the experienced behaviors of those same audiences. In response to these clashes, the NYSF gave up producing Shakespeare for the MT after the 1968 summer season.

The MT's programming thereafter focused extensively on crafting theatrical fare geared toward younger audiences and audiences of color. Some of this might be attributed to the opening of the Public Theater in October of 1967—the MT became something of a testing ground for new work at this multitheater complex and vice-versa—but also, perhaps the NYSF learned a difficult lesson about producing Shakespeare on a moveable stage. Civic and community spaces are charged and marked by the public in ways that must be respected and honored. The crucible the MT navigated—with a blend of naivete, idealism, and hubris—between 1964 and 1968 yielded difficult but necessary insights into the opportunities and limitations of their audience-building project and producing "Shakespeare for all."

Notes

1 "New York Shakespeare Festival Board Minutes," September 5, 1963, Series I, Box 14, folder 32, New York Shakespeare Festival Records (New York: New York Public Library for the Performing Arts).

2 Joseph Papp, Letter to Robert Moses, December 5, 1956, Series I, Box 1, folder 12, New York Shakespeare Festival Records. See also: "Provisional Charter for Shakespeare Workshop," 1954, Series I, Box 1, folder 1. New York Shakespeare Festival Records.

3 "New York Shakespeare Festival: Dates List," October 28, 1987, Series VIII, Box 7, folder 11, New York Shakespeare Festival Records.

4 Joseph Papp, Letter to Newbold Morris, July 25, 1963, Series I, Box 14, folder 27, New York Shakespeare Festival Records.

5   Sam Zolotow, "Mobile Theatre Rallies Neighborhoods," *New York Times*, July 2, 1964.

6   Sophronus Mundy, "New York Shakespeare Festival—Summer, 1964. Mobile Theater Tour of A Midsummer Night's Dream. Some proposals for our public relations campaign," Spring 1964, Series I, Box 22, folder 7, New York Shakespeare Festival Records.

7   Susan Bennett, *Theatre Audiences*, 2nd ed. (London: Routledge, 1997), 139.

8   Mundy, "New York Shakespeare Festival."

9   Stuart Little, "A Bus, a Truck, a Dream, a Youthful Cast," *New York Herald Tribune*, June 2, 1964.

10 "Free Shakespeare Is Here" (MT flier), Series I, Box 22, folder 7, New York Shakespeare Festival Records.

11 Erving Goffman, *Behavior in Public Places* (New York: Simon & Schuster, 1966), 215.

12 Erving Goffman, *Frame Analysis* (New York: Penguin Books, 1976), 131.

13 Goffman, *Frame Analysis*, 43–4.

14 Gregory Bateson, *Steps to an Ecology of the Mind* (Chicago: University of Chicago Press, 1972), 180.

15 Baz Kershaw, "Oh for Unruly Audiences! Or, Patterns of Participation in Twentieth Century Theatre," *Modern Drama* 44, no. 2 (2001): 136.

16 Edward S. Casey, "Boundary, Place, and Event in the Spatiality of History," *Rethinking History* 11, no. 4 (December 2007): 508.

17 "List of Housing Projects Near Sites," undated (ca. Spring 1964), Series I, Box 25, folder 21, New York Shakespeare Festival Records.

18 "New York Shakespeare Festival—Annual Report," Series 1, Box 23, folder 1, New York Shakespeare Festival Records.

19 Nathan Caldwell, Jr., "Wire to the Mayor-Mobile Unit," July 15, 1964, Series I, Box 32, folder 6, New York Shakespeare Festival Records.

20 "Ushers—Delacorte Mobile Theater, New York Shakespeare Festival," 1964, Series I, Box 22, folder 7, New York Shakespeare Festival Records.

21 "New York Shakespeare Festival, Stage Manager's Daily Performance Report," July 14, 1965, Series I, Box 32, folder 10, New York Shakespeare Festival Records.

22 Goffman, *Frame Analysis*, 45.

23 "Venues-Mobile Theater circa 1964–1970," Series XII, Box 35, folder 5–10, New York Shakespeare Festival Records.

24 "New York Shakespeare Festival, Stage Manager's Daily Performance Report," July 15, 1965, Series I, Box 32, folder 10, New York Shakespeare Festival Records.

25 Images and photographic proofs are preserved in the company's records: "Venues-Mobile Theater circa 1964–1970," Series XII, Box 35, folder 10–15, New York Shakespeare Festival Records; "Delacorte Mobile: Shots of Preparation and Set-up for A Midsummer Night's Dream," 1964, Joseph Papp Public Theater/New York Shakespeare Festival Moving Image Collection, New York Shakespeare Festival Records.

26 "New York Shakespeare Festival: Stage Manager's Daily Performance Report," July 3, 1966, Series I, Box 41, folder 20, New York Shakespeare Festival Records.

27 "New York Shakespeare Festival: Stage Manager's Daily Performance Report," July 3, 1966, Series I, Box 41, folder 7, New York Shakespeare Festival Records.

28 "Shakespeare in New York," CBS-TV (New York, 1966).
29 "New York Shakespeare Festival: Theatre Manager's Daily Report," August 9, 1966, Series I, Box 41, folders 14, 7, New York Shakespeare Festival Records.
30 "New York Shakespeare Festival: Stage Manager's Daily Report," August 10, 1966, Series I, Box 41, folder 13, New York Shakespeare Festival Records.
31 During the August 9, 1967, performance of *Volpone* cited above, for example, a man told the theater manager to take the play out of the park because he felt it was "corrupting the minds of Black American Youth." "New York Shakespeare Festival: Theater Manager's Daily Report," August 9, 1967, Series I, Box 53, folder 16, New York Shakespeare Festival Records.

Bibliography

Bateson, Gregory. *Steps to an Ecology of the Mind*. Chicago: University of Chicago Press, 1972.

Bennett, Susan. *Theatre Audiences*, 2nd ed. London: Routledge, 1997.

Casey, Edward S. "Boundary, Place, and Event in the Spatiality of History." *Rethinking History* 11, no. 4 (December 2007): 507–12.

Goffman, Erving. *Behavior in Public Places*. New York: Simon & Schuster, 1966.

Goffman, Erving. *Frame Analysis*. New York: Penguin Books, 1976.

Kershaw, Baz. "Oh for Unruly Audiences! Or, Patterns of Participation in Twentieth Century Theatre." *Modern Drama* 44, no. 2 (2001): 133–54.

Little, Stuart. "A Bus, a Truck, a Dream, a Youthful Cast." *New York Herald Tribune*, June 2, 1964.

New York Shakespeare Festival Records. New York: New York Public Library for the Performing Arts. Archive boxes.

Zolotow, Sam. "Mobile Theatre Rallies Neighborhoods." *New York Times*, July 2, 1964.

10 Imagined Theater
Why Fan Audiences Matter

Louise Geddes

FantasticallyFoolishIdea's 2016 fanfic, "Old Wounds, New Wounds," is a Bencutio slash fanfic in which Benvolio and Mercutio experience a frustrated evening at home after Benvolio returns, bruised and battered, from meeting Sampson and Gregory in the marketplace of Verona.[1] This representation of Benvolio and Mercutio's off-stage relationship is a fairly unremarkable fanfic narrative of the "hurt/comfort" genre, but its paratexts reveal more about the fic than we might expect. The work was written in response to a prompt posted on the popular fan site Tumblr and was written for another user, named whowantsafriend. In the notes, FantasticallyFoolishIdea admits that their fic is influenced by their experience as a fan of the filmed production of *Romeo and Juliet* at the Globe:

> I usually imagine the characters as portrayed by Phil Cumbus and Jack Farthing in the production of the Globe Theatre in 2009. I adore that version mostly because of how utterly comfortable they are with each other, their horsing around and all the gratuitous touching. Also, it fits quite nicely with my headcanons.[2]

FantasticallyFoolishIdea here identifies as an audience member, sharing their experience with a friend who may or may not have also seen the 2009 production (either online or in London). The fanfic, and the questions of how the text on which it is based has been accessed, suggest that the understanding of audience has changed, as (likely) digital viewers continue to regard the screening as a singular performance. Moreover, as this production lingers in the mind of FantasticallyFoolishIdea, blending with their "headcanons" (which is fan parlance for the ways in which a fan imagines particular themes, characterizations, ideas, or relationships in a text to feel true, with little clear textual basis), it creates an impressionistic performance that expands on that which has already occurred onstage, integrating the show with popular media and/or fannish tropes such as slash. In this instance, Dominic Dromgoole's production has served to validate FantasticallyFoolishIdea's perception of the homoerotic relationship between the men of *Romeo and Juliet*, and the resulting fanfic offers the opportunity to understand how at least one audience member absorbed the Globe's production and used it to create new performances for their shared community.

"Old Wounds, New Wounds" expands the parameters of how Shakespeare scholars understand audiences and illustrates how, enhanced by digital and DVD screenings, productions linger in the minds of theatergoers. Acknowledging FantasticallyFoolishIdea's fanfic as a representation of spectatorship, then, suggests the necessity of new metrics by which an audience is defined.[3] The vectors of audience research are shifting away from mere attendance, and, as Jennifer Radbourne, Hillary Glow, and Katya Johanson note, "rather than measuring demand metrics in order to demonstrate the success or failure of arts productions, we should look at *how* audiences are engaged with the performance."[4] Over fifteen years ago, communication studies began to theorize television audiences as users, recognizing the extent to which the convergence of media has altered the way in which programming is consumed.[5] Although media studies has recognized the value of fandom as one of the means by which we might understand audience formation, theater studies has been slow to reconceptualize its understanding of audience and delve more deeply into what audiences do with their experiences as spectators. Fan studies understands consumption primarily through acts of production (or perhaps, *re*production), and this offers performance studies the opportunity to acknowledge the shared qualities of fandom and audiences and think about theatrical events as a longer, ongoing process.

In the twenty-first century, fandom is a communal activity.[6] Fan production, manifest through a combination of "universal archives, community archives, and alternative archives," illustrates how fandoms are characterized by a shared sense of discovery, by "the pleasure of realizing that a solitary activity could be a group activity, that they were not alone in inventing original stories about borrowed characters."[7] Abigail DeKosnik expands this feeling of camaraderie to suggest that it is organized around a text and that it "allow[s] users to access the documents that constitute the cultural tradition of a community."[8] Like many theater communities, fandoms are openly affective. "Fan" is no longer a derogatory term to attach to a zealot, but more carefully defined as an affective sensibility, one that varies in levels of enthusiasm and commitment, but nonetheless enables us, as fans, to redefine our own identity out of the relations among our differences; fans, Lawrence Grossberg notes, "actively constitute places and forms of authority (both for themselves and others) through the mobilization of affective investments."[9] That is to say, I am a Shakespeare fan, with a preference for Shakespeare over Eugene O'Neill, and this affective investment is manifest in the shows that I see, the media I consume, and the scholarship that I produce. The larger result of this subjective, affective engagement is an audience that is experienced in putting its own needs first, that is comfortable with the assumption that it can create what has not been made available by the commercial producers of the cultures it digests.

Radbourne, Glow, and Johanson identify four qualities to assess as a means of understanding audience engagement: knowledge, risk, authenticity, and collective engagement. Knowledge is defined as the "understanding, intellectual stimulation, and cognitive growth" that is earned as part of the experience; risk is the "gap between expectation and perception" as it pertains to the audience's understanding of the expectations placed on them and their understanding of their place in the "spectacle," evidenced by their willful complicity in the event; authenticity is the active search for "truth and believability, artistic authenticity and emotional engagement"; and finally, collective engagement defines the audience's relationship not only to the performers, but to other members of the audience.[10] These criteria are effective for homogenizing a diverse community of individuals into an audience, and these terms are strikingly similar to the qualities of a fandom.

A fandom is a community of individuals drawn together by shared experience of a media franchise, who exhibit an openly subjective position in relationship to their fan objects, maintain participatory expectations, and, through this participation, demonstrate a sophisticated understanding of the formal qualities of their chosen media. Moreover, fans, like audience members, exhibit their imaginative willingness to accept the fan object in accordance with its own logical rules (its "canon" in fan parlance). At its most basic level, Grossberg's affective sensibility is the suspension of disbelief that is often indicative of the minimum threshold for theatrical participation, and is, at its most enthusiastic, manifest in applause and an emotional investment in performance that might be visible through laughter or weeping. In a "real-life" context, the qualities that define a fan would be welcomed in the theater. If we conflate these two communities, we might understand fan production—memes, fan art, and fanfic—as imaginary performances. By creating speculative microperformances, fans affirm their role as keepers of cultural memory and assert themselves as creative consumers, requiring a conceptual adjustment of our definition of the Shakespearean audience as it navigates between the ephemeral and the embodied.

Shakespeare Audiences as Fans

In order to equate a Shakespeare audience with fandom, we must move away from a neoliberal taxonomy of those who buy a single ticket, attend a performance, or log onto YouTube, in favor of repeat or regular participants who might not always obtain access commercially (or legally). Defining such a collective is challenging for two reasons: (1) we must acknowledge the extent to which Shakespeare's cultural capital invites a captive audience in the most literal sense—one that attends events out of obligation or educational requirements; (2) it depends on the Shakespearean fan object—the text—being readily visible and identifiable. Unlike, for example, the straightforwardly generalizable Stephen

Sondheim, Susan-Lori Parks, or Ivo van Hove audience, a Shakespeare audience has no unifying principle, beyond its connection to the larger "transmedial set of objects" that we identify as Shakespeare.[11] There is no definitive Shakespearean aesthetic or philosophy, no accessible original cast around which an audience might coalesce; even the text itself does not exist in a sufficiently organized unit for an audience to uniformly claim it. The most cursory comparison between the two major British Shakespearean theater companies—The Royal Shakespeare Company and Shakespeare's Globe—illustrates enough differences in performance philosophy, ideology, and aesthetic to undercut the assumption that one can define the Shakespeare audience by an examination of who subscribes to Shakespeare-oriented companies.[12] As such, consumers form a heterogeneous community whose members make different demands on Shakespearean theater while still being categorized as part of a Shakespeare audience. For those participants driven to the theater by their affective desire, Shakespearean theater involves sifting through diverse aesthetics, forms, and media, and accommodating variants as part of a broader conceptualization of Shakespearean performance.

Defining a Shakespearean audience, then, depends on a shifting, unstable concept of the text that enables a conceptual framework for Shakespearean theater as an imaginative construct that comes into existence through acts of comparison. We might define a member of the Shakespeare audience as we would a member of a fandom—as someone who not only consumes but does so discriminately and voraciously. The fan is the audience member who attends enough performances that the disparate fragments of the unstable Shakespeare text coalesce into a personalized, subjective understanding of what a character, or play, is to them. It is someone who has built their own headcanon out of a widespread consumption of Shakespearean theater. In this sense, a Shakespeare audience member might be similar to a *Star Trek* fan in the way in which they can accommodate platform and media changes, or to a *Doctor Who* fan defined by their simultaneous preference for one Doctor over another and affection for the show at large. In all instances, audience members commit to following a franchise as it sprawls across time and media with few fixed reference points. In theory, following this model, the more Shakespearean theater a fan accumulates, the more the plays themselves come into focus. For example, they might be drawn to the lean aesthetic of Maxine Peake's 2014 portrayal of Hamlet, or the less glamorous 1992 production featuring Alex Jennings. They might embrace the vulnerability of Michael Maloney's 1999 performance at the Greenwich Theatre, or the warmth of Paapa Essiedu's 2016 portrayal to consolidate their own understanding of the Danish Prince. They might assemble and reject embodied characteristics, or light on a production, as FantasticallyFoolishIdea did, and recognize it as representative of how they imagine the text to be in performance. A real-life audience member, or Shakespeare aficionado, often embraces this practice of assemblage and comparison as intellectual play, which Anne Ubersfeld terms "brico-lage," and this process is often shaped by the context within which it is intentionally shared.[13] In professional communities, such comparative actualization is often the mark of authority in, for example, the reviews of *The Guardian* or *The New York Times*, or postshow bar talk, where it is offered as a show of connoisseurship, constructing a hierarchical valuation structure from which to evaluate theater dispassionately. In such participatory spaces as Web 2.0, however, this work, manifest as fan activity, is much more haphazardly approached, emerging as a glut of confluences that collide and intersect with one another.

As media access evolves, the disaggregation of an audience has the effect of further diffusing the immediacy of the theatrical event. That is to say, if one defines the Shakespeare audience in terms of fandom, one understands the audience as something that self-identifies as such and can therefore exist before and after the playhouse experience has occurred. Digitized live (and encore) streams, in cinemas and in databases such as *Digital Theatre* (not to mention pirated versions that freely circulate online), allow an audience to exist asynchronously, and the capacity to rewatch live screenings undermines our ability to define a theatrical per-formance as an event shared between a community physically present at a location for a specified period of time. Although traditional "live" Shakespeare audiences are steeped in what Susan Bennett suggests is "a shifting vector of nostalgia, memory, and tradition," digital audiences engage in a more speculative practice, beginning with the very suspen-sion of disbelief that allows a viewer to imaginatively place themselves in an event that might have already happened or is currently happening on the other side of the world.[14] As Daniel Sack notes in his introduction to *Imagined Theatres*, in this digital age, "new technologies might allow us to write code that literally lives or to fashion performances that out-live the organic body," and the role of the performer or director may be reoriented to reflect this new reality, reminding us that the starting point of the theater is not the stage, but the space of imagination.[15] Shakespeare's audiences, then, in the digital age, not only look forward to anticipate new desired productions but also askance, imagining productions or theater that never happened, and in some cases, could never happen. As Sack has observed elsewhere, performance is boundless potentiality.[16] To accept performance's move away from physical embodiment toward ephemera allows for the validity of imagined performances as the outer limits of the theatrical event. Imagined performances are no less theatrical because they are not real.

To identify the Shakespearean audience as "fannish" is to accommo-date conceptually the multiplicity of the Shakespearean performance text—to recognize it as a thing that exists in the minds of theatergoers through the generative process of comparison and expands to aggregate newer iterations. Abigail DeKosnik defines media texts that can only exist as unstable, transmedial variants as "archontic." She suggests that such media texts accumulate their own archive, inviting their audience in to roam, explore, and contribute to the texts' archontic growth. DeKosnik's suggestion that we identify "mass media, *as* an archive, as an ever expanding collection of archives that exist for their use, that contain the raw matter for their generation for new narratives, new connections, new significations," implies that fan productivity can be accessed in much the same way as a YouTube performance, sought out of an online repository and expanded by way of a "like," shares, or a comment, or a responding fic.[17] By defining archontic production as an activity that both draws from and contributes to the archive, DeKosnik carves out a space for audience consumption to be made visible through fan activity and imagines archontic production as akin to performance. These iterative practices of Shakespearean theater that are reconstituted as new performance objects suggest a shared Shakespearean archive in which the "embodied memory" of repertoire exists in the fannish audience members' network of affective associations.[18] DeKosnik further characterizes archontic accretion as a

> process by which audience/receivers of mass-produced and mass-distributed cultural texts ... seize hold of these commodities as a vast archive of usable resources, from which they select desirable parts as the raw material for their own revisions and variations.[19]

Because of language such as "revisions and variations," DeKosnik's theory appears to lean toward appropriation and seemingly eschews the notion of performance in its dismissal of repertoire based on an assumption of its immateriality. The prevalence of memes and fanfics, however, illustrates not only the archontic nature of the Shakespearean audience, but suggests a desire of the audience to create more stable markers of the performance, to seek out its material elements by translating these comparative accretions of cultural memory into fictional microperformances that accommodate both the archontic nature of theater and the material traces of spectatorship that an audience leaves behind.

By recognizing the Shakespearean performance text as a fan object that allows fans to stake a participatory claim on the text, and by accepting fannish appropriation as acts of imagined theater, it is possible to acknowledge the ephemerality of performance and redistribute the theatrical process of "filling in the gaps" more equitably between the performer and the audience. Moreover, to thus validate audience members, defined by their imaginative engagement, is to upend the traditional scholarly assumption that theater is an event that can only occur in a shared physical space. Online, Shakespearean theater fans, who speculate about performances in digital spaces, reverse the traditional "real-life" paradigms of performance by constructing the audience first and imagining a performance to suit. This irregular twenty-first century audience, then, is made up of what Johannes Birringer terms "spect-actors," who presume an entitlement to engage with performance on their own terms, processing the experience through new acts of creation that reveal much about how performance works in a digital age.[20] For fans, memes, fanfic, fan art, and other fan productions, such as mashups, allow us to become spect-actors in the most active sense imaginable and speculate what Shakespeare performance could be, as it is shaped with popular culture and fan tropes—in short, by the affective sensibilities of its audience.

Memes as Microperformances

In 2018, an entertaining meme began circulating on social media, in which Shakespeare plays are defined by screen-captures from popular television sitcoms, including *Parks and Recreation*, *The Office*, *Arrested Development*, and *It's Always Sunny in Philadelphia*. This trend was triggered by a previous meme that imagined Shakespeare plays as headlines from the satirical website *The Onion*, and contributors to a Twitter feed presented captioned images that they thought embodied the crux of the play, under the titles of individual plays. In one *Arrested Development* meme titled "*Coriolanus*," for example, Lucille, the demented, alcoholic matriarch of the Bluth family, tells her son Michael, "I happen to be a more caring mother than most" (Figure 10.1).[21] In a *The Office*-themed meme, inept manager Michael Scott represents *Twelfth Night* in a screencap that shows him looking down at his body and ruefully admitting that "it was a weird day. I accidentally crossdressed."[22] These memes are created by those who love both Shakespeare and these particular sitcoms and they acquire their potency from our willingness to look at these little images as miniature, imaginary theater spaces in which a Shakespeare play is being performed. Absurdity (and mild nihilism) is characteristic of this genre. They offer embodiment without bodies, asking us to cast fictional characters as other fictional characters, and as such, enact Sack's potentiality, offering the promise of an experience that we must fulfill with our own imagination.

I happen to be a more caring mother than most.

Figure 10.1 Shakespeare Theatre Company, *Coriolanus*. Screengrab.

Guys love it when you can show them you're better than they are at something they love.

Figure 10.2 @alisonlsloan, *The Merchant of Venice,* tweet, July 18, 2018.

While some memes exist as merely brief play summaries, others represent an interpretive stance that allows one source to act as paratext to another. For example, in the *Parks and Recreation*-themed screencap titled "*The Merchant of Venice*," Leslie Knope, small-town council heroine and chronic overachiever, is dressed in hunting gear standing in a forest, while she brightly announces that "guys love it when you're better than they are at something they love," while her office partner, Ron Swanson, stands stone-faced in the background, rifle in hand (Figure 10.2).[23] In this instance, the meme conflates Knope's over-zealous idealism and obsession with perfectionism with Portia's decision to attend the Venetian trial of Antonio. Moreover, a more considered attention to the larger plot of *Parks and Recreation* draws attention to the Shakespeare play's ending. For many of the early seasons, Knope's inadequate love-life is accounted for by her propensity to over-plan and her well-meaning, yet overwhelming, desire to determine each step of her relationships. Knope's blithe indifference to Swanson's probable irritation and very different set of priorities is foregrounded in the meme and facilitates ways to think about the gender separation as emblematic of insurmountable differences in perspectives. These attributes encourage the viewer to mentally perform an ending in which Portia's involvement in Antonio's trial is a well-intentioned blunder that accentuates the problematic degree of control that she attempts to maintain over personal and professional relationships, ignoring the extent to which her involvement is not welcome. The sly comedy that characterizes *Parks and Recreation* therefore implicitly recasts Portia as a representation of the naive optimist Leslie Knope, who would likely not realize that her new husband may, in fact, be both gay and in love with someone else.

These fictional microperformances extend existing practices of Shakespearean theater. Even though Leo Benedictus notes that for some theater lovers, "the mire that mainstream theatre has sunk in" is a natural by-product of a celebrity culture, his remark ignores the ways in which Shakespeare's audiences have been defined by the affiliations between Shakespeare and celebrity since Garrick's time.[24] In 2011, for example, Josie Rourke's production of *Much Ado About Nothing* cast former *Doctor Who* costars David Tennant and Catherine Tate as Benedick and Beatrice. In casting these two actors, the production consciously exploited the comedically tense relationship that the two developed when they played The Doctor and his companion, Donna Noble. The mirroring that the production facilitated allowed the audience to expand speculatively their knowledge of Shakespeare by substituting what they knew (or maybe imagined) about Donna and The Doctor's relationship for that which Shakespeare does not reveal. Michael Billington's review for *The Guardian*, for example, notes that this was "a marriage that, if not made in heaven, is certainly cemented by television."[25] Under these conditions, Donna and The Doctor's well-documented antagonism allowed a fannish audience to accept Shakespeare's lovers' sparring as part of a longer trajectory of their relationship and potentially tied into the pleasure of fan shipping when Beatrice acknowledged that Benedick gave her his heart "and I gave him use for it, a double heart for his single one" (2.1.255–6). The extension of these imaginative invitations also occurs through paratextual marketing materials, such as the social media production strategy for Ian McKellen and Patrick Stewart's 2013 Broadway double bill of *Waiting for Godot* and *No Man's Land*, which saw the two men out and about town, eating hotdogs, visiting landmarks, and generally engaging in touristy activities. These promotions invite us to "pretextually poach" and speculatively consume theater, reconceptualizing the event beyond a singular performance that "translates" the text.[26] These imaginative acts are theatrical in that they strive for "efficaciousness not authenticity" and complicate theater's status as a "richly materialized semiosis, one that enforces an intellectual, sensory, affective encounter with an estranged worldliness."[27]

On some level, theater thrives on affective networks and their affiliations; Marvin Carlson's now-famous definition of the haunted theater suggests that the palimpsest of associations is inescapable for the audience.[28] Ghosting utilizes the paratextual embodiment of such tangible qualities as the actor's body, topical set design, and celebrity, and extending the theatrical event to accommodate imagined performance allows fictional characters to carry equal weight with these tangible qualities and validate the claims of the fannish audience. Fanfic in particular thrives on the practice of ghosting, formalizing it as part of a practice called "crossover." In Singofsolace's 2019 fanfic, "Sir, Spare Your Threats," the leading characters of Netflix's show *The Chilling Adventures of Sabrina* rehearse a production of *The Winter's Tale* that is cast with freshly divorced couple

Zelda Spellman and Faustus Blackwood playing Hermione and Leontes, with their families in the supporting roles. Singofsolace constructs an imaginative production that generates a sense of danger by putting "real-life" characters from *The Chilling Adventures of Sabrina* into fictional roles where they may either work out or exacerbate their tensions. At one point, the director, Lillith, observing a rehearsal of 2.1, expresses her anxiety because the performance is a little too successful:

> It wasn't until Faustus entered the stage that she was struck by a sense of foreboding. She couldn't quite put her finger on it, but it was as if the energy in the room and on the stage had completely shifted from the warm, domestic scene it had previously been to something … else. When he went to take Judas away from Zelda, it felt like the cast, both onstage and in the wings, were collectively holding their breaths.[29]

Singofsolace's description of the scene is interwoven with Shakespeare's lines, inviting the fanfic reader to imagine the production in accordance with their vision. Moreover, their narrative positioning, which accommodates both performer and audience member, efficiently encapsulates the fan's place as both producer and consumer of culture. The comments suggest a community of both *Sabrina* and Shakespeare enthusiasts, with "applause" in the form of kudos (Archive of Our Own's equivalent of "likes") from fans of both media franchises.[30] One commenter, Moonshine Madam, announces that "this intro is absolutely amazing and I think 'The Winter's Tale' is going to be the next Shakespeare I'll read," presumably now imagining the play through the prism of *The Chilling Adventures of Sabrina*.[31] Unlike FantasticallyFoolishIdea, Singofsolace was unable to find a "definite" production of *The Winter's Tale* and so they simply imagined one, creating both production and theater and inviting in their audience to watch and respond. Like FantasticallyFoolishIdea's fanfic, "Sir, Spare Your Threats" is also a gift to a shared community, but Singofsolace is not clear to whom this is dedicated, simply announcing that this is "Madam Spellman Shakespeare AU [alternate universe], as promised."[32] Many of the comments refer to the author's Tumblr account as the starting point for their discovery of the fanfic, suggesting ways in which this shared community has formed in anticipation of this imagined performance.

All of the imagined microperformances cited in this chapter meet Radbourne, Glow, and Johanson's criteria for audience engagement. They all advance our knowledge of the text, particularly through the type of crossover that invites us to think more critically about the works they use and to recognize these microperformances as acts of theater in their own right. Fandom, particularly as it pertains to imagined theaters, facilitates risk, as audiences are invited to participate in accepting the premise of the performance and risk degrees of participation by sharing or adding to the meme. The fanfics, written in response to kudos or at the request of other fans, share a similarly communal point of origin to the memes, which were collected as threads and archived on webpages but began life as a crowdsourced thread on Twitter that enabled audience members to share and add on new entries as replies to the original tweet. In the case of these meme microperformances, risk is encouraged because this ephemeral body of work exists on a platform that is as inviting to participation as a black box theater. All of these works depend on a working knowledge of fan canon—my own lack of knowledge of *It's Always Sunny in Philadelphia* was a barrier to my participation as an audience member in that particular set of memes. Finally, the circulation of these microperformances generates applause in the shape of "likes," shared links, and other forms of exchange around social media. As such, these texts circulate as tiny speculative performances viewed and collected by a community of users that we might define as an "audience."

Such thinking holds many possibilities for audience studies as it conflates with fan studies. Performance studies is invested in the ephemerality of the theatrical experience. As Valerie M. Fazel and I argue elsewhere, the Shakespeare text has always been an archontic object, but there is much to be gained from thinking about performance itself as archontic.[33] Perhaps paradoxically, we can trace audiences' imaginary participation through reconceptualizing our understanding of embodiment in the world of Web 2.0 and conceptualizing the audience as a community that might well continue to engage with a performance, five, ten, or twenty years after the event.

Notes

1 FantasticallyFoolishidea, "Old Wounds, New Wounds," Archive of Our Own, February 20, 2016. https://archiveofourown.org/works/6069613.
2 FantasticallyFoolishidea, "Old Wounds, New Wounds."
3 Despite likely accessing these productions online, fans continue to identify as audience members, evidenced by the categorization of fanfics as "theater" and tags such as "RSC compliant" that emphasize performance.
4 Jennifer Radbourne, Hillary Glow, and Katya Johannes, "Knowing and Measuring the Audience Experience," in *Audience Experience*, eds. Jennifer Radbourne, Hillary Glow, and Katya Johannes (London: Intellect, 2013), 5 (my italics).
5 See Sonia Livingstone, "The Challenge of Changing Audiences, Or What is the Audience Researcher to do in the Age of the Internet?" *European Journal of Communication* 19, no. 1 (2004): 75–86.
6 Obviously, this consolidation of an audience into a unified community is an idealistic observation. Fan studies is particularly adept at interrogating the extent to which the act of defining an audience as asynchronous invites "untroubled (and often idealistic) geotemporal convergence" by eliding the critique of "how and why communities of affect and belonging are constituted" as political and ideological entities. Lori Hitchcock Morimoto and Bertha

Chin, "Reimagining the Imagined Community: Online Media Fandoms in the Age of Global Convergence," in *Fandoms: Identities and Communities in a Mediated World*, eds. Jonathan Gray, Cornell Sandvoss, and C. Lee Harrington, 2nd ed. (New York: New York University Press, 2017), 174, 175. See also Rukmini Pande, *Squee, From the Margins* (Iowa City: University of Iowa Press, 2018).

7 Abigail DeKosnik, *Rogue Archives* (Cambridge, MA: MIT Press, 2016), 134, 137.

8 DeKosnik, *Rogue Archives*, 137.

9 Lawrence Grossberg, "Is there a Fan in the House? The Affective Sensibility of Fandom," in *The Adoring Audience: Fan Culture and Popular Media*, ed. Lisa Lewis (London: Routledge, 1992), 59.

10 Grossberg, "The Affective Sensibility," 8–9.

11 Douglas M. Lanier, "Afterword," in *Shakespeare/Not Shakespeare*, eds. Christy Desmet, Natalie Loper, and Jim Casey (New York: Palgrave Macmillan, 2017), 276.

12 Within the Shakespeare audience-as-fandom, it is possible to define subcultural fan audiences that coalesce around these diverse companies and their spaces.

13 Anne Ubersfeld, "The Pleasure of the Spectator," trans. Pierre Bouillaguet and Charles Jose, *Modern Drama* 25, no. 1 (1982): 131.

14 Susan Bennett, *Performing Nostalgia* (London and New York: Routledge, 1996), 17.

15 Daniel Sack, "A Constellation of Imagined Theatres: Technology and Performance," *Theatre Journal* 68, no. 3 (2016): 380, 382.

16 See Daniel Sack, *After Live* (Ann Arbor: University of Michigan Press, 2015).

17 DeKosnik, *Rogue Archives,* 279. See also Valerie Fazel's chapter in this book (Chapter 11).

18 Diana Taylor, *The Archive and the Repertoire* (Durham: Duke University Press, 2003), 20.

19 Taylor, *Archive and Repertoire*, 277.

20 Johannes H. Birringer, *Performance on the Edge* (London: Bloomsbury, 2002), 69.

21 "Every Shakespeare Play Summed Up in a Quote from *Arrested Development*," Shakespeare Theatre Company, accessed September 15, 2019. www.shakespearetheatre.org/watch-listen/every-shakespeare-play-summed-quote-arrested-development/.

22 Meeeeesh, "37 Hysterical Times 'The Office' Perfectly Depicted Shakespeare Plays," CHEEZburger, accessed September 15, 2019. https://cheezburger.com/6834437/37-hysterical-times-the-office-perfectly-depicted-shakespeare-plays.

23 Elizabeth Entemen, "A Clever Twitter User Summed Up Shakespeare Plays with *Parks and Rec* Quotes, and It's Absolute Perfection," Hello Giggles, July 23, 2018. https://hellogiggles.com/reviews-coverage/shakespeare-plays-parks-and-rec-quotes-twitter/.

24 Leo Benedictus, "What to Say About … Much Ado About Nothing," *Guardian*, June 2, 2011. www.theguardian.com/culture/2011/jun/02/much-ado-david-tennant-catherine-tate.

25 Michael Billington, "*Much Ado About Nothing*—Review," *Guardian*, June 1, 2011. www.theguardian.com/stage/2011/jun/01/much-ado-about-nothing-review.

26 Matt Hills, "Location, Location, Location: Citizen Fan Journalists' 'Set Reporting' and Info-War in the Digital Age," in *Popular Media: Fans, Audiences, and Paratexts*, ed. Lincoln Geraghty (New York: Palgrave Macmillan, 2015), 165.
27 Taylor, *The Archive and the Repertoire*, 13; W. B. Worthen, *Shakespeare Performance Studies* (Cambridge: Cambridge University Press, 2014), 50.
28 See Marvin Carlson, *The Haunted Stage* (Ann Arbor: University of Michigan Press, 2001).
29 SingofSolace, "Sir, Spare Your Threats," Archive of Our Own, July 25, 2019. https://archiveofourown.org/works/19978774/chapters/47297026.
30 Matt Hills has noted that Shakespeare is the ultimate media franchise. See *Fan Cultures* (London: Routledge, 2002).
31 Miss Moonshine, "On Chapter 1." Archive of Our Own, July 25, 2019. https://archiveofourown.org/works/19978774/chapters/47297026.
32 SingofSolace, "Sir, Spare Your Threats."
33 Valerie M. Fazel and Louise Geddes, *The Shakespeare Multiverse* (London: Routledge, 2021).

Bibliography

@AlisonSloan. "The Merchant of Venice." Tweet. July 19, 2018. https://twitter.com/alisonlsloan/status/1020045730902310912?s=20.
Benedictus, Leo. "What To Say About … Much Ado About Nothing." *Guardian*, June 2, 2011. www.theguardian.com/culture/2011/jun/02/much-ado-david-tennant-catherine-tate.
Bennett, Susan. *Performing Nostalgia: Shifting Shakespeare to the Contemporary Past*. London: Routledge, 1996.
Billington, Michael. "*Much Ado about Nothing*—Review." *Guardian*, June 1, 2011. www.theguardian.com/stage/2011/jun/01/much-ado-about-nothing-review.
Birringer, Johannes H. *Performance on the Edge*. London: Bloomsbury, 2002.
Carlson, Marvin. *The Haunted Stage: Theatre as Memory Machine*. Ann Arbor: University of Michigan Press, 2001.
DeKosnik, Abigail. *Rogue Archives: Digital Cultural Memory and Media Fandom*. Cambridge, MA: MIT Press, 2016.
Entenman, Elizabeth. "A Clever Twitter User Summed up Shakespeare Plays with *Parks and Rec* Quotes, and It's Absolute Perfection." Hello Giggles. July 23, 2018. https://hellogiggles.com/reviews-coverage/shakespeare-plays-parks-and-rec-quotes-twitter/.
FantasticallyFoolishIdea. "Old Wounds, New Wounds." Archive of Our Own. February 20, 2016. https://archiveofourown.org/works/6069613.
Fazel, Valerie M. and Louise Geddes. *The Shakespeare Multiverse: Fandom as Literary Praxis*. London: Routledge, 2021.
Grossberg, Lawrence. "Is there a Fan in the House? The Affective Sensibility of Fandom." In *The Adoring Audience: Fan Culture and Popular Media*, edited by Lisa Lewis, 50–65. London: Routledge, 1992.
Hills, Matt. "Location, Location, Location: Citizen Fan Journalists' 'Set Reporting' and Info-War in the Digital Age." In *Popular Media: Fans, Audiences, and Paratexts*, edited by Lincoln Geraghty, 164–8. New York: Palgrave Macmillan, 2015.

Hills, Matt. *Fan Cultures*. London: Routledge, 2002.

Lanier, Douglas M. "Afterword." In *Shakespeare/Not Shakespeare*, edited by Christy Desmet, Natalie Loper, and Jim Casey, 293–306. New York: Palgrave Macmillan, 2017.

Livingstone, Sonia. "The Challenge of Changing Audiences, Or What is the Audience Researcher to do in the Age of the Internet?" *European Journal of Communication* 19, no. 1 (2004): 75–86.

Meeeeesh. "37 Hysterical Times 'The Office' Perfectly Depicted Shakespeare Plays." CHEEZburger. Accessed September 15, 2019. https://cheezburger.com/6834437/37-hysterical-times-the-office-perfectly-depicted-shakespeare-plays.

Miss Moonshine. "On Chapter 1." Archive of Our Own. July 25, 2019. https://archiveofourown.org/works/19978774/chapters/47297026.

Morimoto, Lori Hitchcock, and Bertha Chin. "Reimagining the Imagined Community: Online Media Fandoms in the Age of Global Convergence." In *Fandoms: Identities and Communities in a Mediated World*, 2nd ed., edited by Jonathan Gray, Cornell Sandvoss, and C. Lee Harrington, 174–90. New York: New York University Press, 2017.

Pande, Rukmini. *Squee, From the Margins: Fandom and Race*. Iowa City: University of Iowa Press, 2018.

Radbourne, Jennifer, Hillary Glow, and Katya Johannes. "Knowing and Measuring the Audience Experience." In *Audience Experience: A Critical Analysis of Audience in the Performing Arts*, edited by Jennifer Radbourne, Hillary Glow, and Katya Johannes, 1–14. London: Intellect, 2013.

Sack, Daniel. *After Live: Possibility, Potentiality, and the Future of Performance*. Ann Arbor: University of Michigan Press, 2015.

Sack, Daniel. "A Constellation of Imagined Theatres: Technology and Performance." *Theatre Journal* 68, no. 3 (2016) 379–403.

Shakespeare Theatre Company. "Every Shakespeare Play Summed up in a Quote from *Arrested Development*." Accessed September 15, 2019. www.shakespearetheatre.org/watch-listen/every-shakespeare-play-summed-quote-arrested-development/.

Singofsolace. "Sir, Spare Your Threats." Archive of Our Own. July 25, 2019. https://archiveofourown.org/works/19978774/chapters/47297026.

Taylor, Diana. *The Archive and the Repertoire: Performing Cultural History in the Americas*. Durham: Duke University Press, 2003.

Ubersfeld, Anne. "The Pleasure of the Spectator." Translated by Pierre Bouillaguet and Charles Jose. *Modern Drama* 25, no. 1 (1982): 127–39.

Worthen, W. B. *Shakespeare Performance Studies*. Cambridge: Cambridge University Press, 2014.

Observing Audiences

11 "A vulgar comment will be made of it"

YouTube and Robert Weimann's *Platea*

Valerie M. Fazel

The montage of scenes from Franco Zeffirelli's *Romeo and Juliet* (1968) streams by as British countertenor Barratt Waugh croons his classically arranged 2000 rendition of the film's theme song, "A Time for Us." Within moments Waugh's gender-ambiguous tones fade to the background, upstaged by my interest in the audience's response ("he's incredible, I always thought it was a woman singing!," "just a timeless and beautiful song"). Remarks about Zeffirelli's recent death, actor Zac Efron as a Leonard Whiting lookalike, 40-year-old Waugh, Nino Rota's song, and the nostalgic pulse of people's past experiences with this filmed adaptation of Shakespeare's tragedy catch my attention one by one. I register statements such as, "Still the absolute best *Romeo and Juliet* movie of all time," "RIP Zefferelli," "Why did they change the original lyrics of 'What is a Youth?' They spoiled it!," and "This is my favorite play by Shakespeare."[1] Not everyone in the audience recognizes the tune, nor has everyone seen Zeffirelli's film in its entirety. Many have never heard (of) Waugh before this experience, while others express their annoyance with other people's remarks. Everyone in this audience seems compelled to be a critic, a pedant, and/or an actor of sorts. All this I note as I lean forward from the "best seat in the house"—in front of my laptop screen—scrolling through the comment section of stumblingChaos's YouTube Shakespeare video mashup, "A time for us Romeo and Juliet 1968."[2] Although I am merely a lurker situated in stumblingChaos's "diffused audience," one of countless dispersed spectators who in today's media-saturated society is "continually surrounded by [Shakespeare] representations,"[3] through YouTube, I experience "a collective sense of participation,"[4] albeit virtually, and within the privacy of my home.

The emergence of YouTube in 2005 ushered in a new paradigm of audiovisual viewing, storage, and sharing—one that manifested Web 2.0's promise of dynamic internet pages, user-generated creative content, and social interaction affordances (including collaboration and sharing).

That Shakespeare appeared early in YouTube's history is substantiated through Luke McKernan's curated videos on Bardbox.net and a compact, but essential, body of critical work on YouTube Shakespeare that emerged in academic publications in the late 2000s.[5] Fast forward to 2020, and YouTube Shakespeare shows no sign of waning. Stephen O'Neill's claim that "YouTube is now one of the dominant media through which Shakespeare is iterated, produced and received in the twenty-first century" is evinced by fans, students, and teachers who unapologetically turn to YouTube in their pursual of Shakespeare videos as entertainment, tutorials, and performances of the plays and poetry.[6] Second only to Google's search engine in popularity, the video-sharing platform is virtually accessible through most contemporary screens, including laptops, smart TVs, and handheld devices like tablets and smartphones.[7] Better-than-ever broadband internet speeds and mobile app access mean that YouTube's participatory affordances of uploading or viewing videos and the acts of liking, lurking, and posting comments are "always-on" and can be put into immediate service by YouTube users.

As YouTube Shakespeare videos continue to draw the critical and casual attention of a wide range of users, imperative to the future of YouTube Shakespeare study is a richer theorization of the website's interface, particularly in the ways its interactive affordances activate and manifest audience participation. This chapter maps onto YouTube Robert Weimann's theory of flexible dramaturgy and his postulations for the imaginary and interactive spaces of performance he designates *locus* and *platea* in the Elizabethan theater. As concept-rich terms, Weimann's *locus* and *platea* serve as apt analogies in the theorization and codification of YouTube's interface. This chapter draws most heavily on Weimann's claims for the *platea*, arguing specifically that YouTube's interactive affordances, particularly its comment feature, bear comparison to actor–audience interactivity that took place in Shakespeare's Elizabethan theater. Comments in YouTube's *platea* engender for the audience a sense of immediacy with the performance[8] and an imagined community[9] of viewers who, through their comments, influence video reception. As Balthasar's words in this chapter's title suggest, people's talk—their "vulgar" comments (3.1.100)—has the power to shape perception, a certainty Antipholus acknowledges as he reins in his own actions in response to his friend's advice.

Theorizing YouTube's interface as analogous to the spaces of performance in the Elizabethan playhouse draws attention to the way performance presentation and representation in virtual space is shaped, as in Shakespeare's playhouse, via a remarkable correspondence "between experimentation, innovation, and revitalization."[10] As social-cultural venues for performance, both the Elizabethan theater and YouTube emerged during liminal periods of technological change. In the early modern period, this technological change was the construction of purpose-built professional playhouses designed as spaces for profitable entertainment. In the twenty-first century, technological change is represented by widespread engagement with digital tools and the influence of social media, often with an eye toward future profitability.[11] These analogously corresponding thresholds, where performance and reception straddle old and new paradigms, and at their very essence afford(ed) "great adaptability in ... the endless assimilation of new subjects, themes, and modes of verbal and mimetic expression," encourage critical thinking about the commonalities between live performance in the Elizabethan theater and YouTube's video-sharing, social media platform.[12]

For instance, in her essay, "(You)Tube Travel: The 9:59 to Dover Beach, Stopping at Fair Verona and Elsinore," Barbara Hodgdon proclaims that one of YouTube's "multiple roles" is as a space of performance not entirely unlike theater.[13] With "participatory culture its core business," Hodgdon argues, YouTube "operates as a self-organized, totalizing 'public' in that it is made up of a crowd of users witnessing themselves in a visible space (as with a theatrical public, which brings strangers into relation with one another)."[14] Hodgdon's thinking about the "critical distinctions between liveness and mediation and between the archive and the repertoire" rightly downplays notions of YouTube as merely a repository for Shakespeare videos.[15] Rather, she highlights the acts of posting and responding to Shakespeare appropriations and remediations as a transformation both in the ways the public plays a role in the creation and dissemination of Shakespeare and in the ways Shakespeareans should come to think of YouTube's entire interface as a performance medium.

Hodgdon more specifically asserts that via their interactivity on YouTube, users function as transient, "privileging bodies," the kinds of bodies associated with live performance theater.[16] Anticipating potential debates over virtual versus "live" bodies, she cites Philip Auslander's claim that "physical bodies may be a sufficient cause for liveness, though not a necessary one."[17] In this same argumentative vein on embodiment, Hodgdon argues that YouTube Shakespeares exhibit the essential qualities of the repertoire as defined by Diane Taylor. For Hodgdon, Taylor's definition of repertoire is evinced by the ways YouTube viewers respond to the video *and* interact with other users:

> Viewers see themselves as present and as perceiving (embodied) performances as they take place but they also ... imagine themselves as sharing a (bodied) space with performers. However much they may know that they are engaged in second-hand experience, viewers *behave* as though they are witnessing live performances and participate in the kinds of knowledge-making associated with having "been there."[18]

Hodgdon speaks not of YouTube Shakespeare as repertoire per se but as repertoire in the post-production, post- and para-viewing interactivity that takes place on YouTube's interface. Hodgdon's claims for user interactivity suggest that the actions that take place on YouTube's interface (in its individual frames and in its entirety) *are* the performance. However, any claim for YouTube as a space of user-embodied performance calls for a conceptual and theoretical understanding of where those "bodies" are represented on YouTube's interface, a key fissure in Hodgdon's reading of YouTube. This gap draws to mind Robert Weimann's 1978 and 2000 postulations on the conceptual spaces of performance in the Elizabethan theater, and his claims for *locus* and *platea*.

Flexible Dramaturgy: *Locus* and *Platea*

Weimann's theory of flexible dramaturgy draws attention to the relationship between actor, audience, and performance in the Elizabethan theater and postulates that particular modes of performance and uses of dramatic space connected an elevated early modern literary culture with the vernacular words and gestures of the everyday population. Defining the playhouse's conceptual spaces figuratively rather than by physical location, Weimann argues that different "purposes of playing" and the "function of (re)presentation ... suggest certain parameters of interaction" took place during a play's performance.[19] Representational aspects of performance evoke imaginary characters, locations, and situations in the *locus*, and presentational modes encouraged actor–audience interactivity in the *platea*. Weimann explains:

> The *locus* as a fairly specific imaginary locale or self-contained space in the world of the play and the *platea* as an opening in *mise-en-scene* through which the place and time of the stage-as-stage and the cultural occasion itself are made either to assist or resist the socially and verbally elevated, spatially and temporally remote representation.[20]

Weimann's *locus* is the representational mode of performance whereby the actor remains in character, focused completely on the fictive illusion of dramatic action/location of the play. Weimann's *platea* is the presentational performance mode whereby the actor, through direct audience address—word, gesture, look, or another embodied sign—incorporates audience response *as* the performance.[21]

Yet Weimann's *platea*, Stephen Purcell reminds us, "is not so much a specific zone of the stage as [it is] a space that is brought into being by the actor's relationship with the audience and the here-and-now of performance."[22] Pascale Aebischer's interpretation likewise asserts that Weimann's claims for the *platea* are premised less on where, but more on when and how, performance spurs or includes audience interaction:

> The *platea* is the conceptual space which, while unlocalised in relation to the fiction of the play, is located in the here and now of the performance. And this here and now, whether in early modern

London or today, happens in front of a specific set of emancipated spectators who bring to the performance their individual and collective extratheatrical experiences and who, through their collaborative engagement ... [are able] "to do something about" an event for which they share responsibility.[23]

The emphasis Weimann, Purcell, and Aebischer place on the *platea* as engendering a sense of performance immediacy and a disposition of audiences "to do" or to say something in response—the *platea* activated as "here-and-now"—are all key to understanding situated audience response in shaping performance reception both on the Elizabethan stage and, as Aebischer and I each argue, via Web 2.0 technologies.

Conceptualizing the *platea* as "iconographically and symbolically" fluid, Weimann insists that the *platea* is where "the responsiveness of spectators was implicated" and anticipated as shaping the performance experience.[24] Susan Bennett similarly notes that in the early seventeenth century "there was a flexibility in the relationship between stage and audience worlds which afforded, in different ways, the participation of those audiences as actors in the drama."[25] Aebischer, citing Tiffany Stern, affirms that such actor-audience interaction "had a potentially material impact on the play, which could be later dropped from the repertoire or ... revised 'directly after the first night, in the light of the audience's criticism.' "[26] Weimann's concept of flexible dramaturgy, therefore, effectively theorizes how and why reception impacts dramatic (re)performance and underpins claims that performance shifts shape a new and unique dramatic experience for performers and audiences. More to the point, the rising view-counts of some videos and continuation of uploading new YouTube Shakespeares are testimony to the ongoing engagement by producers and audiences in viewing, discussing, and creating new ways of appropriating, and responding to, Shakespeare. As O'Neill argues, "responses to Shakespeare on YouTube variously suggest an intervention in or contribution to meaning."[27]

YouTube's *Platea* and Audience Comments

YouTube's "dynamic and cluttered" interface analogously evinces Weimann's imaginary *locus* and interactive *platea*.[28] The video serves as an approximation to Weimann's *locus*, and all other spaces on YouTube's interface, particularly the user interactive affordances, are analogous to claims for the "here and now" interactive experience of the *platea* in the Elizabethan theater. In the Elizabethan theater, Aebischer claims, Shakespeare had at his "disposal a dynamic set of conventions in which modes of performative interaction ... orient[ed] spectators towards the performance in ways that facilitated a range of modes of spectatorship."[29] So too, YouTube's interface is absolutely loaded with a "dynamic set of conventions," user-selected information options that impact viewers' "spectatorship" and reception of the video performance: the video title, the name of the uploader, information about the video, embedded hyperlinks to other related videos and to advertisements on the page, and, below the video, the comment section, where users post their responses.

By posting comments, YouTube's viewers become enmeshed in a paradigm of performance reception. Each comment, link, and image on YouTube's interface has the potential to influence the viewing audience in some (in)tangible way, much the same way silence, laughter, applause, grumbling, cracking nuts, and shuffling, throat-clearing bodies impacted responses to performance within the Elizabethan theater.[30] YouTube comments may express a wide range of viewer emotions, including confusion, outrage, and nostalgia, and spur pedagogical, philosophical, or practical discussions about Shakespeare, users, and the video. Comments might invoke a particular Shakespeare performance or actor, or they may query the process of a particular remix or the accuracy of statements made about Shakespeare. Equally significant is that comments leave visible traces of user response and these, for subsequent viewers, have the power to shape, activate, or merge with their experience of reception.

A case in point are the responses to the animated summary of *The Tempest* created and uploaded by @thebooktutor, where commentator @yone initiates discussion critiquing the artist's interpretations of Shakespeare's play as incomplete or inaccurate:[31]

@YONE: you need to get your facts straight though, there were several errors. It was as if you haven't read the play or seen it performed.

Immediately clear is that @yone has objections to @thebooktutor's interpretation of Shakespeare's play, and their comment spurs queries and responses from viewers who follow, beginning with a question on how the video fails to summarize Shakespeare with accuracy:

@JOHN: What were the mistakes

Unfortunately for @John, no direct response is forthcoming; @yume, however, agrees with @yone, indirectly answering John, but then immediately shifts the conversation into a critique of Prospero's character and actions:

@YUME: I was cringing at how bad this synopsis was for anything but the most superficial elements. First of all Prospero is such a bastard at the start ... he just treats [the spirits] better than Caliban whom is nothing but a lowly tortured slave
@SARA: @yume, the reason he treats Caliban so poorly is bc he tried to rape miranda, so it's not entirely unjustified
@JILL: @yume I agree, right from the beginning I was like "this isn't right??", but Miranda is actually the one that taught Caliban

(although her monologue is sometimes given to Prospero, so it depends on which version read/saw) [I'm playing Miranda right now, that's why I'm picky about that monologue:)]

Responses to this animated rundown of *The Tempest* suggest that viewers feel it is their responsibility to do or "say" something about @thebooktutor's perceived inaccurate synopsis, to shape for other members of this imagined community a right or "correct" understanding of the play. @yume and @jill challenge @thebooktutor's synopsis, with @sara and @jill agreeing with @yume in their exasperation toward @thebooktutor's rendering. Each brief analytical remark informs and shapes understanding and reception of this particular *Tempest* appropriation, as well as its source text. Such pedantic discourse occurs frequently in YouTube Shakespeare comments, and it is not uncommon for viewers to debate the video's fidelity to the text with other commentators.

Comment threads often reveal an era's cultural zeitgeist. For example, in many Zeffirelli-inspired YouTube *Romeo and Juliet* mashups and film clips, one particular conversation thread appears time and again: the striking resemblance between popular thirtysomething American heartthrob Zac Efron and Zeffirelli's 1968 Romeo, then seventeen-year-old English actor Leonard Whiting. Asking the question "does anybody else think romeo looks like Zac Efron?" on the aforementioned stumblingChaos's 2009 comment section, viewer @abic invites other viewers of the video to enter a mode "of spectatorial engagement that [is] specific to that space and to the present historical moment."[32] Yet before and after @abic's posting, remarks comparing the two actors abound:

@KAIL: omg he looks lyk zac efron!

@AISH: I like him better than Zac Efron though, his hair is different:] … Romeo is the dude from Austin Powers, right?

@KARI: yes, he does look a little like Zac. Zac's eyes are a little more radiant

@FEEW: I think it's more unfortunate that Zac Efron looks like Leonard Whiting

@FINF: Romeo and Juliet is a great story but I hate that the fact that the actor who plays Romeo looks like Zac Efron

@LYSJ: no way that's not zac efron. Hollywood must have some secret time machine stashed away[33]

At face value, this lighthearted textual exchange might appear too insubstantial to inform contemporary academic criticism, particularly in an era when a wealth of always-present user-generated content and the audience responses they engender are just a few taps of the fingers away. Yet to gloss over users' everyday reactions as simply mundane implicitly and undesirably upholds a hierarchy of authority. It further undervalues the *ethos* of participatory culture—the sharing of content and/or creating something meaningful together with others—in which Shakespeare is crowdsourced and crowd-shared. And as messy, spontaneous, glorious, and un-critical as such sourcing and sharing of viewpoints may seem to be, they mark Shakespeare's relevancy for this particular audience. Certainly, the genre of "Efron as Whiting" discussion trivia could be seen as little more than cocktail party chatter, yet as Patrick Davidson has argued, because YouTube comments are "wildly heterogenous textual specimens," they are also semiotic markers of people's response to the cultural phenomena that are significant in their individual lives within the context of that specific historical moment.[34] Such discussion "specimens," I noticed, that touched on Efron were all posted in the English language. A further investigation of website comments (on YouTube or other social media platforms) might explore how celebrity flourishes or is simply lost in translation for transnational audiences.

This draws attention to ways in which a study of YouTube Shakespeares might turn its attention to the participation (or lack thereof) of varied linguistic communities and their responses to (trans)national Shakespeare appropriations. As an illustration, I turn to the YouTube video "Beedi (Video Song)," the six-minute, energetic song-and-dance scene from *Omkara*, Vishal Bhardwaj's 2006 Hindi-language appropriation of *Othello*.[35] Comments in the video's *platea* are made up of many languages: Hindi, Bengali, Brazilian Portuguese, Spanish, Russian, Thai, and Arabic. Postings include the usual suspects: fan-gushing for particular actors/actresses ("Bipasha is queen of Bollywood"); enthusiasm for the scene or song ("Супер песня!");[36] and the occasional reminder "Omkara is based on Shakespeare's Othello." One of several key themes among "Beedi" commentators is that the Bollywood film tune also serves as the title theme song for the popular 2009 Brazilian telenovela, *Caminho das Índias*.[37] Several YouTube comments affirm that "in Brazil this song was in the soundtracks of a very famous soap opera," which perhaps spurs @ayan's remark, "Looks like foreigners have enjoyed this song more than us (the indians)." Specifically, a conversation between a non-Portuguese speaker, @indo, who claims to use Google Translate to post their queries in Portuguese, and @bian, who communicates in Portuguese, discusses the transnational popularity of "Beedi." Repeating their query in five separate posts, @indo seeks to understand why so many Portuguese language speakers are drawn to this video. @bian's reply comes as two separate, but consecutive responses, "Brasileiro é um povo apaixonado por ritmos fortes. Amo as músicas indianas, fervem a alma" and "e essa música também é de uma novela muito famosa no brasil."[38] To remark that YouTube's *platea* engenders multilingual interactivity between users seems to state the obvious, but more opaque is what Shakespeare researchers might do with such cultural evidence. It is also worth noting that responses to "Beedi" include insults pointing at the film actors' skills, hostile flame-throwing among commentators, and overtly racist insults, all of which support studies that have "concluded that an individual's mood as well as the surrounding context of an online discussion can trigger almost anyone to engage in ... aggressive online behavior."[39] How might such YouTube comments inform a study of social media Shakespeares/Shakespeare appropriation? Furthermore, disparaging remarks warrant critical attention as they could open up new arenas of Shakespeare reception study that might explore gender, age, race, ethnicity, literacy, and more.

YouTube comments register historical popular culture interests in past Shakespeare appropriations, especially because YouTube blurs conceptual binaries of storage/use when whole films (or video clips) are drawn from a limited-access archive of the past.[40] *Angoor*, a classic 1982 Bollywood based on the "Gr8est comedy Inspired by Shakespeare's 'Comedy of Errors,'" draws comments from individuals voicing nostalgia, their love for the film, and/or their fandom for its award-winning star, "phenomenal and the legendary" Sanjeev Kumar, who died in 1985 at age 47. Several full-length versions and film clips from *Angoor* are available on YouTube, but comments for most are similar: how the film owes its origins to Shakespeare's *The Comedy of Errors*; Kumar as beloved, favorite, or talented actor; the hilarity of the film; and a sense of sanctity for films prior to the 2000s.[41] @desh comments, "People of this era and eras before this were very lucky to be able to watch such sweet, simple, and beautiful films like this unlike today's generation who are obsessed with vulgarity and violence".[42] The linguistic range here includes English, Devanagari, and Hindi or Bengali written in the Roman alphabet.[43] Curiously, within *Angoor's platea*, few debates or conversational exchanges occur; most of the nearly 200 comments are directed at the film and its actors. The demographics of *Angoor* viewers indicate an older audience, as the close reading of the audience comments suggests. Certainly, the overarching tone in responses is one of nostalgia, and overall the comments seem less aggressive than those posted under "Beedi." At the risk of assuming too much without employing further ethnographic methods, I hypothesize that this YouTube Shakespeare is attractive to a localized viewer, an audience member whose (maybe diasporic) ties to India are both more immediate and historical, whose gaze oscillates between the film's past and social media's "here and now," and seems fixed on the film as if sharing the space in the cinema—aware of others, but not intruding into other audience members' reverie. But this hypothesis would be for a quantitative study at another time, another place, the "here and now" of another research agenda.

So far, this chapter has expanded on YouTube's similarities to Weimann's *platea*. Arguing for the ways YouTube Shakespeares evince Weimann's postulations for *locus* is a little more challenging because the website is purposefully designed for explicit participatory practices. But YouTube users might choose *not* to engage with YouTube's *platea* by simply clicking on the video's "fill the screen" button. When this occurs, the expanded video hides YouTube's interactive affordances and functions analogously like the imaginary space of Weimann's *locus*. The video performance establishes an imaginary space, the performance world of the narrative immediately visible and yet remote behind the fourth wall of the screen all at once—it cannot signal anything beyond its own localization within its dramatic moment. The film clip is recorded, crystalized to play the same frames in the same sequence over and over again, and therefore ostensibly unchangeable (but of course, in the hands of someone else, like the director/producer of a mainstream production, might be downloaded and subjected to manipulation and remix). Captivated by the streamed video, the YouTube viewer is situated in ways that are unsurprisingly similar to a film or television viewing audience immersed in their viewing bubble: they simply watch. Or do they? Media reception theories argue that watching is a complicated activity.

As E. Deidre Pribram argues, a viewing experience is shaped as "the result of various discourses put in play by the text, but also the subject of social, economic, and political practices beyond the text, which are brought to bear at the moment of screen/viewer interaction."[44] This experience "may render the spectator as anything along a barometer of viewership from passive imbiber of pre-packaged ideology to active and successful resistent [*sic*] of these same oppressive, psychic, discursive, and socio-historical forces."[45] Watching the video in YouTube's *locus*, like viewing scenes performed in the dramaturgical *locus* of the early modern theater, does not preclude interaction or receptive impact from outside forces. The levels of activity in the reception of that same video content are dependent, as Aebischer proposes with audiences viewing streamed performance, on users' cultural experiences. Furthermore, the video, unlike performance in the Elizabethan theater, is subject to buffering, stops, starts, and rewatches. In my viewing experience, I stopped and started each YouTube video I screened multiple times, popping off to read or watch something else, or to respond to an email, or to teach a class. I viewed the first ten minutes of *Angoor* dozens of times, fascinated by its chorus-like opening and portrait-like shot of "Shakespeare." With headphones clamped to my ears as I wrote, I replayed "Beedi" countless times (engendering the most marvelous earworm). In each instance of returning to the video, my perspective was influenced, shaped and reshaped, by the outside-the-viewing-experience forces that impacted my mood, awareness, attentiveness, and the perpetual curiosity that returns me to viewing. The acts of stop and start, rewind and fast forward, of walk-away and return, as well as the viewer's rhetorical situation, all impact how the viewer receives and perceives the video performance. In other words, the video is a fixed performance, so our interactivity with the YouTube affordances tied to the video cannot *change* the video's content at the moment of viewing, but the conditions that influence reception can alter how we see it with each reviewing. Arguably, then, the space of the imaginary is subject to the influences of a remarkable audience *inner*activity, as well as interactivity. And this is at the heart of Weimann's postulations. The *locus* as applied to the Elizabethan theater is also never truly entirely contained or separate; the audience never becomes invisible, nor is the audience remote from the *inner* performance within the performance—the space of the imaginary cannot exist without imagining the audience's engagement and reception.

Conclusion

In his opening chapter of *Author's Pen and Actor's Voice*, Weimann ruminates over the shifts in the ways the "majority of people" today encounter Shakespeare "not through reading what he wrote, but through watching certain electronically processed images of filmed performances."[46] He voices concerns about the appropriation of Shakespeare's playtext in media as "bringing forth 'representative modes' of reception that are even more remote from cultural 'intervention, participation, direct action,'" qualities he attributes to live theater.[47] Though he did not, perhaps could not, have anticipated the particular interactivity that takes place on social media platforms like YouTube, he affirms the potentiality of "textual assimilation of the classic [as a] new poetics of cultural response."[48]

Weimann's conceptualization of early modern performance, Stephen Purcell observes, "has had a major impact on critical thinking about Elizabethan stage space."[49] The metaphorical boundary between *locus* and *platea*, and the distinctions Weimann makes between both modes of performance, (re)tested by digital performance and platform affordances, may have a "major impact" on how we come to think of performance's "here and now" as live/not live and the embodied audience as not needing any *body* in sight. Although YouTube comments may lack the hermeneutic density desired of popular culture appropriation study, they have a role to play in the future of Shakespeare adaptation and appropriation through digital technologies. Weimann's theories on the uses of space, of *locus* and *platea*, and the shaping of performance as interactive condition between actor and audience, offer Shakespeareans a theoretical framework for understanding and approaching the disparate yet interactive audiences of social media platforms such as YouTube.[50]

Notes

1 Videos are cited by title; the name of the video channel host, when mentioned, is accurate at the time of writing, but direct quotations from YouTube's comment section (*platea*) when cited are by only the first four characters of commentators' YouTube identities. Not all comments in a discussion thread are quoted, and identities are cited only when transcribed discussion between commentators appears in this chapter or a comment is translated into English.

2 stumblingChaos, "A Time for Us Romeo and Juliet 1968," YouTube video, June 4, 2009, www.youtube.com/watch?v=4FHpmn-KYec.

3 Dennis Kennedy, *The Spectator and The Spectacle* (Cambridge: Cambridge University Press, 2009), 7.

4 Peter Kirwan, "Cheek by Jowl: Reframing Complicity in Web-Streams of *Measure for Measure*," in *Shakespeare and the "Live" Theatre Broadcast*, eds. Pascale Aebischer, Susanne Greenhalgh, and Laurie Osborne (London: Bloomsbury, 2018), 162.

5 See Luke McKernan, "About," on Bardbox.net, and, for instance, Lauren Shohet, "YouTube, Use, and the Idea of the Archive," *Shakespeare Studies* 38 (2010): 68–76; and Christy Desmet, "Paying Attention in Shakespeare Parody: from Tom Stoppard to YouTube," *Shakespeare Survey* 61 (2008): 227–38.

6 Stephen O'Neill, *Shakespeare and YouTube: New Media Forms of the Bard* (London: Bloomsbury, 2014), 2.

7 Two billion website visits each month and one billion hours of viewing occur daily in ninety-one countries and eighty languages. See YouTube, "About," accessed July 21, 2020.

8 Pascale Aebischer, *Shakespeare, Spectatorship, and Technologies of Performance* (Cambridge: Cambridge University Press, 2020), 13.

9 Lori Hitchcock Morimoto and Bertha Chin reimagine Benedict Anderson's theory of "imagined communities" as foregrounding "the trans-border, transnational reach of the Internet in creating a sense of simultaneous, shared popular cultural experience." See Morimoto and Chin, "Reimagining the Imagined Community: Online Media Fandoms in the Age of Global Convergence," in *Fandom: Identities and Communities in a Mediated World*, 2nd ed., eds. Jonathan Gray, Cornel Sandvoss, and C. Lee Harrington (New York: New York University Press, 2017), 1.

10 Robert Weimann, *Shakespeare and the Popular Tradition,* trans. Robert Schwartz (Baltimore: Johns Hopkins University Press, 1978), xvii.

11 At the time of writing, the social media influence/influencer zeitgeist is the subject of both popular and academic publication. For instance, see works in the bibliography by Crystal Abidin (2016), Karina Sokolova and Hajer Kefi (2020), Julia Hautz et al. (2014), and Henry Jenkins, Sam Ford, and Joshua Green (2013).

12 Weimann, *Shakespeare and the Popular Tradition*, xvi.

13 Hodgdon, "(You)Tube Travel: The 9:59 to Dover Beach, Stopping at Fair Verona and Elsinore," *Shakespeare Bulletin* 28, no. 3 (2010): 313.

14 Hodgdon, "The 9:59 to Verona," 314.

15 Hodgdon, "The 9:59 to Verona," 314.

16 Hodgdon, "The 9:59 to Verona," 319.

17 Auslander qtd. in Hodgdon, "The 9:59 to Verona," 319.

18 Hodgdon, "The 9:59 to Verona," 319 (italics and parentheses original).

19 Robert Weimann, *Author's Pen and Actor's Voice* (Cambridge: Cambridge University Press, 2000), xvi, 11.

20 Weimann, *Author's Pen and Actor's Voice*, 181.

21 In addition to my own sketch of Weimann's *locus* and *platea*, I include Pascale Aebischer's more elegant summary:

> On early modern stages, the *locus* corresponded to the self-contained, fictional world of the higher-ranking characters who, confined within approximations of specific locales such as a presence chamber, a bedroom, garden or closet, remained incapable of communicating directly with the

audience. The *platea*, meanwhile, translated into the outer margins of the stage, the liminal and unlocalised zone into which lower-class characters could step forward to address the audience, engaging in a much more self-consciously theatrical, performative mode of characterisation.

Aebischer, *Shakespeare, Spectatorship, and Technologies*, 10–11.

22 Stephen Purcell, "*Locus* and *Platea* in Modern Shakespearean Performance," in *The Arden Research Handbook to Shakespeare and Contemporary Performance*, eds. Peter Kirwan and Kathryn Prince (London: Bloomsbury, 2021), 91.

23 Aebischer, *Shakespeare, Spectatorship, and Technologies*, 13.

24 Weimann, *Author's Pen and Actor's Voice*, 22.

25 Susan Bennett, *Theatre Audiences*, 2nd ed. (London: Routledge, 1997), 3.

26 Aebischer, *Shakespeare, Spectatorship, and Technologies*, 13.

27 O'Neill, *Shakespeare and YouTube*, 9.

28 O'Neill, *Shakespeare and YouTube*, 30.

29 Aebischer, *Shakespeare, Spectatorship, and Technologies*, 14.

30 Audience disruption of London stage performances has been frequently reported in the 2010s. For further details, see Kirsty Sedgman's excellent book, *The Reasonable Audience* (London: Palgrave Macmillan, 2018).

31 TheBookTutor, "The Tempest by Shakespeare," YouTube video, April 24, 2018. www.youtube.com/watch?v=KVsQjZxLqTY.

32 Aebischer, *Shakespeare, Spectatorship, and Technologies*, 16.

33 stumblingChaos, "A Time for Us." Not all responses are included here, nor do they appear in sequential order. Comments transcription date: May–September 2019.

34 Patrick Davidson, "On Avril Lavigne's Missing YouTube Comments," *Critical Quarterly* 55, no. 4 (2013): 82.

35 Eros Now, "Beedi (Video Song)/Omkara," YouTube video, September 29, 2009, www.youtube.com/watch?v=XLJCtZK0x5M&vl=en. Eros Now is an OTT (over the top) subscription service that provides streamed Indian film selections via the internet.

36 @andr, comment under ErosNow, "Beedi." Google Translate: Russian to English, "super song."

37 See Swapnil Rai and Joseph Straubhaar, "Road to India—A Brazilian Love Story: BRICS, Migration, and Cultural Flows in Brazil's *Caminho Das Indias*," *International Journal of Communication* 10 (2016): 3124–40, for an overview of *Caminho das Índias*.

38 @bian, comments under ErosNow, "Beedi." Google Translate: Brazilian to English, "Brazilian is a people in love with strong rhythms. I love Indian songs, [they warm] the soul"; "this song is also from a very famous soap opera in Brazil."

39 George Veletsianos, et al. "Public Comment Sentiment on Educational Videos," *PLOS ONE* 13, no. 6 (2018): 3.

40 Shohet, "YouTube Archive," 71.

41 VideoPalace, "अंगूर | Angoor Full Movie, Classic Hindi Comedy Movie, Sanjeev Kumar, Deven Verma, Moushumi," December 16, 2016, www.youtube.com/watch?v=tKzUWsA0hFw

42 @desh, comment under VideoPalace, "अंगूर | Angoor Full Movie."

43 Also, *patois* of English and Hindi.

44 E. Deidre Pribram, "Spectatorship and Subjectivity," in *A Companion to Film Theory*, eds. Toby Miller and Robert Stam (Hoboken: John Wiley & Sons, 2004), 159.
45 Pribram, "Spectatorship and Subjectivity," 162.
46 Weimann, *Author's Pen and Actor's Voice*, 3.
47 Weimann, *Author's Pen and Actor's Voice*, 3.
48 Weimann, *Author's Pen and Actor's Voice*, 3.
49 Purcell, "*Locus* and *Platea* in Modern Shakespearean Performance," 4.
50 My gratitude to both Pascale Aebischer and Stephen Purcell for generously sharing their soon to be published works with me. Their distinct approaches to Weimann's theory were of inestimable help to my thinking about YouTube. Many thanks also to Peter Kirwan and Matteo Pangallo for their helpful responses to the early version of this chapter.

Bibliography

Abidin, Crystal. "'Aren't These Just Young, Rich Women Doing Vain Things Online?': Influencer Selfies as Subversive Frivolity." *Social Media Society* 2, no. 2 (2016): 1–17. https://journals.sagepub.com/doi/pdf/10.1177/2056305116641342.

Aebischer, Pascale. *Shakespeare, Spectatorship and Technologies of Performance.* Cambridge: Cambridge University Press, 2020.

Bennett, Susan. *Theatre Audiences: A Theory of Production and Reception.* 2nd ed. London: Routledge, 1997.

Davison, Patrick. "On Avril Lavigne's Missing YouTube Comments." *Critical Quarterly* 55, no. 4 (2013): 81–92.

Desmet, Christy. "Paying Attention in Shakespeare Parody: from Tom Stoppard to YouTube." *Shakespeare Survey* 61 (2008): 227–38.

Eros Now, "Beedi (Video Song)/Omkara." YouTube, September 29, 2009. www.youtube.com/watch?v=XLJCtZK0x5M&vl=en.

Hautz, Julia, Johann Fuller, Katja Hutter, and Carina Thurridl. "Let Users Generate Your Video Ads? The Impact of Video Source and Quality on Consumers; Perceptions and Intended Behaviors." *Journal of Interactive Marketing* 28, no. 1 (2014): 1–15. doi.org/10.1016/j.intmar.2013.06.003.

Hodgdon, Barbara. "(You)Tube Travel: The 9:59 to Dover Beach, Stopping at Fair Verona and Elsinore." *Shakespeare Bulletin* 28, no. 3 (2010): 313–30. doi:10.1353/shb.2010.0010.

Jenkins, Henry, Sam Ford, and Joshua Green. *Spreadable Media: Creating Value and Meaning in a Networked Culture.* New York: New York University Press, 2013.

Kennedy, Dennis. *The Spectator and the Spectacle.* Cambridge: Cambridge University Press, 2009.

Kirwan, Peter. "Cheek by Jowl: Reframing Complicity in Web-Streams of *Measure for Measure*." In *Shakespeare and the "Live" Theatre Broadcast*, edited by Pascale Aebischer, Susanne Greenhalgh, and Laurie Osborne, 161–76. London: Bloomsbury Publishing, 2018.

McKernan, Luke. "About." Bardbox.net, https://bardbox.net/about/.

Morimoto, Lori Hitchcock and Bertha Chin. "Reimagining the Imagined Community: Online Media Fandoms in the Age of Global Convergence." In

Fandom: Identities and Communities in a Mediated World, 2nd ed., edited by Jonathan Gray, Cornel Sandvoss, and C. Lee Harrington, 174–88. New York: NYU Press, 2017.

O'Neill, Stephen. *Shakespeare and YouTube: New Media Forms of the Bard.* London: Bloomsbury, 2014.

Pribram, E. Deidre. "Spectatorship and Subjectivity." In *A Companion to Film Theory*, edited by Toby Miller and Robert Stam, 146–64. Hoboken, NJ: Wiley, 2004.

Purcell, Stephen. "*Locus* and *Platea* in Modern Shakespeare Performance." In *The Arden Research Handbook to Shakespeare and Contemporary Performance*, edited by Peter Kirwan and Kathryn Prince, 82–98. London: Bloomsbury, 2021.

Rai, Swapnil, and Straubhaar, Joseph. "Road to India—A Brazilian Love Story: BRICS, Migration, and Cultural Flows in Brazil's *Caminho Das Indias.*" *International Journal of Communication* 10 (2016): 3124–40.

Sedgman, Kirsty. *The Reasonable Audience: Theatre Etiquette, Behavior Policing, and the Live Performance Experience.* London: Palgrave Macmillan, 2018.

Shohet, Lauren. "YouTube, Use, and the Idea of the Archive," *Shakespeare Studies* 38 (2010): 68–76.

Sokolova, Karina, and Hajer Kefi. "Instagram and YouTube Bloggers Promote It, Why Should I Buy? How Credibility and Parasocial Interaction Influence Purchase Intentions." *Journal of Retailing and Consumer Services*, 53 (March 2020), https://doi.org/10.1016/j.jretconser.2019.01.011.

stumblingChaos. "A Time for Us Romeo and Juliet 1968," YouTube, June 4, 2009. www.youtube.com/watch?v=4FHpmn-KYec.

TheBookTutor. "The Tempest by Shakespeare-Summary." YouTube, April 24, 2018, www.youtube.com/watch?v=KVsQjZxLqTY.

Veletsianos, George, Royce Kimmons, Ross Larsen, Tonia A. Dousay, and Patrick R. Lowenthal. "Public Comment Sentiment on Educational Videos: Understanding the Effects of Presenter Gender, Video Format, Threading, and Moderation on YouTube TED Talk Comments." *PLOS ONE* 13, no. 6 (2018). doi.org/10.1371/journal.pone.0197331.

VideoPalace, "अंगूर | Angoor Full Movie, Classic Hindi Comedy Movie, Sanjeev Kumar, Deven Verma, Moushumi," December 16, 2016, www.youtube.com/watch?v=tKzUWsA0hFw.

Weimann, Robert. *Author's Pen and Actor's Voice: Playing and Writing in Shakespeare's Theatre.* Cambridge: Cambridge University Press, 2000.

Weimann, Robert. *Shakespeare and the Popular Tradition in the Theater.* Trans. Robert Schwartz. Baltimore: Johns Hopkins University Press, 1978.

YouTube. "About." Accessed July 21, 2020. www.youtube.com/about/.

12 Shakespeare's Digital School Audience

Agency and Control in the Reception of an RSC Schools' Broadcast

Rachael Nicholas

For many of us, school was where we became part of Shakespeare's audience for the first time. Shakespeare's enduring dominance on syllabi and curricula across all levels of education and in many different countries has meant that watching a Shakespeare performance of some kind, whether live or mediated, has become a staple feature of English literature and drama education.[1] It has also meant that for publicly funded theaters producing Shakespearean work, such as the Royal Shakespeare Company (RSC), schools constitute an integral, and commercially important, part of their potential audience. During the 2010s, digital forms of distribution gave these theaters and their growing education departments new ways to access that school audience. The development of digital streaming platforms designed for the educational market, such as Digital Theatre Plus (DT+) and Drama Online, provides teachers and students with on-demand access to recorded performances, opening up new possibilities for the use of performance within the classroom. For theaters, distribution to schools offers an economical way of reaching a school audience by repurposing material initially filmed for cinema or online broadcast, with Shakespeare's Globe, the RSC, and even the UK's National Theatre (NT), which has taken pains to emphasize the importance of liveness and communality in the marketing of its cinema broadcast program, making their cinema broadcast recordings available on-demand to schools and universities.

While some of these recordings are accessed through paid subscription services, many are free for UK state-funded schools, leading Susan Bennett to argue that such projects are primarily motivated by a commercial need to develop future audiences for Shakespearean theater and so are "an exercise in lifelong brand recognition."[2] Courtney Lehmann and Geoffrey Way have been similarly skeptical of the burgeoning relationships between business and Shakespeare education that these projects represent, arguing that they position young audiences in relation to a complex set of commercial transactions, including sponsorship deals with corporate companies, in which they have little option but to participate (2017).[3] However, as Amy Borsuk has highlighted, the ways in which the producers of these digital services envisage their products working and the ways in which they are actually put to use in the classroom may differ.[4] Borsuk suggests that the producers of these digital platforms "must understand not only what content teachers at different education levels need, but *how* teachers and students interact with the material."[5] Similarly, if we are to understand the dynamics between theater companies and students generated by these digital offerings, we need to understand how they are actually put to use and experienced by teachers and students within classrooms.

This chapter begins to explore these uses of digital performance by drawing on an observation conducted at a UK secondary school as the students participated in the RSC Schools' Broadcast of *Twelfth Night* (recorded and broadcast to cinemas in 2017; broadcast to schools on March 8, 2018). The RSC Schools' Broadcasts distinguish themselves from other digital educational services by making a previously recorded production available to stream "live" for UK schools over the course of a particular morning so that all schools are watching simultaneously. All schools participate for free but must sign up in advance to receive a link to access the broadcast, with a teaching pack and suggested pre-broadcast classroom activities also provided by the RSC. On the morning of the *Twelfth Night* broadcast I joined a group of students and their teacher to observe how the experience was framed for students and how students themselves watched, and reacted to, the broadcast.

This research was conducted as part of a wider investigation that employed audience research methodologies to explore the reception of digitally distributed Shakespeare performance across cinemas, schools, and online. Unlike the investigations into cinema and online audiences, where it was necessary to survey and interview audiences to get a sense of their experiences, school groups made for an unusually visible, and vocal, theater audience, making observation a particularly fruitful way of researching their experiences. From notes taken during the observation, I created a thick description, which formed the basis of an interpretative analysis of the experiences that these broadcasts create, and the relationships they forge between the RSC, teachers, and students. This was supplemented by an analysis of the tweets that students and teachers were encouraged to send during the broadcast, which helped to build a wider picture of reception across schools.

In the remainder of this chapter, I provide an edited version of the thick description from the observation of *Twelfth Night*, setting out the viewing contexts and describing key moments from the broadcast. This is followed by a discussion that focuses on how the observation sheds light on the different levels of agency and control at work in these experiences. The RSC Schools' Broadcasts are particularly interesting in this respect as, unlike on-demand platforms that users can access at any time, the RSC seeks to retain some control over the mode of reception by streaming live. While demonstrating the ways in which the RSC worked to control attention, this case study also exemplifies the key, but often overlooked, role played by teachers in framing reception for students.

The wider investigation into school reception also included an observation of the RSC's Schools' Broadcast of *Macbeth* at a different UK secondary school (in central London, with a group of 14- to 15-year-olds), and while I do not explore this broadcast in depth here, I make reference to it in discussing how Twitter functions as a potential tool for students to exercise agency. I examine the impact that multiple levels of control had on the students' own agency to actively shape their experiences, and I argue that, beyond being an exercise in audience development, these broadcasts constitute complex encounters in which experiences of Shakespeare are framed and managed not only by those producing and distributing theater, but by teachers, other students, and the interpretative framework of the school.

Watching *Twelfth Night* at School: March 8, 2018

I observed the broadcast of *Twelfth Night* at a co-educational state-funded secondary school in a small town in north Cambridgeshire. The school teaches students from the ages of 11 to 18 and has the highest percentage of students on free school meals in the area.[6] Students are taught two Shakespeare plays in Key Stage 3 English (ages 11–14) to prepare them for the study of another play in Key Stage 4 (ages 14–16) for their English GCSE examinations.[7] Live performance is not an integral part of the teaching of Shakespeare at the school, and the majority of students have little or no experience of performance outside of school. Although teachers work hard to organize theater trips, uptake is often low due to the cost of travel and tickets.

For this school, then, the RSC Schools' Broadcasts present an opportunity to introduce live performance, and Shakespeare, to students by negating the barriers of distance and cost. The school had previously participated in the RSC Schools' Broadcast of *Julius Caesar* (2017), which had been set up and facilitated by the deputy head of English; following the success of this first broadcast, the deputy head arranged for fifty-five students from across Key Stage 3 (aged 11–14) to participate in the *Twelfth Night* broadcast. This broadcast was not linked directly to any curriculum work, and the students had been specially invited to participate, selected by the teacher either because they had been identified as "gifted and talented" in English, because they had recently shown outstanding effort in English classes, or because they were a member of the school's "Friday Shakespeare Club." The group was mixed in age, ability, and enthusiasm, and in their prior knowledge of Shakespeare and performance. Some of the students present had also attended the broadcast of *Julius Caesar* and were therefore familiar with the screening format.

The broadcast was an opportunity to reward students' efforts, and this was reflected in the fairly relaxed atmosphere set up for the viewing. The students were "off-timetable" and were told in advance that they could bring snacks, setting the broadcast up as an experience outside of usual school routine. The broadcast took place in the school's "Learning Resource Centre," a multifunctional space with a library and IT suite, with movable school chairs set up in rows facing a pull-down screen onto which the broadcast was projected. The broadcast itself was accessed via a unique link emailed to the teacher, which opened a web page containing an embedded YouTube Live video. As the students filtered in from around 8:30 a.m., trailers played on the screen, which were then replaced with a holding screen that played music and showed a countdown clock, building up anticipation for the performance.

Disrupting the RSC's attempt to create an atmosphere for the broadcast, the music was muted in order for attendance to be taken before the teacher initiated an activity from the broadcast guide provided by the RSC. The guide, which is a distillation of the "Teacher's Pack" created to support the 2017 RSC production of *Twelfth Night*, stresses that it is essential students are pre-prepared in order to have a positive experience of the broadcast, and suggests that students undertake a series of activities the day before the broadcast to help them understand the plot, characters, and basic context of the play.[8] The teacher explained that it was only possible to devote the four lessons on the day of the broadcast to preparing for and watching the play at the school, leaving only twenty minutes before the broadcast to introduce students to plot and character. Working in groups, students were given either a short scene from the play or a character description, asked to discuss or act out what was in their section, and to provide feedback to the whole group.

This activity ran over the first part of the live introduction to the broadcast, which included presenter Ayo Akinwolere introducing Sophie Hobson, an RSC Education practitioner, and Matthew Dann, the assistant director of the production. The activity finished in time for the students to tune in to a specially created animation that ran through the plot of the play, which was followed by an introduction to the characters, including photos that focused on the costumes that the characters would be wearing so that students could identify and understand the various gender swaps in order to follow the plot.

The screening itself was split into three sections of around one hour each, with two fifteen-minute breaks, none of which coincided with the interval in the theater. The teacher dimmed the lights as part one began, although, as a multipurpose space where other people continued to work, the degree to which lighting could be controlled was minimal. Despite it being 9:00 a.m., the students began eating their snacks as soon as the first part of the play started and, taking full advantage of the permission to eat sweets and junk food not usually allowed on school premises, continued eating throughout the screening. The students sat mostly in friendship groups and with those from their own year groups. The teacher sat at a table behind the students, marking papers as she watched, but provided interventions and commentary at key points. When Viola (Dinita Gohil) appeared in disguise as Cesario, the teacher spoke over the production to clarify that the character was actually Viola, prompting them to "remember they all think she's a man."

The students' reactions to moments of intended comedy often differed from that of the filmed audience, with the laughter on-screen not always mirrored by the student audience. While a loud fart from Sir Toby Belch (John Hodgkinson) prompted laughter from the (mainly adult) theater audience, it was met with stony silence from the students. They did, however, find the physical comedy from the actor playing Sir Andrew Aguecheek (Michael Cochrane) absolutely hilarious, responding verbally by talking to each other about the drunken song scene and particularly laughing at Sir Andrew falling over and passing out drunk at the end of the scene. The music in this scene, and throughout the production, provoked movement and talking, with some students even moving seats and dancing. Malvolio's "my masters, are you mad?" was met with laughter and a few shouts of "YES!" from the students. Generally, the students felt able to react physically and verbally to the production and mostly this behavior was not curbed by the teacher, apart from occasional shushing to signal that students should refocus on the production.

The transition into the first interval feature was very abrupt and there was no time for applause. Students were encouraged to watch a live Q&A session, in which the music in the production was discussed, and were encouraged by Akinwolere to tweet about the show before a break in the stream. Going against usual rules about mobile phone use at school, the teacher also encouraged the students to join in by tweeting their questions about the production, and a few attempted to do so, although a question from one student to the teacher—"do you get how Twitter works?"— indicated that this was not a familiar mode of communication for at least some of the students. A short documentary was shown on screen during the break, but this was eclipsed by the arrival of more snacks provided by the school, and the resulting commotion meant that no attention was paid to this, with the students talking over the beginning of part two.

Students took much more time to settle into watching the second part, requiring more direction from the teacher for quiet, and a request for students to put their phones away unless they were tweeting about the play. The break also initiated movement, with some students sitting or lying on the floor in front of the seats. The decision to stage a kiss between Orsino and Cesario in the second part of the play provoked a huge reaction from the students, generating gasps and a number of wolf-whistles. A few students at the back turned around to seek clarification about the nature of the kiss from the teacher, who confirmed that this was an addition by the director and that Orsino still thought Cesario was a boy, prompting them to ask directly whether or not Orsino was gay. At this point the teacher focused attention back onto the production, leaving the students to interpret the meaning of the moment for themselves.

The production's choices in regard to the sexualities and gender identities of the characters provoked a lot of interest from the students throughout the play, although the live Q&A in the second break, with the actors playing Viola (Dinita Gohil) and Orsino (Nicholas Bishop), mostly avoided discussing this in any detail. The questions asked by the presenter were often fairly simplistic and focused on plot and character motivation—"Why was Viola on the ship?" "Why doesn't Olivia love Orsino?" —and although the students were initially focused on the Q&A, their attention began to slip as they became bored by questions like "Why is Malvolio so grumpy?" The teacher made a number of interventions during the final scenes of the play to explain the complex identity mix-ups. While the students were chatty, they seemed to be talking mostly about the broadcast, with some delayed laughter at moments that suggested to me that they were making their own jokes about what they were seeing on screen, rather than always responding to any intended comedy in the production.

The end of the production transitioned rather abruptly into another Q&A session, again leaving no time for applause. The students chose to ignore this and clapped over the beginning of the twenty-minute session. After a few moments of applause, the teacher encouraged the students to focus on the Q&A, although, perhaps understandably after watching a three-hour production, they only gave it partial attention. The exceptions to this were students who had tweeted in questions and were eagerly waiting for them to come up. There was real disappointment when their questions did not get chosen, with one student exclaiming that he had "tweeted eleven things!" As the Q&A ended, the credits rolled, showing the names of participating schools. The students watched this intently, giving a massive cheer when they saw the name of their school.

After the screening, the teacher asked the students to sit in a large circle, introducing an activity that she explained would help them when studying a new Shakespeare play. She distributed a handout with a speech from the play on it and asked students to read it aloud around the circle, with one student offering an emotion and the next applying that emotion to their reading of the line. They then split into groups and were asked to decide on the emotion of the speech as a whole and to work on a short performance of the speech with that emotion in mind. A few of the groups were asked to perform their interpretations, with the others giving feedback. The students performed confidently, and there were a number of varied interpretations of the speech that did not seem to be overly determined by the production they had just seen. Before dismissing the students for lunch, the teacher asked them what they had enjoyed about the broadcast. Their answers ranged from parts of the production—"the part with the statue" (a reference to the production's staging of Malvolio's gulling)—to the experience itself—"eating food."

Beyond "Brand Recognition": Agency in the Classroom and Online

The observation described above clearly demonstrates that, while the RSC makes attempts to determine and shape experience by suggesting preparatory activities, controlling the temporality of the stream, and providing introductory paratexts and Q&As, the way students actually experience the broadcast also depends on the physical space and context in which they watch, and, perhaps most importantly, how the broadcast is framed by the teacher. Here, the broadcast was framed as a treat for students; with the students invited to participate, attending the session "off-timetable," and allowed to bring snacks into school, the framing of the event by the teacher and school signaled that this was a special, valuable, and fun experience away from the "work" of the usual school day. The sense of occasion was heightened by the fact that the broadcast was not directly linked to any curriculum work and took place in a flexible space that not only allowed students to move physically, or even lie down, during the production, but also permitted them to participate in performance-based activities before and after the broadcast. This was in stark contrast to my observation of the *Macbeth* broadcast, where older students were studying the play for their GCSE exams and were not allowed to move, chat, or use their phones during the broadcast, and where there were no pre- or post-broadcast activities.

Participation in the broadcasts relies on individual teachers who are motivated enough to organize screenings—a process that may involve liaising with senior staff and advocating for the importance of dedicating a whole morning to watching a Shakespeare production. Recognizing that teachers are the gatekeepers of student attention, RSC Education has made working with teachers one of its key strategies, providing a range of continued professional development programs for teachers focused on teaching Shakespeare, along with workshops and educational offerings designed for students.[9] Building relationships with teachers is not only important for facilitating access to students but also plays a key part in the "brand recognition" function that Bennett identifies as a motivation for the broadcasts. At the school in north Cambridgeshire, the teacher's own enthusiasm for the RSC and its particular approach to Shakespeare was clear, as she engaged with the suggested activities provided in the broadcast pack, directed students to watch the introductory material and other paratexts, and encouraged them to tweet questions.

In some ways, then, the teacher here can be seen as facilitating the RSC's mission of creating future audiences. There were, however, moments in which the teacher exercised her own agency, shaping reception in ways that sometimes worked against the RSC's intentions. Only able to dedicate twenty minutes to preparing students for the broadcast, rather than the hours advised by the RSC, her own activity ran over the introduction to the broadcast, and the decision to provide snacks in the first break created a commotion that won out over watching the Q&A. At the *Macbeth* broadcast, the majority of the RSC's paratextual material was muted, with the final twenty-minute Q&A cut completely. Instead, the teachers provided their own introduction to the play, framing it in the way most appropriate to their own students and their needs. While RSC Education wields control over when schools are able to access the stream, it is ultimately the teacher, or relevant adult, who determines exactly how students watch and engage with these school broadcasts, acting as cultural intermediaries by determining and positioning the cultural value of the broadcasts and Shakespeare for students. The experiences students have with the broadcasts are, therefore, not just of the RSC's making, but differ in relation to the localized conditions of reception, dependent on the physical reception space, the actions of their teachers, and the specific educational contexts in which they watch.

With both the RSC and teachers working to control their attention, students themselves appeared to have little control or agency over how they participated. Paratextual material, teacher packs, and verbal interventions all demonstrate the perceived need to guide student spectatorship of Shakespeare that Jan Wozniak has argued is endemic in Shakespeare performances for young people. These performances, he suggests, subject students "to an interpreter who tells them how they should think about and understand the texts" rather than allowing young audiences to "consider their own meanings in relation to Shakespeare's text."[10] The mechanism by which the impulse to guide spectatorship and interpretation can curb student agency was evident in the way that students were able, or unable, to respond to and engage with the broadcast especially through Twitter. Students were prompted at the start of the production to use an official hashtag to tweet their questions, which were answered by cast members during live Q&A sessions during the intervals. Seeing potential in this digital interactivity, Geoffrey Way has suggested that through live Q&As and the use of Twitter, the RSC Schools' Broadcasts engage students by "having them become active participants" in their experiences.[11] The "interactive, hypermediated aspects of the broadcasts," he suggests, distinguish the Schools' Broadcasts by "focusing not just on bringing performances to remote audiences, but actively engaging them to participate in the theatrical event."[12]

In practice, however, the use of Twitter alongside these broadcasts did not straightforwardly offer students a space where they could become active participants in their own experiences. There was some evidence of active engagement through Twitter, although this was limited to a small percentage of the total audience, with just 200 tweets quoting the hashtag #RSCTwelfth or #RSCTwelfthNight between March 7 and 9, 2018.[13] The majority of tweets from students took the form of running commentary, along with some direct questions designed for the Q&A. As mentioned above, the *Twelfth Night* production's portrayal of gender and sexuality was a particular topic of interest. While some students tweeted direct questions such as "Is Orsino bi?" or "Is Antonio Sebastian's sugar daddy?" others clearly had no doubt in their minds about the portrayal of Orsino's sexuality, writing "I appreciate the amount of homosexuality in this" and that "Orsino thinking he's in love with Olivia is like me in Y7 [Year 7, 11- to 12-year-olds] insisting I'm straight." The interest students showed in exploring these elements of the production was mirrored in the classroom, where students sought clarification from their teacher when Orsino and Viola, disguised as Cesario, shared a kiss on stage. Seeking further information, one of the students tweeted to find out more, asking "Why did you choose to do the kiss when so many other productions don't?" While the observation and the tweets demonstrate a clear interest from students in this aspect of the production, the live Q&A avoided discussing the production's portrayal of gender and sexuality. Instead, the questions selected tended to focus on quite basic issues of plot and character motivation, which, although perhaps appealing to younger audience members, largely bored the group of 11- to 15-year-olds with whom I was watching.

In comparing the tweets with the questions read out on screen, it appears that questions were chosen in order to steer the conversation away from themes that may have been regarded by some adults as unsuitable for younger audience members. This came at the cost of a missed opportunity to engage older students with some of the elements of the production that they found most interesting. Questions such as "why is Malvolio so grumpy?" meant that students missed out on what could have been a productive and insightful discussion with relevance beyond the play, sparked by questions such as, "Do you think the play would have been different if Sebastian had been the one to switch genders?" which was posed by a student on Twitter.

Although the Q&A did not touch on the way same-sex relationships and desire were portrayed in the production, it did include discussions of heterosexual relationships by including questions such as "Why doesn't Olivia love Orsino?" As well as being problematic on a wider political level, the lack of engagement with this topic meant that the online conversation and audience community bore very little connection to the live Q&A sections of the broadcast. Rather than speaking back to the Twitter conversation, the Q&A tended to speak across it, leaving the desire for recognition, which motivated a number of the tweets, largely unrealized. Unlike an in-person Q&A or a radio phone-in, in which the speakers must deal with the questions asked, the broadcast performed the concept of audience interactivity and participation by encouraging audiences to use Twitter but largely ignored them once they were there, selecting questions in a way that minimized the audience's agency in shaping how the broadcast was framed and received. The RSC's apparent reluctance to engage with the topic of diverse relationships suggests that they may have been wary of prevailing and continuing prejudice against inclusive relationship education in UK schools, and the potential for some schools and parents to react negatively to the broadcast, putting them off future participation.[14] If so, in their anxiety to mitigate complaints, brand management was prioritized over fostering genuine student engagement.

The chasm between the way students engaged on Twitter and the way that the RSC presented those engagements complicates the idea that increased interactivity with a digital education offering necessarily results in greater student agency. Twitter provided the potential for students to exert agency over their experiences, but an anxiety over "inappropriate" lines of discussion and a rigid Q&A format meant that this agency was curbed and controlled by the RSC. One student tweeted during the *Macbeth* broadcast, asking, "When you gonna realise school kids will just meme the shit out of this play?" The tweet nods to the enjoyment students had in using the platform—perhaps in a deliberately disruptive way—as part of their experience and reveals the rift between the RSC's imagined vision of a productive, engaged, community of reception across schools and the reality, which also includes reluctant spectators and dissident voices.[15] However, by "memeing the shit out of the play," students demonstrated complex spectatorship skills, remixing what they were watching in real time with GIFs and photos, often commenting on and interpreting the production in ways that differed from the guidance given by the RSC and teachers, demonstrating the ability of students to speak, as Wozniak puts it, "appropriately about Shakespeare" without the need for tutoring.[16] Relaxing the anxiety around young people's reception of Shakespeare, trusting in their ability to spectate and speak about Shakespeare with less direction, and engaging with new forms of (digital) spectatorship as they evolve seem central to recognizing and encouraging student audiences in these experiences.

Conclusion: Shaping Value

Exploring how the Schools' Broadcasts are received in schools provides insight into how such broadcasts can create multiple experiences that are shaped by the educational contexts in which they are encountered as well as by the shifting relationships between theaters, schools and teachers, and students. While this one observation can only provide a snapshot of reception, it nevertheless provides new insight into how student experiences are not only determined by the RSC but also shaped by teachers who act as intermediaries between the theater and the students. The potential for teachers to exert their own agency over these experiences offers a source of hope for those concerned about the commercial relationships that these projects set up between theaters, schools, and students.[17] However, observing the broadcasts in schools paints an ambivalent picture of student agency. Rather than being active participants in their experiences, students are doubly controlled by the RSC and by teachers, both of whom seek to define the limits of their participation. Their online engagement is curbed or ignored by a format that prioritizes creating an experience that fits with the curriculum over fostering genuine engagement or exploring students' own personal and political responses to Shakespeare. Looking closely at how students actually use and experience digital performance also demonstrates the need to be cautious about assuming that inter-activity is a gateway to agency and highlights a pressing need to continue to interrogate the power dynamics at play when students are asked to speak back to Shakespeare through digital media. By carefully managing participation in order to appear as apolitical as possible, the RSC exerts its own forms of political control over the experience, promoting its brand along with its own pedagogical and political agendas.

The way that theaters such as the RSC are attempting to access the classroom through digital distribution underscores how important the school is as a site for determining how young (and potentially future) audiences value Shakespeare and how they understand their role as theatrical consumers. For the majority of their student audiences, these broadcasts are likely to be among their first encounters with Shakespeare in performance and represent key experiences around which ideas about valuing and viewing Shakespeare in performance are formed. Despite framing the experience differently, both the *Twelfth Night* and *Macbeth* broadcasts tended to reinforce the sense that watching Shakespeare (especially performed by the RSC) was, if not an "elite" activity, then a privileged and prestigious act of learning, even when that experience was framed as "fun" or a treat. Such ideas are likely to shape how audiences approach any future encounters with Shakespeare in performance. Understanding the models of value instilled by school encounters with Shakespeare performance is therefore important for understanding Shakespeare's twenty-first-century audience more broadly. School broadcasts not only teach students about watching Shakespeare in the theater, but train them in digital modes of spectatorship. It may be that with the development of new kinds of digital engagement, in which audiences have a greater degree of agency, young people will forge different kinds of relationships with Shakespeare, relationships that companies such as the RSC will need to accommodate and embrace if they want to continue building new audiences for the future.

Notes

1 In England, Shakespeare was the only named author for required study on the first National Curriculum for English in 1989, and the study of Shakespeare's plays remains a National Curriculum requirement across both Key Stage 3 (ages 11–14) and Key Stage 4 (ages 14–16). For a comprehensive overview of Shakespeare's place in the English education system, see Sarah Olive, *Shakespeare Valued* (Bristol: Intellect, 2015). Similarly, in the United States, Shakespeare is the only named author for grades 9–12 (high school) on the federally designed Common Core State Standards for English Language Arts; one of the "reading standards" for grades 11–12 is to analyze a "recorded or live" production of a Shakespeare play. Common Core State Standards Initiative, "Common Core State Standards for English Language Arts & Literacy in History/Social Studies, Science, and Technical Subjects," June 2, 2010, www.corestandards.org/wp-content/uploads/ELA_Standards1.pdf.

2 Susan Bennett, "Shakespeare's New Marketplace: The Places of Event Cinema," in *Shakespeare and the "Live" Theatre Broadcast Experience*, eds. Pascale Aebischer, Susanne Greenhalgh, and Laurie E. Osborne (London: Bloomsbury, 2018), 52.

3 Courtney Lehmann and Geoffrey Way, "Young Turks or Corporate Clones? Cognitive Capitalism and the (Young) User in the Shakespearean Attention Economy," in *The Shakespeare User*, eds. Valerie M. Fazel and Louise Geddes, (Cham: Palgrave Macmillan, 2017), 63–79.

4 Amy Borsuk, "Digital Visions and Revisions: An Interview with and Response to Robert Delamere," *Research in Drama Education: The Journal of Applied Theatre and Performance* 25, no. 1 (2020): 35.

5 Borsuk, "Digital Visions," 36.

6 Free school meals are provided in England by the government for pupils whose families may otherwise struggle to pay for them. The eligibility criteria differ by local authority but are often related to the amount and types of governmental financial aid that the pupil's household receives. In January 2019, 15.4% of all school students in England were eligible for free school meals. Department for Education, "Schools, Pupils and their Characteristics: January 2019," London: Department for Education, June 27, 2019, www.gov.uk/government/statistics/schools-pupils-and-their-characteristics-january-2019.

7 In a recent survey of Shakespeare teaching in the UK, Victoria Elliott and Sarah Olive found that while teachers have free choice of which plays to teach, they are often guided by awarding bodies who set plays for examination and that students in the UK are "likely to have studied at least one of a small number of plays," including *A Midsummer Night's Dream*, *The Tempest*, *Macbeth*, and *Romeo and Juliet*, with *Hamlet*, *Othello*, and *King Lear* also taught regularly at advanced level. "Secondary Shakespeare in the UK: What Gets Taught and Why?" *English in Education* (2019).

8 The teacher's pack for the broadcast was supplied directly to the teacher by the RSC and is not publicly available. The teacher's pack for the 2017 production is available on the RSC website at www.rsc.org.uk/twelfth-night/education.

9 Joe Winston, *Transforming the Teaching of Shakespeare with the Royal Shakespeare Company* (London: Bloomsbury, 2015), 6.

10 Jan Wozniak, *The Politics of Performing Shakespeare for Young People* (London: Bloomsbury, 2016), 61.

11 Geoffrey Way, "Together, Apart: Liveness, Eventness, and Streaming Shakespearean Performance," *Shakespeare Bulletin* 35, no. 3 (2017): 397.

12 Way, "Together, Apart," 400.

13 Tweets for both the *Twelfth Night* and *Macbeth* broadcast were collated and analyzed manually. They were categorized into tweets from students, teachers/school, and other, as well as by content. To maintain anonymity, I do not name accounts when quoting tweets.

14 Recent protests outside of a number of UK schools over inclusive relationship education reveal that such prejudice still exists. TES Reporter, "Relationship Education Protests Spread to Third Primary," *Times Educational Supplement*, July 22, 2019, www.tes.com/news/relationship-education-protests-spread-third-primary.

15 While it was not such an issue in the *Twelfth Night* broadcast, over one quarter of student tweets during the *Macbeth* broadcast contained inappropriate, irrelevant, or offensive content, demonstrating the challenge of using an external platform where the tweets sent by students cannot be edited or deleted by teachers or the RSC. While some students tweeted from accounts with their names, a number of students also set up anonymous accounts to tweet during the broadcast. The greater percentage of disruptive content in the *Macbeth* tweets compared to *Twelfth Night* may have been a result of the fact that there were more participants, many of whom would have been studying *Macbeth* for compulsory GCSE examinations and so were generally older (ages 14–16) and potentially less engaged, than the audience for *Twelfth Night*.

16 Wozniak, *Politics of Performing*, 204.

17 These issues are raised by Bennett, "Shakespeare's New Marketplace." Lehmann and Way have expressed concern over the neoliberal agenda of school broadcast projects. "Young Turks."

Bibliography

Bennett, Susan. "Shakespeare's New Marketplace: The Places of Event Cinema." In *Shakespeare and the 'Live' Theatre Broadcast Experience*, edited by Pascale Aebischer, Susanne Greenhalgh, and Laurie E. Osborne, 41–58. London: Bloomsbury, 2018.

Borsuk, Amy. "Digital Visions and Revisions: An Interview with and Response to Robert Delamere." *Research in Drama Education: The Journal of Applied Theatre and Performance* 25, no. 1 (2020): 26–37.

Common Core State Standards Initiative. "Common Core State Standards for English Language Arts & Literacy in History/Social Studies, Science, and Technical Subjects." June 2, 2010. www.corestandards.org/wp-content/uploads/ELA_Standards1.pdf.

Department for Education. "Schools, Pupils and their Characteristics: January 2019." London: Department for Education, June 27, 2019. www.gov.uk/government/statistics/schools-pupils-and-their-characteristics-january-2019.

Elliot, Victoria, and Sarah Olive. "Secondary Shakespeare in the UK: What Gets Taught and Why?" *English in Education* (2019). DOI: 10.1080/04250494.2019.1690952.

Lehmann, Courtney, and Geoffrey Way. "Young Turks or Corporate Clones? Cognitive Capitalism and the (Young) User in the Shakespearean Attention Economy." In *The Shakespeare User: Critical and Creative Appropriations in a Networked Culture*, edited by Valerie M. Fazel and Louise Geddes, 63–79. Cham: Palgrave Macmillan, 2017.

Olive, Sarah. *Shakespeare Valued: Education Policy and Pedagogy 1989–2009.* Bristol: Intellect, 2015.

Royal Shakespeare Company. "Teacher Pack: *Twelfth Night*." Royal Shakespeare Company, 2017. Accessed July 22, 2020. www.rsc.org.uk/twelfth-night/education.

TES Reporter. "Relationship education protests spread to third primary." *Times Educational Supplement*, July 22, 2019. www.tes.com/news/relationship-education-protests-spread-third-primary.

Way, Geoffrey. "Together, Apart: Liveness, Eventness, and Streaming Shakespearean Performance." *Shakespeare Bulletin* 35, no. 3 (2017): 389–406.

Winston, Joe. *Transforming the Teaching of Shakespeare with the Royal Shakespeare Company*. London: Bloomsbury, 2015.

Wozniak, Jan. *The Politics of Performing Shakespeare for Young People: Standing up to Shakespeare*. London: Bloomsbury, 2016.

13 For Everybody

Casting, Race, and Audience Engagement in The Public Theater's Mobile Unit

Emily Lathrop

In 1957, Joe Papp started the Mobile Theater with a production of *Romeo and Juliet*, touring to each of New York City's five boroughs. Looking back on the early days of The Public, Papp stated that "I wanted to bring Shakespeare to the people, that was the whole idea. I had to reach the thousands of people who lived and died in their neighborhoods."[1] For Papp, Shakespeare was a form of sustenance: "To me, he's the symbol of everything that's great on the stage—a marvelous, nourishing greatness. Everything else seems a diet of thin gruel: actors and audiences can't grow on that, they'll be undernourished."[2] Papp's Shakespeare is familiar—a universal figure whose works improve the lives of those who read and view them. However, as Vanessa I. Corredera argues in her essay "How Dey Goin' To Kill Othello?! *Key & Peele* and Shakespearean Universality," this Shakespeare can be quite dangerous, as claims of universality "gloss over Shakespeare as an alienating entity—a shibboleth for approved 'high' culture often imagined as white."[3] Even so, Papp's dedication to Shakespeare and his need to bring it to the people remain central to The Public's Shakespeare programming and, to an extent, the institution as a whole, even as it has evolved.

For much of the institution's history, its casting practices could be described as "colorblind" or casting that hires the "best" person for the role, regardless of race, often doing this by ignoring the impact race has on the production, its cast members, and its audience. Joe Papp and Shakespeare in the Park became almost synonymous with color-blind casting in the twentieth century and affected the casting practices of theaters across the country. The term colorblind is fraught, as it not only implies that casting directors, theater artists, and audiences do not see race (which, of course, they do), glossing over a performer's race to presume blanket whiteness, but also because it risks ableism, presuming that an audience member's main mode of experiencing race and the production is sight.[4] Over the past decade, The Public has continued to develop Papp's ideology and has moved toward "color-conscious" casting, which acknowledges the impact casting decisions have on individual characters, their relationships, and the play as a whole. This casting practice recognizes that theater audiences are not only aware of

race on stage, but that their experience of both the production and institution will be affected by it.[5]

Taking this progression into account, this chapter discusses The
Public's 2019 Mobile Unit production of *Measure for Measure* alongside the institution's history of casting practices and audience engagement
initiatives. In this chapter, I work from firsthand experience of the Mobile
Unit's production, professional reviews, official marketing from The
Public, and interviews with The Public's staff members. The cast for this
show was comprised entirely of Black women and travelled across the
boroughs of New York City before landing at The Public for a short run.
This production's use of color-conscious casting, combined with audience
engagement practices, centered Black women and offered a new way to
think about Shakespeare and his audiences. The Mobile Unit makes an
intervention into Shakespearean performance and American theater by
providing a model of engagement that places the impetus on community
want, need, and identity.

As Ayanna Thompson has argued, the field of reception studies has
long relied on the anecdote to discuss audience reactions.[6] Though I do
include a few anecdotes about audience response that I observed during
this production, my focus is more on how the Mobile Unit thinks about
its multiple audiences and then provides space to listen to them during the
show, as well as before and after. I also recognize that it is impossible for
me to remove my experience as an audience member from this chapter.
I participated in each of these exercises, spoke with staff members, posted
my playbill on Instagram, and filled out the end-of-show survey. I am not
a New Yorker and this production was not made with me in mind. I was
in attendance as a Public member, as an academic who has studied The
Public's history and interviewed its staff members, and as a theater practitioner, and I attended the show with plans to write about it in the future.

The Mobile Unit is one of many initiatives at The Public aimed at
making theater accessible. Joe Papp's original Mobile Theater program
eventually evolved into Shakespeare in the Park, one of the pillars of
The Public Theater. In 2010, Artistic Director Oskar Eustis decided to
resurrect the program as the Mobile Unit, taking inspiration from Papp's
original program and the Ten Thousand Things Theater in Minneapolis,
Minnesota, founded by Michelle Hensley. As Hensley explains, she
created this form of theater because "in addition to noticing how many
people theater excluded" she "sensed that so many people who actually
did come to theater didn't want to be there."[7] The program uses a 14-by-
14-foot square playing space with chairs around all sides and does not
use theatrical lighting or sound systems but does allow for costumes and
props. Music and sound effects are played live, usually by actors. This
style of theater is built to travel and everything for the production fits
inside of a cargo van. Associate Director of the Mobile Unit Roxanna
Barrios explained to me that "we learned this from her [Hensley] and
then we adopted it and adapted it to work for us. The bare bones of it are

still there."[8] The Mobile Unit travels to every borough in New York City, performing free Shakespeare at libraries, community centers, homeless shelters, and correctional facilities. Funding for the program comes from The Public's budget, as well as the Ford Foundation, The Andrew W. Mellon Foundation, The Doris Duke Charitable Foundation, Open Society Foundations, and Denise Littlefield Sobel.[9] For the 2019 fall show, the Mobile Unit decided to repeat a play for the first time, restaging the show that relaunched the initiative in 2010, *Measure for Measure.*

This production of *Measure for Measure*, directed by LA Williams, was set in New Orleans in 1979, during a police strike that caused the cancellation of Mardi Gras festivities. Though single-sex ensembles are not uncommon in productions of Shakespeare, they tend to be male and are often overwhelmingly white. Producing *Measure for Measure* can be tricky, especially in 2019, almost exactly a year after the confirmation hearing of Brett Kavanaugh to the Supreme Court. However, by utilizing color-conscious casting and a female ensemble, Williams produced a version of Shakespeare's play that was deeply concerned with the violence inflicted upon Black women. As Jose Solís pointed out in his review for *The New York Times*, this production came after Kenny Leon's Shakespeare in the Park production of *Much Ado About Nothing* featuring an all-Black cast, and ran at The Public at the same time as Leah C. Gardiner's revival of Ntozake Shange's *for colored girls who have considered suicide/when the rainbow is enuf.* As he stated, both *Measure for Measure* and *for colored girls*, "showcase the plight of women who must adhere to rules created by men who bend them according to their whims and desires."[10] This production of *Measure for Measure* put the bodies and feelings of Black women front and center and asked its audience to do the same. As Patricia A. Cahill and Kim F. Hall express in their introduction to *Shakespeare and Black America,* "Shakespeare continues to be part of American racial politics, a prominent lightning rod for anxieties about cultural change."[11] By casting a play concerned with wrongful imprisonment, abuse of power, and sexual violence with a cast of Black women, the Mobile Unit recognized the lightning rod Cahill and Hall discuss, giving audience members space before and after the performance to process and to reflect.

When I spoke with Roxanna Barrios about the process of choosing and casting *Measure for Measure* and about the approach the Mobile Unit takes to Shakespeare she said:

> If we're doing our jobs right, if we're crafting the shows right, there's a lot of clarity and storytelling that can happen as a result. A lot about human nature is wrapped up in these stories from hundreds and hundreds of years ago. There's this suspension of disbelief because this isn't written by a modern playwright so people kind of feel like it's a thing that is malleable, that you can put your own interpretation on without the fear or the threat of someone telling you, "you can't

do that this way." There's a lot of freedom in how to express it and we don't have to ask to be able to cast to represent a slice of New York City. We are sort of free to do what we need to do.[12]

Barrios and the Mobile Unit team leveraged not only the cultural capital that comes with producing Shakespeare—something that assuredly helps raise money for funding the Unit—but also the fact that Shakespeare does not come with limitations. While continually producing Shakespeare does run the risk of promoting universality, Shakespeare is out of copyright. There is not an estate that can withhold rights and dictate acceptable casting choices—theater practitioners are free to cast the show however they see fit without legal consequences. The casting for this production was intentional and sought to present audiences around the city with an ensemble and crew that represented them. As Director of the Mobile Unit Karen Ann Daniels stated in the playbill for the production, "I love the Mobile Unit because as a person of color, they're among the only times in NYC where I get to be surrounded by other POC."[13] The Mobile Unit uses this approach to representation both onstage and off, investing in extensive pre-show and postshow engagement.

Part of the Mobile Unit's ethos is to create the most welcoming environment possible for each of its audiences, regardless of where the performance is taking place. I was lucky enough to see the production at Weeksville Heritage Center in Brooklyn, a "multidisciplinary museum dedicated to preserving the history of the 19th century African American community of Weeksville, Brooklyn—one of America's many free black communities."[14] Once the audience was inside the space, staff interacted with them, introduced themselves and invited everyone to partake in the pre-show activity.

In the center of the stage (in the middle of the room, surrounded on all sides by audience chairs), the teaching artist and host placed two glass cylinders, both containing Mardi Gras beads. Staff instructed audience members to grab and wear beads from either jar, depending on whether they would rather live in a world full of mercy or one full of justice, and audience members were asked to explain their decision. This question served as a frame for the show, as many audience members wore their beads of mercy or justice during the performance. In addition to asking audience members why they chose mercy or justice, the host and teaching artist introduced everyone to the themes in the play, asking us to agree or disagree with a series of statements by giving a thumbs up or down. These statements included: "I love Brooklyn," "I'd rather be feared than loved," "I would support my family no matter what," and "shows should have a teachable moment." Once everyone had voted yes or no, the host went around and asked audience members why they had voted the way they had, making the audience integral to the performance before the production had even begun as well as putting these questions at the front of everyone's minds.

It is nearly impossible to watch *Measure for Measure* in 2019 and not think of the #MeToo movement. LA Williams's production deepened the conversation surrounding this play and its other recent productions, including those of Josie Rourke at the Donmar Warehouse (2018) and Cheek by Jowl (2013–) by highlighting intersections of race and gender within the play. According to the Maryland Coalition Against Sexual Assault, Black girls and women experience higher rates of sexual assault than women of other races and "40–60% of black women report being subjected to coercive sexual contact by age 18."[15] In addition, "four in ten black women have been subjected to intimate partner violence in their lifetimes" and "40% of confirmed sex trafficking survivors in the Unites States are African-American."[16] These numbers are staggering and only include those who have *reported* sexual crimes. While multiple people have written about *Measure for Measure* in the age of #MeToo, this production emphasized how whiteness and white people can take over movements and silence those who are at the center.[17] As Angela Onwuachi-Willig argues in "What about #Ustoo?: The Invisibility of Race in the #Metoo Movement,"

> The recent resurgence of the #MeToo movement reflects the longstanding marginalization and exclusion that women of color experience within the larger feminist movement in U.S. society. This marginalization of women of color has occurred within the #MeToo movement despite the fact that a black woman, Mechelle Vinson, was the plaintiff in the very first Supreme Court case to recognize a cause of action under Title VII for a hostile work environment created by sexual harassment; despite the fact that #MeToo began with a woman of color; and despite the fact that women of color are more vulnerable to sexual harassment than white women and are less likely to be believed when they report harassment, assault, and rape.[18]

By casting a Black woman as Isabella (Jasmine Batchelor), this production not only put the assault of a Black woman at the center of the play but also allowed her the space to express the hurt and anger she felt with both the characters on stage and with the audience.

Throughout the production, Jasmine Batchelor portrayed Isabella as the complex character she is. She consistently moved away from the sexual gestures of other characters and held her rosary often. Batchelor masterfully portrayed the switch from Isabella as a trusting and, at times, naïve woman to a woman who has endured a traumatic experience and feels deep resentment for being wronged. When Angelo attempted to assault her, she laughed in his face, proclaiming:

> Ha! Little honour, to be much believed,
> And most pernicious purpose. Seeming, seeming!
> I will proclaim thee, Angelo; look for't.

Sign me a present pardon for my brother,
Or with an outstretched throat I'll tell the world aloud
What man thou art.

(2.4.149–54)

She threatened to expose his deeds with such conviction it was hard to think that anyone would dare discredit her. When she turned to each side of the audience, asking "To whom should I complain?" (2.4.171), a sorrow settled into the character that stayed throughout the rest of the performance, an acknowledgment that like so many other women of color, Isabella would not receive justice for Angelo's crimes against her. Pascale Aebischer has written about audience complicity in relation to *Measure for Measure*, arguing that by having Angelo and Isabella use direct address, productions interpret the audience as being "deeply compromised by their silent acquiescence to his corruption."[19] By utilizing universal lighting, direct address, and by staging this production in the round, LA Williams asked audience members to reckon with their own complicity.

Adrian Kiser's performance as Angelo highlighted one of the many things gained by having an all-female cast for this show. Women are keenly aware of the threat Angelo poses to Isabella and Kiser's delivery reflected that, both in the character's speeches and in the actress's body language. Kiser as Angelo knows precisely what the character is asking of Isabella, the harm it will cause her, and asks her anyway. When Angelo all but spat "Who will believe thee, Isabel?" (2.4.154) at Isabella, multiple audience members groaned (myself included), recognizing the echoes of so many powerful men in that statement. This was echoed again when the Duke forced Isabella to accept him, claiming, "What's mine is yours, and what is yours is mine" (5.1.537). Though the performance ended with an ensemble dance, the final moment of Isabella turning to stare at each side of the playing space after the Duke's exit forced the audience to choose either to look away or to make eye contact with her, to acknowledge this injustice and to potentially recognize it in their own communities.

In the postshow check-in, the host asked audience members to describe how they felt about the show and their experience. A few of the responses were "deep," "timeless," "funny," "welcoming," "hip," "unsettling," and "entertaining." The range of responses spoke to the complicated nature of the play and to the talent of the ensemble and the direction by LA Williams. The final question of the night asked the audience members to check in with themselves and to reassess the question of mercy versus justice. Many audience members stuck with their original choice, but a good number switched from justice to mercy. When the host inquired why, multiple people mentioned being unable to trust the justice system, equating the idea of justice with the legal sphere. This distrust of the judicial system in the United States is entirely warranted.

According to the National Association for the Advancement of Colored People (NAACP),

> African Americans are incarcerated at more than 5 times the rate of whites. The imprisonment rate for African American women is twice that of white women. Nationwide, African American children represent 32% of children who are arrested, 42% of children who are detained, and 52% of children whose cases are judicially waived to criminal court.[20]

The question of mercy or justice not only served as a frame for the play but also provided space for the production's audience of predominantly people of color to discuss openly the systematic oppression they are subjected to on a regular basis by the state.

When I asked Roxanna Barrios about audience response to *Measure for Measure* and the Mobile Unit more broadly, she emphasized that the most common survey notes had to do with gratitude:

> Things like, "Thank you. Thank you for coming to my neighborhood. Thank you for making the arts accessible. Thank you for your cast of nine black women." People being really thankful for the representation, the fact that we showed up, and that's usually the case. Just a lot of gratitude, which is very humbling.[21]

I want to linger on the idea of gratitude here. The Mobile Unit is doing important work and is intentional about the work they do with and within communities. It makes sense for an audience member to thank the people who have performed for them. However, in the responses quoted by Barrios, there is still a sense that The Public has given these communities something that they might not have gotten elsewhere. Institutions need to hold themselves accountable so audiences of color no longer need to feel gratitude for representation. How can institutions and theater practitioners switch the power dynamic actively and intentionally toward audience members, particularly those of color? While The Public as an institution seems to be working toward this goal, the Mobile Unit and Public Works, who share many community partners, seem to be getting the closest because of the time and effort the staff take to meet with community members and to give them the space to voice their opinions, both in person and on paper.

One simple way the Mobile Unit prioritizes audience engagement is by carving out time at the end of the show for the audience to fill out surveys. In our interview, Barrios also mentioned the fascinating nature of surveys, which in many ways give theaters the opportunity to track emotional responses to each show. Ayanna Thompson has discussed this in her essay, "(How) Should We Listen to Audiences? Race, Reception, and the Audience Survey," in which she tracks direct and coded responses to race and casting at Oregon Shakespeare Festival:

> Using these data, I want to explore if and how scholars should read, interpret, and employ theatre-administered audience surveys with regard to the reception of non-traditional casting. In a sense, I want to ascertain if and how we can understand audience members' reactions to use of non-traditional casting when they are not explicitly asked to respond to questions about race. Can we accurately gauge an audience's reception of something if their answers are neither directed towards nor direct about that topic? Part of the reason I am stressing these methodologies' guiding questions is that theatre companies are loath to directly engage their audiences about the semiotics of race onstage.[22]

As Thompson argues, the methodologies for discussing audience response can be messy, and postshow surveys offer critics and historians written reception from which to gather evidence. Though the Mobile Unit's postshow survey only explicitly asks about race in terms of audience demographics, Barrios has stated that it came up regularly in survey responses. Many of these responses seem to stem from audience members seeing themselves represented onstage and it is clear that race was something audiences thought about in their reception of the production.

Theaters are often hesitant to directly address race with audiences, due in part to an inherent nervousness about speaking frankly with audiences. It is much easier to provide space for open reflection than it is to facilitate meaningful dialogue about tough issues. This hesitancy is also due to a lack of training. When I spoke to former Public Forum producer Drew Broussard about postshow discussions, he referenced a moment when an audience member posed a question about white supremacy that the facilitators were not prepared to answer. When I asked about how that affected plans for future postshow discussions, he said, "Institutionally there has been a discussion of 'Right, we can use post show talkbacks as this …' We'd have to prepare people if that's what we're going to do."[23] Though theater practitioners and administrators are getting better at understanding and speaking about race due to programs like artEquity, most theater staff do not go through training about how to discuss racism, much less how to be antiracist. However, of all the programs at The Public, the Mobile Unit and Public Forum seem to be the readiest to facilitate these kinds of conversations with the communities with which they partner. Imagine what the survey responses might have been if the Mobile Unit had guided audience members through questions of race, representation, and the themes of the play? How might the responses of audiences on tour have differed from those who saw the show at The Public, which is in many ways a predominantly white institution?

At the end of each tour, the Mobile Unit performs at The Public Theater, in the Shiva Theater. During our interview, Barrios spoke about the differences between these audiences and those for whom the Unit performs on tour:

> It's so so so different. I think that just by nature of when we're in the Shiva Theater, which is the black box, audiences are sort of on auto-pilot when it comes to that sort of engagement and behavior, just by nature of the fact that it is at the Public Theater. Our audiences are sometimes quieter. I will say that for this show, we did not even dim any sort of lights, the house lights are up in the Shiva and everything is in the light as it is in any sort of community center. I feel like that spirit remains the same. That sort of physical touch is really important and so instead of embracing the fact that it's a theater, we're trying to go against the very space itself, which is not easy because it's a black box, it's still painted black all around—floor, ceiling, walls. You have to go to the box office to get your ticket or wait in line and there are ushers. The experience of the event is more traditional. I think people, whether they have been to our theater or not—and for the majority, they are returning to The Public for whatever reason—they have their kind of behavioral patterns. On the road, we might be someone's first play. We definitely have an audience base on the road, but our audiences, I've sensed, are a little bit more engaged on the road.[24]

Physical space and seating configuration affect audience response. At the Weeksville location, the glass wall offered a view into the courtyard and into Brooklyn, making the community into part of the setting—the audience and Brooklyn became part of *Measure for Measure* and vice versa. Though not every tour stop featured windows like these, each stop did take place in a space familiar to its community, potentially having a similar localizing effect. While it is possible the Shiva has this ability for audience members (theater membership is a kind of community), the performances at The Public tied this production of *Measure for Measure* to a history of performances in that space, both institutionally and for the audience. The advantage of the black box theater is that it can change easily, surprising audience members with each production. By seeing the Mobile Unit in this space, returning audience members add another production to their memory of that room. On tour, the production becomes a part of each community's history, though each borough's venue might change from year to year.

The Mobile Unit operates between its touring locations and The Public, producing the same show and often getting very different results with its different audiences. Everyone who saw its *Measure for Measure* can be described as an audience of Shakespeare—they did, in fact, attend a performance of one of his plays. However, the Mobile Unit places its emphasis on each audience's relationship to the show, rather than

Shakespeare's cultural relationship with audiences. Rather than framing Shakespeare as a giant of the canon that is brought to people or that people must come to in order to better themselves, which might align more with Papp's original vision, the Mobile Unit (as exemplified in this production of *Measure for Measure*) frames Shakespeare as something audiences control, change, and own in their own way. Though every show sees different audiences for every performance, the joy of the tour is that the production encounters those different audiences in different communities and spaces every single time. These spaces were likely not created out of a love of Shakespeare, like The Public was, and operate differently than Broadway and Off-Broadway theaters, both in terms of their place in each audience member's life but also in terms of learned and often policed audience behavior.

The performances of *Measure for Measure* at The Public could in many ways be seen as a kind of coming home, a return to the project's parent institution. However, from its inception, the Mobile Unit was built to travel around the city, meeting New Yorkers, shaking hands, and fostering community, presenting a show that not only represents onstage its audience, but that values their voices and makes space for them. LA Williams's production of *Measure for Measure* represents the Mobile Unit at its best. Mainstream theater in the United States remains an overwhelmingly white field, from the cast and crew to producers and board members. Though this production of *Measure for Measure* was produced within this structure, it offered a way to reimagine the current state of the field. Featuring a cast of Black women and designed and crewed by mostly people of color, the production embraced color-conscious casting to make a strong statement about the violence perpetrated against Black women and the trauma that results. The Mobile Unit embraced Papp's original vision and bettered it, creating a version of Shakespeare in collaboration with each of its audiences.

Notes

1 Kenneth Turan and Joe Papp. *Free For All* (New York: Anchor Books, 2010), 99.
2 Turan and Papp, *Free For All*, 61.
3 Vanessa I. Corredera, "How Dey Goin' Kill Othello?! Key & Peele and Shakespearean Universality," *Journal of American Studies* 54, no. 1 (2020): 28.
4 For more on colorblind casting practices, see Ayanna Thompson, *Colorblind Shakespeare* (New York: Routledge, 2006).
5 For more on color-conscious casting, see Lavinia Jadhwani, "Color-Conscious Casting: Three Questions to Ask," *HowlRound Theatre Commons*, December 21, 2014, https://howlround.com/color-conscious-casting.
6 Ayanna Thompson, "(How) Should We Listen to Audiences? Race, Reception, and the Audience Survey," in *The Oxford Handbook of Shakespeare and Performance*, ed. James C. Bulman (Oxford: Oxford University Press, 2017), 158.

7 Michelle Hensley, *All the Lights On: Reimagining Theater with Ten Thousand Things* (St. Paul: Minnesota Historical Society Press, 2014), 3.

8 Roxanna Barrios, "Interview," conducted by Emily Lathrop, December 6, 2019.

9 "Mobile Unit," The Public, accessed July 22, 2020, https://publictheater.org/programs/mobile-unit/.

10 Jose Solís, "'Measure for Measure' Review: No One Is Innocent on Mardi Gras," *The New York Times*, December 2, 2019.

11 Patricia A. Cahill and Kim F. Hall, "Forum: Shakespeare and Black America," *Journal of American Studies* 54, no. 1 (2020): 6.

12 Barrios, "Interview."

13 Program for William Shakespeare's *Measure for Measure,* The Public Theater's Mobile Unit, New York. The Public Theater, 2019.

14 "What We Do," Weeksville Heritage Center, accessed July 22, 2020, www.weeksvillesociety.org/our-vision-what-we-do.

15 Maryland Coalition against Sexual Assault, "African-American Women and Sexual Assault," National Organization for Women, accessed July 22, 2020, https://now.org/wp-content/uploads/2018/02/Black-Women-and-Sexual-Violence-6.pdf.

16 Maryland Coalition against Sexual Assault. "African-American Women."

17 See Tara Isabella Burton, "What a Lesser-Known Shakespeare Play Can Tell Us about Harvey Weinstein," *Vox*, November 15, 2017, www.vox.com/culture/2017/11/15/16644938/shakespeare-measure-for-measure-weinstein-sexual-harassment-play-theater; Nora J. Williams, "Taking Shakespeare's Measure in the Twenty-First Century," HowlRound Theatre Commons, April 3, 2018, https://howlround.com/taking-shakespeares-measure-twenty-first-century; and Abigail Weil, "'Measure for Measure': Shakespeare's #MeToo Moment," *The Theatre Times*, October 27, 2018, https://thetheatretimes.com/measure-for-measure-shakespeares-metoo-moment/.

18 Angela Onwuachi-Willig, "What about #Ustoo?: The Invisibility of Race in the #Metoo Movement," *Yale Law Journal Forum* 128, no. 105 (2018): 107.

19 Pascale Aebischer, "Technology and the Ethics of Spectatorship," in *The Oxford Handbook of Shakespeare and Performance*, ed. James C. Bulman (Oxford: Oxford University Press, 2017), 308.

20 NAACP, "Criminal Justice Fact Sheet," National Association for the Advancement of Colored People, accessed July 22, 2020, www.naacp.org/criminal-justice-fact-sheet/.

21 Barrios, "Interview."

22 Thompson, "(How) Should We Listen," 163.

23 Drew Brousard, "Interview," conducted by Emily Lathrop, July 15, 2019.

24 Barrios, "Interview."

Bibliography

Aebischer, Pascale. "Technology and the Ethics of Spectatorship." In *The Oxford Handbook of Shakespeare and Performance*, edited by James C. Bulman, 302–20. Oxford: Oxford University Press, 2017).

Barrios, Roxanna. "Interview." Interview by Emily Lathrop. December 6, 2019.

Broussard, Drew. "Interview." Interview by Emily Lathrop. July 15, 2019.

Burton, Tara Isabella. "What a lesser-known Shakespeare play can tell us about Harvey Weinstein." *Vox*, November 15, 2017. www.vox.com/culture/2017/11/15/16644938/shakespeare-measure-for-measure-weinstein-sexual-harassment-play-theater.

Cahill, Patricia A., and Kim F. Hall. "Forum: Shakespeare and Black America." *Shakespeare and Black America*, special issue of *Journal of American Studies* 54, no. 1 (2020), 1–11.

Corredera, Vanessa I. "How Dey Goin' Kill Othello?! *Key & Peele* and Shakespearean Universality." *Shakespeare and Black America*, special issue of *Journal of American Studies* 54, no. 1 (2020), 27–35.

Hensley, Michelle. *All the Lights On: Reimagining Theater With Ten Thousand Things*. St. Paul: Minnesota Historical Society Press, 2014.

Jadhwani, Lavina. "Color-Conscious Casting: Three Questions to Ask." *HowlRound Theatre Commons*. December 21, 2014. https://howlround.com/color-conscious-casting.

Maryland Coalition Against Sexual Assault. "African-American Women and Sexual Assault." National Organization for Women. Accessed July 22, 2020. https://now.org/wp-content/uploads/2018/02/Black-Women-and-Sexual-Violence-6.pdf.

NAACP. "Criminal Justice Fact Sheet." National Association for the Advancement of Colored People. Accessed July 22, 2020. www.naacp.org/criminal-justice-fact-sheet/.

Onwuachi-Willig, Angela. "What about #Ustoo?: The Invisibility of Race in the #Metoo Movement." *Yale Law Journal Forum* 128, no. 105 (2018), 105–20.

Public Theater. "Mobile Unit." The Public. Accessed July 22, 2020. https://publictheater.org/programs/mobile-unit/.

Public Theater Mobile Unit. *Measure for Measure* theater program. New York. The Public Theater, 2019.

Solís, Jose. "'Measure for Measure' Review: No One Is Innocent on Mardi Gras." *The New York Times*, December 2, 2019. www.nytimes.com/2019/12/02/theater/measure-for-measure-review.html.

Thompson, Ayanna, ed. *Colorblind Shakespeare: New Perspectives on Race and Performance*. New York: Routledge, 2006.

Thompson, Ayanna. "(How) Should We Listen to Audiences? Race, Reception, and the Audience Survey." In *The Oxford Handbook of Shakespeare and Performance*, ed. James C. Bulman, 157–69. Oxford: Oxford University Press, 2017.

Thompson, Ayanna. *Passing Strange: Shakespeare, Race, and Contemporary America*. Oxford: Oxford University Press, 2011.

Turan, Kenneth, and Joe Papp. *Free For All: Joe Papp, The Public, and the Greatest Theater Story Ever Told*. New York: Anchor, 2010.

Weeksville Heritage Center. "What we do." Accessed July 22, 2020. www.weeksvillesociety.org/our-vision-what-we-do.

Weil, Abigail. "'Measure for Measure': Shakespeare's #MeToo Moment." *The Theatre Times*, October 27, 2018. https://thetheatretimes.com/measure-for-measure-shakespeares-metoo-moment/.

Williams, Nora J. "Taking Shakespeare's Measure in the Twenty-First Century." *HowlRound Theatre Commons*. April 3, 2018. https://howlround.com/taking-shakespeares-measure-twenty-first-century.

Index

For Product Safety Concerns and Information please contact our EU
representative GPSR@taylorandfrancis.com
Taylor & Francis Verlag GmbH, Kaufingerstraße 24, 80331 München, Germany